T0354548

SUPER TROOPER

JOHN YOUNG

authorHOUSE®

AuthorHouse™
1663 Liberty Drive
Bloomington, IN 47403
www.authorhouse.com
Phone: 1-800-839-8640

Published by AuthorHouse 07/23/2012

ISBN: 978-1-4772-2049-8 (sc)
ISBN: 978-1-4772-2048-1 (hc)
ISBN: 978-1-4772-2050-4 (e)

Library of Congress Control Number: 2012910821

chapters

Introduction   ix
Application   1

1. Patrol Cadet   7
2. The Academy   23
3. Standard Issue Uniform   39
4. Weapons   43
5. Assigned Patrol Vehicle   47
6. Trooper Conduct   55
7. The Coaching Trip   59
8. Shift Work   73
9. Patrol Preparation   83
10. First Assignment (Probationary Year)   87
11. Quotas/Profiling   121
12. Judicial System   127
13. Weather Conditions   137
14. Most Annoying Violators   149
15. Investigating Traffic Accidents   163
16. Fatality Accidents   181
17. Halo Effect   217
18. Use of Radar   221
19. Speeders   233
20. Drunk Drivers (DWI/DUI)   245
21. Chases/Pursuits   285
22. Army Dust Off Program   305
23. Aircraft Enforcement   311
24. Use of Deadly Force   323
25. Patrol Car Accidents   335
26. Unusual events and
    embarrassing moments   347
27. Epilogue   379

Preface

I was a Washington State Patrol Trooper for 27 years. I have been retired for 19 years, and still remember the good old days. There are times, when my wife and I are out for a drive, when I suddenly recall, "I know this spot." My wife asked, "What are you talking about?"

"This is where I investigated my first fatality accident. Three people were killed instantly in this one car. I had only been a Trooper for seven months when it happened."

I babble on, remembering it as if it were yesterday. After all these years, I still recall every detail involving that investigation.

Over the past few years I have begun to recall many things that happened to me, and situations involving other Troopers. Some were educational, many exciting, a few frightening, some humorous, and others, downright gross. One day, an old acquaintance suggested my stories were interesting and unusual enough that I should write a book about them.

With that in mind I put together a few of the experiences that were part of my normal workday as a State Trooper. Without a doubt, my stories are no different or better then those of Troopers who served before or after my years of service. The reader may consider the situations in which I was involved unusual and unsettling; however, they were simply part of a normal way of life for me for several years of working the "beat."

My first few years as a State Trooper were probably the most interesting and educational years of my life, but certainly not unusual for the job.

Ever vigilant,

Super Trooper

Introduction

Even though State Troopers work a forty-hour week, they are subject to working different shifts, and often work weekends. The pay is reasonable, so no one complains about working a graveyard shift, two or three times a year, a month at a time.

It is an absolute rule that a Trooper report for duty on time, with no exceptions. The reason is, there are so few Troopers. If a shift begins at 7 a.m., and the Trooper assigned to that shift is sick, and the next Trooper doesn't report to work until 9 a.m., who will fill the two-hour void?

Emergencies and accidents happen whether Troopers are working or not. The bottom line is, every Trooper feels he or she really can't afford to be sick. Who's going to replace that Trooper? We all know this and feel the pressure to be at work, regardless. Sick or not, we sign into service and go on patrol.

A Trooper works a nine-hour shift and is entitled to two twenty-minute coffee breaks and one hour for lunch. Unfortunately, we can't go to the break room to take that break, or to have lunch. When we want to take a break it has to be on the beat, with easy access to a freeway in case we have to respond to an emergency or traffic accident. If the Trooper's home is away from his assigned beat, then he's required to have lunch on the beat at his expense. This is just part of a somewhat complicated, but normal job.

There is no routine to this job; Troopers not only have to respond to emergencies at any given moment, they must also be vigilant about their surroundings. They should always be monitoring potential traffic issues, and other criminal matters. Never are they allowed a moment in their nine-hour shift to relax, to sit back, have a cup of coffee or a cigarette, and contemplate the meaning of life.

An ordinary day for a Trooper likely puts him in contact with ten to twenty different people and personalities. These people will often not be in a good mood, nor happy to be talking with him. The job requires that he deals with them, regardless, and be on his best behavior when doing so. All he can do is hope each interaction ends well.

For the purpose of this book I will be using the male gender when referring to Troopers, since there were no female Troopers at the time of my service.

Application

During my teen years I had decided on two career choices. I knew I was destined to be a fighter pilot, no doubt about it. However, my grades were not at all good at the time, so until I could get my act together to qualify for the Air Force flight program, my backup plan was to be a State Trooper.

Why the dramatic shift of choices you might ask. Well, my dad was a State Trooper, and I respected him for what he did, and the reputation of his organization. The Washington State Patrol at the time was considered to be one of the top three state police organizations in the country.

When push came to shove, I realized I wanted to be a Trooper, more than a pilot. So, I had to wait until I turned twenty-one before I could be hired. Although I knew the hiring standards were difficult, I put all my eggs in one basket and felt if I failed at this, I didn't have a clue of what I would do next. I was confident, but with a certain amount of apprehension.

Historically, a large percentage of the Troopers hired for the Washington State Patrol were either related to a current or former Trooper, lived next door to one, or personally knew a Trooper. My father was a Washington

1

State Trooper, and I was hoping that would mean something.

To qualify to become a State Trooper, you had to be at least six feet tall, with your weight proportionate to your height, and you had to be a high school graduate. I felt confident because I was 6'2", and I had finished two years of college. I did qualify for the first stage to be interviewed by the State Patrol personnel staff.

In my interview they told me I was too skinny (155 lbs.) and if I wanted to "cut it" as a Trooper, I had to gain fifty more pounds. I promised I would if they hired me. Prior to being accepted into the Academy training program, I consumed about two pounds of protein tablets every day to gain weight, but it never happened. This was an absolute waste of money, and the supplements tasted terrible.

I made it through the interview with flying colors, and did well on the typing test—all that remained was the background check. The Department's internal investigator interviewed almost everyone I had ever come into contact with in my entire life. He checked my military record, interviewed my high school teachers, past employers, everyone. I was told if I passed muster and I had a clean record, I probably would be hired within three or four weeks.

The wait to hear back would turn out to be the longest four weeks of my life. I finally received a call from the State Patrol personnel section informing me I would be hired, but not until they had some openings. I had to wait three more months before they began hiring again.

*   *   *

Once I received notice of my acceptance, I was on cloud nine. I had no clue what was next in store for me, and I couldn't wait to quit my current job at Boeing. Unless I screwed up somewhere along the line, I was going to be part of one of the best state police organizations in the country. I was going to be part of law enforcement's elite.

I reported to the Personnel Section and signed papers listing me as a State Patrol Cadet. I would be assigned to work as a radio dispatcher. There were only three positions for a Patrol Cadet—radio dispatcher, driver's license examiner, and truck-weighing scale officer. It was decided I would be a dispatcher because of my previous experience in the Army, where I had worked with military radios.

Before reporting for duty at one of the State Patrol's district offices, I had to attend a two-week training course to learn how to operate the radio transmitter, and most importantly become familiar with the verbiage used when communicating with Troopers on the road.

One critical component of transmitting over the radio is there must not be any misunderstanding when communicating information to or from Troopers. To avoid confusion, words or license plate information must be spelled out by using the phonetic alphabet. Surprisingly I

3

had difficulty with the alphabet used by law
enforcement. I assumed it would be the same
one I had learned in the Army. I couldn't have
been more wrong. Here's a comparison of the
two different phonetic alphabets.

Military	Law Enforcement
Alpha	Adam
Bravo	Boy
Charlie	Charles
Delta	David
Echo	Edward
Foxtrot	Frank
Golf	George
Hotel	Henry
India	Ida
Juliet	John
Kilo	Kay
Lima	Lincoln
Mike	Mary
November	Nora
Oscar	Ocean
Papa	Peter
Quebec	Queen
Romeo	Robert
Sierra	Sam
Tango	Tom
Uniform	Union
Victor	Victor
Whiskey	William
X-ray	X-ray
Yankee	Young
Zulu	Zebra

To illustrate the importance of working with
this style of alphabet: if a Trooper were to
check to see if a car was stolen, he would
give the Radio officer the license number, KRS

114, by saying, "Check for stolen King Robert Sam 114." The words describe the letters.

It took me a couple of months to work my way through the new alphabet. This alphabet is so ingrained with me now, I can no longer remember how the military one works.

After this training I was sent off to my new assignment. Now I had to find a cheap place to live. My new salary was actually less then what I was being paid at Boeing. I was taking a step forward, but actually a financial step backwards.

Patrol Cadet

When I reported to my first assignment, I had to spend two weeks training with an experienced radio dispatcher to get a feel for listening to, and understanding the radio traffic, learning map locations, and determining which Troopers were assigned to the different areas or zones. This was mind-boggling. I was overwhelmed with information.

When I went home after a shift, I would immediately collapse from the mental exhaustion and fall asleep. It took me several weeks to become comfortable and accustomed to the routine.

Once the radio supervisor felt I wouldn't screw up too badly, he assigned me to the graveyard shift from 10 p.m. to 6 a.m. The reasoning was that nothing really happened after midnight. The assumption was I would make fewer mistakes. Even I was looking for a breather from the hectic day shift, and welcomed being on my own for the first time.

The last Trooper went off duty around 2 a.m. and the next began his shift at 6 a.m. This four-hour gap allowed me to breathe, and correct any mistakes I may have made.

There was no limit to how many mistakes I could make; at least I now had the time to learn from them, without someone looking over my shoulder.

However, even during this supposedly free period of four hours, accidents would happen. If there was an emergency between those hours and I had to call a Trooper from home, the Trooper to call was determined by the hour; the last one off duty would take calls up to 4 a.m. After 4 a.m. the early guy got the call. The early call was the one I dreaded the most.

There was one old-timer who scared the crap out of us Cadets. If he was the early day shift call out guy, we knew we would get yelled at. Since I was the new guy working the late shift, I dreaded the moment when I had to call him out of his warm bed. I prayed for no accidents after 4 a.m. To no avail, they happened more than once.

I recall having to call the old-timer at home around 5 a.m., and when he answered the phone he told me he hadn't had his coffee yet and he would sign in service and be enroute when he damn well felt like it. He didn't just tell me, he yelled at me. Oh well, it was not my place to argue with him. I knew the call was recorded so it was his ass if anything bounced back for him not responding in a timely fashion. Thankfully there was only one of him in the department.

*   *   *

My first memorable moment, working radio, happened on the graveyard shift. I was working alone and it was a very slow evening. I had finished all of my reports and was thinking of having my mid-shift lunch. The only working Trooper on duty called in on the radio asking me to check a car license to see if the car was stolen.

I checked the database and there wasn't any record of the car being stolen. I radioed this information to him, and he acknowledged. That was the end of that. The next night the same Trooper again asked me to check for stolen information regarding the same license plate. I immediately recognized the plate number and was wondering how the Trooper came across the car a second time. I checked the database again and it was not stolen, so I reported this back to the Trooper, ending the transmission.

The third night in a row, he called in again, asking me to check the same car to see if it was stolen. I'm on point now; I don't want to screw up here. I now know this Trooper suspects something is wrong with this car, otherwise he wouldn't have continually asked me to see if it was stolen.

I made a more concerted effort to determine whether this car was stolen or not. I checked all the records available for me to check. I called other city police departments, and the Sheriff's office to see if they had any recent reports of stolen cars that might not have been put on the current hot sheet. There was no way I would screw this up so soon into my new career.

I radioed back to the Trooper, assuring him there were no existing records showing this car to be stolen. In his response over the radio, I could tell by his voice he was clearly disappointed. Damn, I knew he had something on this car, I wished I could have confirmed the car was stolen. I felt bad for the Trooper. I couldn't quit worrying.

A few minutes after the last check, he entered the office and walked up to my workstation and said he really thought this car was stolen. It had been abandoned for three nights in a row and just looked suspicious.

I knew it. He did know something was wrong with this car. I had to ask him—maybe I can learn from this—why did he believe the car was stolen? He told me the car appeared to be relatively new, and was abandoned in a location where no other cars were normally parked. He spotted it three days ago, and every time he drove by, the car was parked like it was abandoned. He checked the interior of the car but didn't find anything unusual. All he saw was some athletic gear inside; otherwise, it appeared to be normal under the circumstances.

I was more than curious now so I asked him where the car was abandoned. The Trooper told me, "It's right in back of our office." I said, "You have to be kidding," I jumped out of my chair ran to the back door and looked out back. Sure enough, there was the abandoned car. The license plates matched the ones I had been checking for several days to see if the car was stolen.

This car was not stolen because it was my car. My hope of attending the next academy class appeared dim at this point because I thought, "I'm so stupid, stupid, stupid."

It took me a few years, working the road, when I began to use this gag on new Cadets whenever I had the chance.

*   *   *

Not too long after my embarrassing moment checking to see if my own car was stolen, I was working the graveyard shift, when I received a telephone call from a man who really sounded drunk. However, he was coherent enough to tell me his car had been vandalized, and almost everything inside had been stolen, including the steering wheel.

My first thought was, this guy shouldn't be driving, so I needed to get more information about where he was and get someone to his location to prevent him from driving. I asked him where he was right then—where did the theft take place. He told me he was at a location that proved to be inside the city limits. This meant the city police had jurisdiction and needed to be notified.

I told the caller to stay with his car, and I would have an officer there immediately to investigate his complaint. I called the local police department and passed the information on to them, knowing they would handle the problem.

About an hour later I got a call back from the city dispatcher who was laughing so hard she couldn't talk. After catching her breath she finally told me, "This drunk who called earlier reporting stuff stolen from his car—you know the missing radio, steering wheel, and glove box, etc.—was not accurate. The drunk driver had gotten in the back seat by mistake." This is a true story that eventually made the newspapers nationally.

*   *   *

After I had been working for six weeks on the graveyard shift, I was assigned to work the swing shift 4 p.m. to midnight. One night the dispatcher I was replacing warned me there was a cold weather front heading into our area from the west and to be prepared for the worst. The county I worked in was hilly with nothing but two lane roads. They are the worst roads to be driving when there's ice and snow.

I was thinking, "What's the big deal; all I can do is dispatch the Trooper on duty to wherever an accident happens. Why worry, there's nothing I can do about it anyway." I looked out the front window from the radio room and saw the snow beginning to fall. I suddenly felt this was not going to be a good night.

All I could do was wait and stare out the window watching the snow accumulate, probably up to two or three inches by now. The phone began to ring off the hook.

I was receiving reports of accidents every fifteen minutes. All I could do was dispatch the lone Trooper to what sounded like the worst ones. For the rest, all I could do was dispatch tow trucks. Most reports only involved cars sliding off into the ditch.

This mayhem had been going on for about an hour when I heard someone knocking on the office front door. The office was closed at this hour so I assumed it was someone wanting to report another accident. As I walked toward the door I could see it was an old high school friend of mine I hadn't see for several months. I let him in and told him to be quiet for a bit as I was busy answering the phone of reports of accidents coming in from throughout the county.

He said not to worry and left me alone. I continued managing the calls with the Trooper who was bouncing around from one accident scene to another. Fortunately, there were a couple of Sheriff's Deputies still on duty who could help out with some of the accident calls. During a slack period I noticed my friend smelled strongly of alcohol. He is a kind of a free spirit so I wasn't surprised.

I told him he shouldn't have been driving, and requested for him to stay with me till he sobered up. He told me he was in the area and wanted to see how I was doing. He didn't know that I was actually working that evening. How he found me I'll never know.

Suddenly the power to the patrol office went off. No more emergency radio and no lights. That didn't mean the telephone quit working—it still did, and it was still ringing off the hook with people reporting accidents.

The problem now was I couldn't use the radio to put out the accident information. I called my supervisor and got him out of bed. He told me there was a patrol car at the office, not being used, and to bring it up close to the front door, and use its radio to call out the accident information, which I did.

After I moved the patrol car to the front, I could see the distance between my telephone and the car was about fifty feet. I asked my guest if he was up to answering the phone for me to yell out the information while I sat in the patrol car, dispatching from that radio. I filled him in on what questions to ask and to write the answers down for me. He thought this was really cool and kind of sobered up.

We did this two-way communication for about two more hours before things began to slow down. About the same time the power came back on. My friend said this was a blast and we'll have to do it again sometime. He was sober now, so he left and went home. I took a big breath and felt I did okay. I never told anyone that I had help. I could not explain my friend's presence. He should never have been there in the first place. Fortunately no one thought to ask how I walked back and forth from the telephone to the patrol car so fast for two hours.

*   *   *

All of us Patrol Cadets were chomping at the bit. We couldn't wait to get selected to attend the next Academy class. When working Radio we heard almost every day about Troopers involved in pursuits, or responding to injury accidents, or being involved in fights, taking prisoners to jail, and running Breathalyzer tests. Instead of hearing it on the radio, or from war stories being passed around the office, we needed an adrenalin fix. The one saving grace is that all Patrol Cadets are required to ride several hours a month with a Trooper.

This required ride-a-long is a training tool for what to expect once we become full-fledged commissioned Troopers. The excitement—we finally are allowed to get out of the office and be where the real action is. Of course this all takes place on our own off-duty time.

I was an eager beaver; I would try to put in at least one eight-hour tour a week, in addition to my regular 40-hour workweek. Not wanting to waste my time, I searched around to find out the best Troopers to ride with—the real hot dogs, the ones who were always where the action was. Patrol Cadets compared notes about the best Troopers. I chose to ride with the younger, aggressive Troopers, not the slow methodical old time Troopers, who seemed not to get excited about anything.

Eventually I learned, or realized, the older Troopers appeared to take things more slowly only because they were a bit more careful. They were smarter, experienced, and committed fewer mistakes; however, this had not registered yet with us hyper—eager Patrol Cadets.

As it turned out, Patrol Cadets are not permitted to choose. The Detachment Sergeant determined which Trooper we could ride with. He took into account our current learning curve, and then found a Trooper whose shift was compatible to our off-duty time. At this point I really didn't care with whom I rode. I just wanted to get going. I wanted the thrill of the ride.

My Pollyanna view of what Troopers were, as I would later learn, was somewhat distorted. They turned out to be normal people doing a difficult job, and were surprisingly not perfect. In a short period of time I was able to ride with every Trooper in the Detachment and a few others in neighboring Detachments. Over time the ride-a-longs exposed me to a lot of different ideas on how to perform the job, and the differences between what was considered good and bad police work.

*   *   *

There was this one Trooper who, when working an evening shift, would always time his mid-shift coffee break by stopping at another off-duty Trooper's house during the dinner hour.

His timing was uncanny; he always knew how to plan his visits when a family was having dessert. He didn't just visit one family, however, there were several others. Every visit depended on how good the cook was, and what dessert they were best noted for serving. I could always tell where we were going to eat by the direction of his patrol routine.

I rode with this Trooper only a few times, but it seemed whenever I did, I gained weight. I was always having a slice of pie, or a piece of cake, or even cookies. For example, he would work his way towards a Trooper's house one evening, knowing the family was having apple pie for dessert. Cadet pay was so low, I could never afford to spend money on having dessert, but riding with this Trooper was pleasurable, eating wise.

*   *   *

Cadets loved riding with "hotdog" Troopers. These are the Troopers who are fairly new out of the Academy, and have maybe two or three years on the road. They are highly energized, aggressive, and fear no evil. They are invincible. They do every thing fast. If they are responding to an accident scene, they never drive prudently or carefully, but rather at the highest speed possible. From a Cadet's perspective, this was a blast. Bring it on. Obviously we didn't know any better at the time.

My first exposure to a "hotdog" Trooper was a guy who had been out of the Academy for about three years. He was noted for being a fast driver and absolutely no one could out drive him. All the Cadets wanted to ride with him for the excitement of going fast, with the red lights flashing and siren flashing. There was no training aspect to this riding assignment; it was strictly an adrenalin kick for us Patrol Cadets.

One evening my hero, "Hotdog," was responding to an accident and was driving too fast for the road conditions. He rolled his brand new patrol car over once while rounding a curve. From his mistake I learned if you do not arrive at the accident scene in a safe and prudent manner, you have not done your job correctly. Do not over drive your skills, and know your limitations. By the way, riding with him really did scare the shit out of me.

*   *   *

When I was first hired, I was told there would be one Academy class a year, consisting of only 25 students. If you didn't make it the first time around, it could take as long as another year before the scheduling of a new class. A close friend of mine from high school was a Cadet for five years before making it to the Academy. I wasn't sure I could be that patient.

To qualify for the Academy would be a dream fulfilled. I forced myself to believe I would not fail. My whole life was in front of me. I had no fallback plan if I didn't make it. It was all or nothing.

Everything depends on whether there is adequate funding in the budget to warrant a class. The competition is great, because there are approximately seventy-five Patrol Cadets in the system, and only twenty-five or so will be selected to attend the Academy. When word filters down there'll be an upcoming class, every Patrol Cadet pushes extra hard to become more familiar with all traffic regulations, state laws, rules of court, and first-aid. Of course, this effort happens on our personal time off.

I felt very fortunate when I received word I was selected for the next class after having served only three months as a Patrol Cadet. The report date was in one month, so I felt I needed to get in as much ride time as I could before leaving my radio assignment. Normally I had been doing ride-a-longs twice a month for a total of sixteen hours.

Now, with only three weeks before leaving, I planned to ride every week, time permitting. I decided to ride only on evening shifts, considered to be the more active, dangerous time of day for a Trooper.

My supervisor felt differently. He recognized why I wanted to ride during the evenings, but thought it best to expose me to the intricacies of working a day shift. He explained there is a routine to working traffic on a day shift, and I should learn how a Trooper really enforces accident-causing violations during heavy traffic periods.

I always felt working traffic on a day shift was beneath my skill level. All the Troopers did during the day was watch for moving violations and on occasion respond to routine minor accidents. Very rarely would one find a drunk driver or happen onto a reckless driver while working a day shift. I felt the only way to get an adrenalin fix was to work evenings. Regardless, my boss set me up for my last workday riding with a day shift Trooper.

Our patrol day went pretty much as expected, routine without much action. We stopped a few violators, but the traffic was unusually light and not much happened. With an hour left to go on our shift, we received radio reports of a two-car injury accident on the local freeway. The accident location was on a new stretch of freeway that just opened up to the public the day before, where it intersects with a county road.

While enroute to the accident scene, the Trooper told me he wasn't surprised there was an accident at this intersection. He said, "I knew the locals wouldn't be used to this new stretch of highway because they would not be familiar with the greater speeds you'll find on the freeway. It was just a matter of time until something happened, and now we're going to see just how bad it can be." The intersection in question was controlled by a stop sign for the county road traffic.

It took us about ten minutes running with the red lights and siren to reach the scene of the accident. The first thing I noticed, as we approached the scene, was a log truck on its side and logs scattered throughout the area. Most of the logs were blocking two of the four lanes of travel on the freeway, and several other logs were in an adjacent field. There was a sedan in the ditch, and the whole right side was caved in.

As we exited the patrol car we saw pedestrians huddled around something on the shoulder of the road so we assumed it was an accident victim. Our assumption was correct, and there was another victim about thirty feet away in a field. The Trooper quickly checked the first one for vital signs and found none. He moved over to the second victim who was also deceased.

Both bodies appeared to have suffered a crushing blow from the log truck hitting their car broadside, and had died instantly of severe internal injuries. The victims were not wearing seatbelts and were ejected from the car. I was instructed to get two blankets out of the patrol car and cover them up.

There wasn't much else we could do other than investigate the accident and wait for the Coroner to arrive. The Trooper had me seek out witnesses and take their statements, and when finished, to assist in getting the traffic flowing again.

We had to wait for two tow trucks and some sort of forklift to remove the logs off the roadway. Once the Coroner arrived we were able to have the bodies removed. The truck driver was not injured even though his truck had flipped onto its side.

Before this accident happened I wondered whether or not I would embarrass myself when actually confronted with something so gruesome. However, this Trooper had me so busy running around helping with the investigation, I never had the time to worry about my lack of experience, nor the blood and gore. After the logs had been removed from the road and the truck and car impounded, our day was almost done.

We still had to go to the office to finish our investigative reports. I made it home five hours after my shift ended. The Trooper's last words to me, knowing I was leaving the next day for the Academy, were, "You did a great job today, just remember this was just another day at the office, so don't go and make a big deal out of it. Go home, get some rest, and later, make me proud." I have never forgotten this day, which was the beginning of my new "normal" life.

I recognized later the reason that Troopers are able to cope with situations like a fatal accident is we are too busy to worry about blood being spilled, severed limbs, and deceased people. A Trooper maintains his sanity because the job forces him to. He must ensure all the facts of the accident have been documented, the scene photographed, measurements taken, witnesses interviewed, deal with highway department personnel, tow truck operators, Medic unit officers, and insurance adjusters.

All this investigating, coordinating and interviewing of people requires reams of paper work. Did I mention how much Troopers hate doing paper work? Too many people want and have a need to know how this accident happened and who was at fault. No mistakes are allowed. The pressure doesn't end here.

The judicial system will eventually play a role and is a stickler for detail. A Trooper's reputation and career can be affected by his attention to detail in his fatality accident investigation reports.

The morning after the accident I woke up, and packed for my trip to the Academy. I could not get the accident out of my mind, but I knew this is what I wanted to do for a career.

All I had to worry about now was how to become a professional racecar driver, a medic, a psychologist, a listener, a doctor, an investigator, and an interviewer. I was sure my new best friends, the instructors at the Academy, would guide me along.

The Academy

I felt an immense sense of relief when I was selected to attend the Academy. The relief I felt lasted until my arrival at the training facility in Shelton, Washington on an old World War II airbase for Navy pilots. We heard war stories from previous trainees about how tough the course would be, but who cared, we made it, that was all that mattered. Once you are assigned to the Academy your status changes from Patrol Cadet to that of Trooper Cadet.

The school's session is twelve weeks in length. Each day begins at 7 a.m., and continues until lights out at 10 p.m. There is an extensive classroom curriculum, specialized physical training in un-armed combat, firearms instruction, accident investigation procedures, advanced first aid, and driving the pursuit course.

The staff instructors are seasoned Troopers and Sergeants, and we looked upon them as our idols. They were the elite, and could do no wrong in our eyes. Only the best of the State Patrol employees were assigned to be instructors.

After two days of orientation, I had an uneasy feeling we were there for the instructor's entertainment. It didn't take long to feel we were just a bunch of screw-ups. I had to learn the hard lesson of how to be tolerant of their criticism and laughter. I knew this was going to be a grind, but all I could hope for was to survive the next twelve weeks.

*   *   *

We began the day with calisthenics. If you were not in shape upon your arrival, you were going to be in a world of hurt. Everyone knew there was a strict adherence to being in shape beforehand, because if you were not, you would more than likely wash out within the first week.

It didn't take long for us to realize we couldn't do anything right. Everyone was caught doing something wrong or inappropriate. Apparently, we only knew how do things the wrong way. We were so discouraged as a group we referred to ourselves as the Misfits' Class.

The training cadre didn't like our nickname, so we even screwed up with that. This lack of judgment required extra physical exercise. Since we were a semi-military organization, most of our mistakes resulted in excessive marching.

*   *   *

The State Patrol Academy has a reputation for having a fantastic mess hall. Anyone who ever has had a meal at the Academy raves about the quality and quantity of the food. As for my class, some of us had some physical weight issues that needed to be addressed.

The selection committee identified quite a few Trooper Cadets who should lose a few pounds, and a handful of others who were thought to be under weight. I was in the latter group. I was 6'2" tall, and weighed 165 pounds. It was determined I should be 180 to 190 pounds. This was fine with me.

The mess hall was quite large because there were other training sessions happening all the time, and it was necessary to be able to feed everyone at once, and as quickly as possible. The food was served in a buffet-style setting. When a Trooper Cadet class was in session, the Cadets were separated in a corner for their meals.

Our class was divided into two separate sections—there were three "fat" tables for those needing to lose weight, and one "skinny" table for those who need to gain weight—I sat at this one. The "fat" table ate a lot of salads. We skinny people ate everything put in front of us. This was like being in heaven. We skinny guys didn't have many friends at mealtime.

*   *   *

Anyone who has had dinner at the Academy on a Wednesday will remember it as the famous "Steak Night." The kitchen staff cooked huge thick 16 ounce steaks to order, along with a giant baked potato and salad. For my class, this was the only time the "fat" table was allowed to chow down something meaningful. I so looked forward to Wednesday nights.

Having been in the training cycle for a few weeks I began to notice the State Patrol headquarters staff would schedule their late afternoon meetings at the Academy on Wednesdays. I wondered why? Wednesday nights were the only times I ever saw the Brass during my training cycle.

*   *   *

The class started with twenty-seven Trooper Cadets. Our class was going to be an experiment in many ways. We were going to be the first class to have weekends off, the first to be issued the new .357 Magnum revolvers, and the first to be issued brand new patrol cars. Obviously these changes didn't sit well with the old timers who survived the earlier days.

In the past there were no weekends off. The reason for changing the old policy was to eliminate injuries. The fifteen-hour workdays, seven days a week, created unbelievable stress on the Trooper Cadets. Going without any down time or break from the routine, resulted in fighting among the Cadets, with too many people being injured.

The Academy staff was somewhat upset over this change because the general feeling was, the Trooper Cadets wouldn't be able to handle adversity after graduating, without experiencing a little stress and tension beforehand. Regardless, being able to have weekends off was just fine with us. Since working Radio, I hadn't had a weekend off for over three months.

The Academy curriculum suffered because there were two less days of training. To counter this loss, the staff implemented a new format, loading us down with study material Friday afternoon before our departure, mostly to keep us busy and out of trouble.

We were required to return to the Academy no later than 8 p.m. Sunday at which time we were to be tested on the study material given us.

I don't know for sure if the weekend-off policy was ever a success, but there was a struggle between the Academy staff's expectations and our lack of dedication to our studies. We would show up on time Sunday evenings, drag our bodies to the classroom and wait for the quiz. Clearly everyone, including myself, had ignored most of the study material since we all kept falling asleep at our desks. Weekends were meant for partying, not studying.

I'm pretty certain there was an 80 percent test failure rate every Sunday evening. Because of our lack of interest in the study material, the class was not permitted to go to our rooms until everyone passed the exam together at the same time. It was funny seeing 20 percent of the class who passed the first time, fail the second. There were a couple of Sundays when the quizzes lasted until midnight before we were able to get a passing grade.

*   *   *

It is worth mentioning that if we were not in the classroom, we were spending enormous amounts of time outdoors. The worst part though, was

our classroom training. We had to memorize the
RCW (Revised Code of Washington) traffic laws
that directly affected us as Troopers on the
road. We were also saddled with the obligation
to become familiar with the Patrol's rules and
regulations manual, and internal policies.

Away from the classroom, we were separated
into several groups; one group might be on
the firing range, another working at a mock
accident scene on investigative techniques, or
boning up on advanced first-aid. While all this
was happening, pursuit course training would
begin. Everyone would admit the course was
always in the backs of our minds. We wanted to
drive, but there were so many rumors floating
around about how difficult the course was, so
there was a sense of apprehension.

*   *   *

The WSP Pursuit Course was one of the premier
law enforcement pursuit courses in the
country. Our instructors were often asked to
teach other state police instructors to become
accredited instructors to, in turn, certify
city police officers and deputy sheriffs for
training on their pursuit course. Almost all
police departments in Washington State receive
pursuit training at the WSP Academy.

Every Trooper Cadet in our class thought he
was a damn good driver, otherwise why would he
want to be a State Trooper? We couldn't wait to
get on the pursuit course to show off. Let me
tell you how I mastered the Pursuit Course.

*   *   *

The instructors first took you around the course in one of the patrol training cars on what was called the orientation ride. This was not a leisurely ride; the speed ranged from 25 mph to 110 mph and was scary as hell. Several times I felt the instructor was going to have an accident. My feet were glued to the floorboards and I hung on for dear life. When I was told I would drive at the same speeds we had just traveled at, I knew this was not going to end well. Suddenly, I lost my confidence and couldn't stop my foot from shaking.

*   *   *

The Pursuit Course was set up on abandoned runways at the Shelton Airport. Even though the course was run on asphalt, there were portions that were driven on water, sand, and gravel. Every segment of the course was a surprise. The instructors showed us what happened with panic stops, and how to control them. For example, while traveling at 35 mph, the instructor might hold a cardboard placard in front of your face so you couldn't see. You were then told to keep your speed steady.

Without warning the instructor pulled away the placard. I immediately saw I was in a lane controlled by traffic cones. Up ahead was a line of cones indicating a wall. My only choice was to quickly turn left. If I went forward and struck the cones, in real life I would have damaged the patrol car. I had to go left.

This maneuver required quick thinking and reflexes. If you hit the brakes, the patrol car would slide out of control. All you could do was steer the car and stay off the brakes. I didn't do well the first two or three times.

The whole purpose of the exercise was for us to learn not to panic, and maintaining speed could be an asset. The other lesson was to feather the brakes, not lock them up. Once they were locked up, you had no more control.

*   *   *

The Academy had a fleet of old tired patrol cars used on the pursuit course. There was an expectation the Trooper Cadets would have accidents during this training period, so why damage a new car if the Cadets were indirectly hell bent on destroying them? As it turned out my class was one of the worst to ever graduate from the Academy.

The lead instructor told us we were so bad, he predicted we all would be involved in accidents before our probationary period ended. As it turned out he was wrong. Two of us were not involved in accidents in our first year on the road.

*   *   *

While on the course, we drove at a variety of speeds. We were told to never deviate from the course speed limits. We should not be one mile above or below those assigned limits, otherwise the driver would be penalized. If a Cadet scored below a certain average, he would be required to repeat the course until the staff was satisfied.

The course began with rapid acceleration, and then you had to slow down for a few curves, then speed up again for the next set of curves, and then slow down for the next. Each set of curves had to be taken at different speeds.

One set of curves was set at 25 mph and 35 mph. The second set at 50 mph and 60 mph, with the final set at 35 mph and 45 mph. It was a constant speeding up or slowing down process, requiring braking hard many times. If you lost your concentration you would crash.

Did I mention when I was on the course there was another car following me? An annoying, rude person was driving a patrol car not less than ten feet from the rear of my car, no matter what speed I was traveling. When I was brave enough to take my eyes off the course and look in the review mirror, all I saw was the grill of the instructor's patrol car. My fear pucker factor was maxed out. I just knew he might rear end my car if I made a mistake, but it never happened. The instructors were too good at this.

No matter what speed I was traveling, the other car was right on my tail. The instructor was yelling over the radio for me to keep my speed up, or stuff like; "You moron, watch your speed, you're going too slow," or "Don't slow down," or "Get your speed up, loser." Why in the hell wouldn't he make up his mind? This was extremely nerve racking. I wished he would just go away and die.

*   *   *

When a Trooper Cadet was actually running the full length of the course, the rest of us were divided up into separate groups. Each group was assigned to practice on different portions of the course in preparation for their turn for the full run. One time my roommate and I were assigned to work the 35/45 mph curves. Whenever a Cadet wasn't on a trial run through our area, we practiced driving through these curves. I went first.

This portion of the course required me to travel at 50 mph before approaching the first curve to the left. I had to get my speed down to 35 mph before entering the curve, then maintain that speed all the way through until I approached the second curve, at which time I would have to quickly accelerate up to 45 mph and maintain it all the way through the second curve. When I exited I would have to accelerate again to the next obstacle.

If you didn't do the first curve correctly, it was impossible to make the second curve at the recommended speed. If you were okay with the first curve, but didn't get your speed up for the second, you'd lose time on the stopwatch. Everything on the course was timed.

Any speed higher then the recommended speed resulted in losing control and sliding off the course. When I went through this series of curves, it felt like the car would break loose at any moment. I was forced to drive at the absolute limit of the car's tires and my driving skills.

I felt the car leaning one way or the other, wanting to slide away, but the experts knew the limitation of the car and its tires. The big question was, did the trainee know and trust the car and his own skills? There was a sense of fulfillment when I was able to do it correctly.

My partner and I took a few practice turns on the curves, and after a few runs realized we were pretty damn good and had mastered this part of the course. Even though we decided it wasn't necessary to practice anymore, we still had twenty minutes of practice time left. Being somewhat bored and not wanting to practice again, my partner's brain short-circuited.

He had this idea of killing time by practicing the curves in the reverse order, or opposite direction. We would get our speed up high enough so we could enter the 45 mph curve, hold that speed, brake down to 35 mph and take the second curve at that speed. His idea sounded harmless to me and it just might have been fun. Plus, I needed to prove I was a better driver than him, so I elected to go first. I should have remembered from my Army experience to never volunteer, but as I mentioned earlier, I'm a slow learner.

I went further down the course, then accelerated and entered the curve at exactly 45 mph, and tried to maintain this speed through the top of the curve. At that moment the patrol car began to slide to the right a little bit as I started to turn left. What I didn't understand earlier, was this was a tighter curve then the 35 mph curve. Not a problem as I lightly touched the brakes to get my speed down for the next curve. This was the exact moment I realized how stupid our plan was.

There is no way in hell this two-curve procedure could be completed in the reverse order. Because of the closeness of the curves to each other, I didn't have the time needed to get my speed down to negotiate the second curve. I slid off the course and came to a stop in a stand of small scrub fir trees. This experience showed me how beautifully the patrol car would slide out of control.

Thankfully there wasn't any damage to the patrol car other then a few scrapes from the branches. I thought, no harm, no foul. The only real difficulty I experienced was trying to ignore my partner's laughter.

*   *   *

The one thing all Troopers hate doing is writing reports. A dreaded procedure we try to avoid, even to this day. The Academy staff recognizes this as a problem, so they look for any excuse for getting the Trooper Cadets involved with learning how to write proper reports.

Writing is one of the most important parts of the job and the staff must find ways to expose us to cop speak. We always had to address the five "W's"; Who, What, When, Where, and Why. Eventually, all Trooper Cadets were getting nailed for minor violations forcing them to write reports about why and how they screwed up.

I had succeeded up to this point not to have to write a report. That is, until my minor accident. My non-descript, non-injury, no damage accident involving no one else, somehow had turned into a fatality investigation. The Academy staff thought it was a great opportunity for me to write about how I single handedly killed several trees and destroyed my patrol car. I was really pissed off about getting caught and having to write a report. As it turned out, my writing style was not acceptable to my counselor; so many re-writes were in order before he was satisfied.

*   *   *

The one truly scary part of the pursuit course and actually my favorite exercise was when we were required to drive between two traffic cones that were set up on a long straightaway. The cones were set apart so that as the patrol car passed between them, there was a clearance of only six inches on either side of the car. Obviously you would have to judge the spacing carefully as you passed through. If you hit a cone, you would have to do it over until you got it right.

This section began when you exited out of a long sweeping curve to the left at 60 mph. As I exited the curve I quickly accelerated to exactly 110 mph. I had to step on the gas pedal and never let up because it had been calculated the patrol car would reach that speed as it entered the area where the cones had been set up.

If I was too fast negotiating the previous curve, I'd spin out of control. If I were too slow coming out of the curve, I'd never get the car up to the required speed of 110 mph before reaching the entry point. I had to be exactly at 110 mph, not one mile per hour less, or more—otherwise I'd be dead meat.

I enjoy speed, always have and always will. However, out on the pursuit course I felt for the first time, speed could be my enemy. Doing 110 mph on the course was somewhat out of the ordinary from what we'd been practicing. Regardless, I was ready for this test.

I didn't have a problem getting up to 110 mph but it was nerve racking knowing the tough part would be trying not to hit the cones. A lot of my classmates had trouble maintaining the 110 mph because they worried they'd hit the cones. That aside, it did take awhile to get used to traveling at 110 mph. In all the runs I made through the course I did my best with the 110 mph exercise.

*   *   *

I always felt serving in the U.S. Army forced me to grow up, become self sufficient, and be responsible for my actions. Through this Academy experience I learned skills I never knew existed.

My new responsibilities were incredible and thought provoking. I would really be on my own. I would be issued weapons, a high performance patrol car, and other equipment to perform the service of a State Trooper.

I also learned it would take a couple of years before I would ever feel comfortable in this job. Whatever course of action I took in the performance of my duties, I would be held accountable by my peer group, management, and the judicial system.

The Academy's incredible teaching staff did their best to prepare me and my fellow classmates to be good at our job, and to be safe. I can never thank them enough for their efforts. Job well done, guys.

Standard Issue Uniform

During our training period we wore khaki-colored shirts and trousers. We also wore an old officer's hat that had floppy sides and was referred to as the 50-mission hat, similar to what pilots wore during World War II. As our Academy training neared the end, the department issued our new Trooper uniforms and equipment. This happened only when the staff felt we'd graduate. This was the day we were all waiting for. The uniform would complete us.

We spent one complete day being measured for and issued uniforms. There are two Smokey the Bear campaign hats, one for summer use made of a straw mixture, the other made with a felt-like fabric. The latter campaign hat is used most often during the winter months and formal functions. The summer hat has more ventilation and is worn most often in eastern Washington where the temperatures are higher.

The actual uniform consists of two heavy and two light weight trousers for winter and summer use. The same seasonable principle applies for having two long sleeve shirts for winter, and two short sleeve shirts for summer wear. We were issued a bow tie and shoes that have a high gloss appearance. The tie is worn when wearing the long sleeve shirt for a more formal look. Most police departments didn't wear ties, so we Troopers wore a bow tie to set us apart from the rest of law enforcement.

We received one winter and one summer jacket. The jackets were unique in that they had special brocade interwoven into the fabric that reflected light—a safety feature for the Troopers when they were out of the car during the hours of darkness. The light from the headlights of cars would reflect off the jackets enabling motorists to see the Troopers. The jackets also had zippers on the sides so the holster was exposed outside of the jacket allowing easier access to the weapon. The only things not issued were underwear, socks, and a wristwatch.

The State Patrol has always prided itself on the appearance of its officers. There were policies dictating how the uniform should be worn, and its maintenance. The uniform shirt and trousers always had to have a crease in them. The campaign hat's brim had to be flat with no wave or wrinkles to it. No pencils or pens could stick out of the shirt pockets. A bow tie had to be worn when wearing the long sleeved shirt. On one side of the shirt, the nametag had to be displayed one half inch above the breast pocket. The Marksman badge had to be one half inch above the nametag. The hat was worn at all times when out of the patrol car.

On the opposite side of the shirt was our badge. At the bottom of the badge was the engraved number we were issued when commissioned. The badges for all Troopers and Sergeants were silver, and for Lieutenants and above, the badges were gold. The hat braid was silver for the lower ranks, and gold for lieutenants and higher.

The number system for the Trooper's badge was determined by rank. Not all of the numbers were used due to lack of personnel. When an officer retires, someone replaces that person and receives a vacant number according to the new position of promotion.

#1	Governor
2	Chief
3	Assistant Chief
4-29	Majors & command staff
21-28	District Captains
50-99	Lieutenants
100-250	Sergeants
251-1,000	Troopers

*   *   *

One other unique difference in the State Patrol uniform other then the campaign hat was the set up of the holster. For all Troopers, whether right or left handed, the holster was worn on the left side, in a cross draw fashion. That is, the butt of the handle was facing forward.

No other police department had this sort of holster set up. I learned to be quick when drawing my weapon, so I never worried about this cross-draw issue. I felt we, as Troopers, were special because of these two unique differences.

Why the cross-draw holster arrangement? The theory I heard from old timers was in the "old days" prisoners would be transported in the front seat of the patrol car. This meant if the weapon were worn on the right side, the passenger would have easier access to it. To avoid this potential officer safety issue, it was decided the revolver would be worn on the opposite side, cross-draw style.

⋆   ⋆   ⋆

The utility belt worn around the waist had all the safety tools needed for the job. On the left side near the opening to the front trouser pocket was the cross draw holster. Behind the holster was a ring or loop that could hold the baton, but it was not always worn. To the right side of the belt buckle were two ammunition pouches. Each pouch held one speed loader with six bullets. To the right of the pouches I positioned my mace canister for easy access. To the right side near the back trouser pocket I had my handcuff case.

We did not have radios attached to the belt. Our only way of communicating with Radio or other Troopers was from the radio mounted on the dashboard in the patrol car. We were pretty much on our own once out of the patrol car. It could get scary under certain circumstances without immediate access to the radio.

Weapons

The weapons issued were for self-defense; the pistol, shotgun, nightstick, and a pepper spray canister. The handgun was a Smith & Weston .357 cal. Magnum revolver. The State Patrol was one of the first departments to issue this weapon. In many ways it was my security blanket.

My class was the first to be issued the .357 Magnum, replacing the standard issue .38 cal. revolver. Supposedly this new revolver was so powerful you could stop a tank with it. We had been firing this weapon on the range almost from day one and were quite familiar with it. Practicing on the range was not fun because my hands were always blistered and bleeding from loading bullets and constant firing. Overall, I must have fired two thousand rounds while practicing.

*   *   *

The shotgun was a Remington 12-gauge. The shotgun shell, instead of holding buckshot, was a bit more lethal because each round had nine to ten .30 caliber pellets each, a real showstopper. If you were within ten to twentyfeet of the target, this shell would completely decimate it. I would rather use the shotgun any day before a revolver or automatic.

It takes awhile to become accustomed to firing the shotgun. With a revolver you just point and shoot. The shotgun has a pretty good kick, so after each shot the user needs to lower the barrel back down and re-aim. You have to anticipate the kick back when firing, and not worry about how it hurts your shoulder every time you fire. The effective distance of a shotgun is probably around fifty feet. A revolver is effective up to fifty yards.

*   *   *

To illustrate how difficult using the shotgun can be, I was involved in a training exercise where we had to exit from a patrol car that was parked parallel to the target of a man, remove the shotgun from its sleeve from inside the patrol car, load a round into the chamber, aim and fire one round from across the front hood of the car.

After the first round, we were to duck down, as if fired upon, behind the front wheel area where the best protection is. We would wait a few seconds, jack another round into the chamber, rise above the hood of the car and fire again. The purpose of this exercise was to get used to exiting the car in a hurry and setting up and firing from the side of the car.

The group I was practicing with did okay; we were all hitting the target and feeling good about it. That is, until one Trooper got excited. He fired his first round fine, but after ducking down, he raised back up to fire the second round, but didn't raise the barrel high enough while aiming at the target. He blew off the right front fender. We were laughing so hard the last two guys couldn't finish the exercise. Needless to say, word of his transgression immediately was sent out to all the other Troopers in the state.

*   *   *

The Mace canister was an effective convincer for those prisoners not wanting to be cooperative. I used it only as an absolute last resort. On a couple of occasions when I had removed it from its holster, I had to make sure it would spray so I shook it first to make sure the charge was good enough to work. The violator seeing this would ask what the hell was I doing? I'd tell him apparently he wasn't going to come along quietly so it was necessary to make sure my Mace was working. That did it, he was more then happy to assist me in taking him to jail.

*   *   *

As for the riot stick and baton, even though I left them in the patrol car, I only felt the need to display them once or twice, but never had to use them. I was instructed to never strike a person with the riot stick on the head, or any place on the body where there is a joint. The best area is the buttock where the pain would be the greatest.

*   *   *

A Trooper's best weapon is probably his radio. Whenever I was involved in a situation where

I felt uncomfortable, either for others, or myself, I informed the communication's center or my fellow Troopers about what was happening and my location. Often we were without backup, so it was necessary for me to be more careful and always keep everyone informed.

Assigned Patrol Vehicle

I did not know that a car was a vehicle until I went to work for the State Patrol. Earlier in my demented world a car was a car, a pickup truck was a truck, and a bus was a bus. Now everything was a vehicle. I take liberty in this book by using the word car instead of vehicle, only because I'm now "normal" again like everyone else.

*   *   *

Historically, the department issued worn, tired patrol cars to the new Academy graduates. As I mentioned earlier, the training staff predicts, and statistics have shown, almost all graduates will be involved in a traffic accident within their first year out of the Academy. So, why issue a new patrol car that likely will be destroyed?

This policy changed with my academy class. Due to the sudden need to increase the department's size by an additional 150 Troopers, the decision was made to begin issuing brand new, shiny, all white patrol cars, and hope for the best. There would never be enough old patrol cars turned in to satisfy the increase in personnel. To do this would take time and money the department did not have. So, the new guys would get new cars.

Previous patrol cars were all blue, so this switch to white was a dramatic change for everyone, more so for the old timers. Additionally, each new car would have a light bar on top, a change from when the emergency lights were installed behind the front grill.

When the change did take place, all emergency vehicles had red lights. Perhaps a couple of years later after I graduated from the Academy, law enforcement switched to blue emergency lights rather then red. The reason was the blue light penetrated better in the dark and under foggy conditions.

There was some anticipation that the motoring public might be confused by this transition from red to blue, so it was decided to have both lights installed, red on one side of the light bar and blue on the other side. There were also a couple more changes involving emergency lights; only fire trucks could display red emergency lights, and the Department of Transportation's emergency vehicles could only display yellow lights.

*   *   *

The siren we used in "my day" was the electric wind-up type, and it took a while for it to wind up to reach its highest pitch. When first started, it groaned like a sick animal. The sound was the same when turned off and winding back down. This type of siren must have been in existence for a thousand years.

From my point of view, using this siren was stressful and a hardship. Once I turned on the switch to activate the siren, I had to push the horn ring on the steering wheel for it to sound. Picture this—I am on an emergency run at a high speed, holding down the horn ring for the siren to work while steering with the other hand. This could be dangerous.

I could not keep the siren at its highest pitch because it would not be heard by hearing impaired motorists. I had to be patient until it reached its pitch, then let off the horn rim for the siren to wind down, and then touch the rim again to raise the sound. For the siren to be effective I had to raise and lower the sound.

If I was driving at a high speed, responding to an injury accident with the siren on, most other drivers couldn't hear it because the patrol car's speed was drowning out the sound. The siren was effective at lower speeds; however, if other drivers had their windows closed and the radio on, they wouldn't hear it.

*   *   *

About the time of the arrival of the blue emergency lights, the original siren was replaced with the electronic du-dah sounding siren. This type of siren was used by police all over Europe and proved to be more effective and a great improvement for us. You had the choice of what sounds worked best for the traffic you might be in. All you had to do was punch a button to activate it. No more hands placed awkwardly on the steering wheel. Perfect!

*   *   *

The patrol cars were equipped with almost everything you could imagine except for the kitchen sink. My first patrol car was equipped with two radios; one for WSP use, and the other to communicate with the highway department. There was a roll bar cage surrounding the driver with a screen separating the front seat from the back seat where prisoners would be contained. The screen was a clear solid plastic, strong enough to resist those prisoners who insisted on protesting their arrest by banging their heads or kicking it with their feet—a common occurrence.

The back doors could only be opened from the outside, because the window and door handles were removed from the inside. In the middle of the front seat there was what we call a jockey box. This was a rectangular-shaped box similar to a center console, held in place by straps.

On the front of the jockey box was a small lamp to use at night, and switches for the siren and emergency lights. Inside the jockey box there was storage for our accident reports, ticket books, candy, and maps. In some instances the patrol radio was attached to the front of the jockey box.

In the trunk of my patrol car I had two thirty-six-unit first aid kits, four wool blankets, two air splints (leg & arm), two boxes of different sized flares or fuses—thirty minutes and fifteen minutes in length. There was also a shovel, folded stretcher, tire chains, and a box full of WSP manuals, extra tickets, and candy. There was too much moisture in the trunk to store donuts.

My patrol car was a new Plymouth Fury with a Hemi engine, considered the best high-powered motor for State Troopers working the freeway. Patrol cars were so heavy with all of the additional equipment they were not that fast. They were quick on acceleration, but the best speed I could reach was around 115 mph.

Speaking of speed, three years later Chevrolet got the bid for the State Patrol fleet. This car came with a 409 fuel-injected engine, allowing us to achieve speeds as high as 140 mph. That was one scary patrol car. There was so much heat generated from the engine it could start melting the rubber mats on the front floorboards.

I missed being issued a Chevrolet patrol car. I was stuck with a Ford at the time that, if traveling down a steep hill with a tail wind, could get my speed up to 100 mph. It was a very demoralizing experience for the two years I had it, until I could trade it in.

In front of the seat was a sleeve that ran the length of the front seat where the shotgun was stored. It could only be removed after the driver's door was completely opened. We were instructed to always have five rounds of Double "O" shells loaded in the weapon. Only in an emergency, when I needed to draw the weapon out, would I load a round into the chamber.

There was one incident when a Trooper, not following procedure, had a shell loaded in the chamber. He quit doing that when he pulled out the shotgun, and it accidently discharged, blowing a hole in the passenger door. Not

good. This resulted in two days off without
pay.

*   *   *

In addition to the size of the engine, the
most important part of the patrol car was the
tires. A combination of speed, weather, and
road surfaces necessitated we had the best
tires available. In the beginning, my patrol
car had Michelin tires. This brand of tire had
what I call hard rubber. They were durable with
great traction, at high speeds and on curves.

I learned from my peer group that if I were
taking corners and curves at very high speeds,
the tires could break loose from the tire
rim. To avoid this, it was recommended I have
higher air pressure in the tire, ten pounds
more than recommended by the manufacturer.
This technique made the tires more stable at
higher speeds, but they would wear out sooner.
I felt my safety came first, and did not worry
about tire longevity to save money.

*   *   *

Departmental policy required I have not less
then half a tank of gas in the patrol car when
signing out of service. I know for a fact with
that much gasoline in the car, if I were to be
called out for an emergency; I could reach any
point in my area of responsibility. I was also
aware I would catch hell if I ever got caught
running out of gas on a public highway. This
never happened to me, and it never will. My
wife, however, doesn't believe in that policy.
Her policy is not to worry about getting gas

until the yellow caution light on the dash comes on.

*   *   *

The lifetime of a patrol car generally ends when it reaches a mileage of around 65,000 to 75,000 miles. There are times a tight budget can force the turn-in mileage to reach as high as 100,000 miles. However, experience has taught the State Patrol the cost of maintenance increases dramatically after the car reaches the milestone of 65,000.

Normally it would take Troopers two to three years of driving on their beat to reach the magic number of 65,000 for a turn-in. The type of beat can dictate how quickly you'll put miles on your patrol car. My beat covered such a large area I could easily put on the maximum miles for a car change in a year and a half. I averaged over 40,000 miles a year with my patrol cars.

*   *   *

My second time around for choosing a new patrol car, I was fortunate to be able to choose the color of the car. My choices were white or blue, and whether or not I wanted the emergency lights on top of the car, or in behind the grill. At the time the color of most patrol cars was blue, but the trend was to eventually have them all white. I decided I wanted a white car without the light bar.

I felt the motoring public was not quite used to white patrol cars yet, and I could be a just a bit less visible and sneakier if my car was white, more so if the blue emergency light was concealed behind the grill, not mounted on the top light bar.

Unfortunately, despite the new car smell, my second patrol car, a Ford, was a piece of crap. I assumed it would be better and faster because it was new. Boy, was I ever wrong. For whatever reason it was slower. From a standing start, it would take me a country mile to get up to a freeway speed of 70 mph. On the top end, I could only achieve a maximum speed of 105 mph, if I had a strong tail wind. Man did I hate this car. I worked extra hard to put as many miles as I could on it to qualify for the next one.

*   *   *

My discontent with the Ford got worse the following year when a close friend of mine in the same detachment was issued one of the new hot Chevrolet cars that had the 409 HP engine. I believe this car was the fastest one ever issued to Troopers before or since. One could easily do 140 mph driving it. This was the dream patrol car for all Troopers. I do recall a few Troopers getting involved in accidents because the car was too hot to handle for the inexperienced.

Quite a few of our Troopers were considered "motor heads," that is, they were always trying to get the best performance out of their engines and cars. I knew one of these "motor heads" had tweaked his patrol car to the point where he had achieved 155 mph. At that speed he may as well have been assigned to the Aviation Division.

Trooper Conduct

The Washington State Patrol has an outstanding reputation because of its intense training curriculum, a nationally recognized pursuit course, and unique color-coordinated uniforms with the unusual cross-draw holster for its Troopers, and the quality of their hiring practices. The WSP was always recognized as one of the top three state police organizations in the country. It also didn't hurt to have everyone six foot or taller. ACLU would eventually require there be no height limitations.

The training we received reflects the motto of the State Patrol; "Service with Humility." We were taught what was considered to be proper personal conduct for law enforcement officers, and it was application in the performance of our duties.

The most important and difficult lesson I learned—and it did take some time before it sank in—was: no matter how serious a situation I was involved in, I was absolutely legally in control of it. How Troopers managed this control was what set us apart from all other police departments. So, if we were in control, then there was absolutely no reason for a Trooper to act in any other way but professionally, and to be courteous and respectful when dealing with those involved.

*　　　*　　　*

Our height requirement—having every Trooper be at least six foot or taller—did create a sense of control or intimidation when working with violators. Without a doubt it was an advantage. In my case, my height was somewhat a saving grace. Even though I was 6'2" tall I only weighed 165 pounds; I was a beanpole. With my short crew haircut, my ears stuck out so far that they functioned as wind brakes so I wouldn't fly away in a strong wind. I still looked like I was eighteen years old even though I was twenty-five. My youthful appearance was a hindrance but my height kind of balanced things out. My point here is that height can command respect if presented in a meaningful humble way.

*   *   *

Troopers must always respect others regardless of the situation or circumstance. The key words that work best for us when dealing with others are, "Yes, Sir and No, Sir." We must respect everyone and hope for the best. It can make the job easier and possibly result in less physical confrontations.

In my profession I did come into contact with quite a few people who had "authority issues." The experts say sixty percent of the motoring public will obey the law whether we are present or not, and another fifteen percent will obey the law if they see us, the remaining fifteen percent will disobey the law whether we are present or not.

*   *   *

I always felt it important to recognize and respect my personal self-worth and shortcomings, especially being a State Trooper. For example, I knew I was not the best driver in the world, that I had a temper but could keep it under control, that I needed to be a better listener, and develop a sense humor. All that aside, I was a damn good speller.

There was so much to learn, it never ceased to amaze me how much I did not know, and had yet to learn. I was constantly learning to respect my instincts and know my limitations.

*   *   *

Troopers must always adhere to the department's personal grooming standards. Supervisors constantly monitored us to ensure we represented the State Patrol in the best way possible with an impeccable presence. The uniform had to be freshly pressed and clean, ballpoint pens or pencils could not be sticking out of the shirt pocket, all shirt buttons had to be fastened, and the equipment attached to the gun belt had to be properly aligned. Also, our hair could not touch our shirt collar, and no earrings. When out of the patrol car, we had to always wear our campaign hat, regardless of how windy it was, or how hard it was raining.

There was one instance when a rebel Trooper reported to work one morning wearing an earring. His supervisor asked "What in hell is that in your ear?"

The Trooper told him, "It's an earring, why, isn't that ok?" "Hell no," his boss replied, and ripped it out of his ear. The Trooper had to wear a Band-Aid until his ear healed. Tough love, but regulations are regulations.

*   *   *

The most important ingredient a Trooper must possess is common sense. Those Troopers lacking, will have a history of either being fired or suspended without pay.

To better illustrate the importance of having sound common sense, there was a time when the department was lacking in the quality of its applicants. To address this problem it was decided to lower the height requirement from six foot to 5'11"—if the applicant had a college degree. This change resulted in the hiring of a lot of students right after graduating from college.

It took a few years with these college-educated idiots working the road, for the department to realize having an education was not necessarily the answer for a well-rounded Trooper. After three or four years it was clear we had hired professional students who had never really worked a day in their life.

Most of these students were never exposed to an eight-hour workday, five days a week. They were simply students for their entire lives, until they hired on with the State Patrol. How does one develop common sense, if you haven't been exposed to a working environment? There were times when I witnessed these professional students make stupid mistakes where common sense should have prevailed.

The Coaching Trip

Once I completed the ten weeks of Academy training, the last hurdle before I received my commission was the two-week Coaching Trip. In a way it's the final test.

If I screwed up, made constant bad decisions, or didn't man up to stressful situations, I could get my marching papers to return home. This would be my first exposure to what I'd be doing for a living as a real State Trooper. If I made it through the Coaching trip, I would get a free pass to being commissioned.

I couldn't wait to get started. I was of the mindset I knew everything and wanted to get this Coaching Trip over with. I felt I was wasting my time, but it was a ritual we all had to go through. I guess two weeks wouldn't seem all that long anyway.

*   *   *

The Troopers selected to be Coaches are seasoned veterans with several years of service, have a great work ethic, and are held in high esteem by their peers. This is a coveted assignment, and if selected to be a Coach, this put you on the fast track for promotion. My assigned Coach had been a Trooper for nine years. I immediately liked the guy. He was very personable and easy going. I will refer to him as Coach Vic.

John Young

He already had my training file from the Academy staff and was familiar with my weaknesses and strengths. Coach Vic had been instructed to push me in the direction of my weaknesses, but at the same time, give me enough leeway to see if I'd screw up. If that happened, which it would eventually, I knew I had better correct those shortcomings quickly or I'd be toast.

Even though I wasn't that interested in doing this trip thing, when faced with it, I felt a certain amount of fear and trepidation. After three months of training, I didn't want to screw up now, but what the hell I thought—"Let's get it on; it's make it or break it time." I just wanted to survive those two weeks and I'd be home free.

*   *   *

When I reported for the Coaching trip, I arrived in my personal car. The district staff issued me a patrol car while training there. I was told whenever I drove the patrol car I must be in uniform. If I wished to drive home on my days off, I had to wear the uniform and take the patrol car. Just the appearance of another patrol car on the road has its advantages; however, I could not stop anyone, because I wasn't yet commissioned.

The patrol car I was issued was waiting to be turned in for auction. Essentially the car's usefulness was over. Truth be known, it was a piece of shit. This car had all the markings of a patrol car, but there was one thing wrong with it—the patrol radio didn't work. No sense fixing the problem if the car was being de-commissioned, right?

*   *   *

I had a great Coach. In only a couple of days we were accustomed to each other and we quickly became friends. I considered Coach Vic to be my mentor, and valued his opinion.

However, almost immediately, in the first two days, a little dissension developed between us. Coach Vic had been put on a strict diet because he was getting a bit pudgy around the waist. He had no problem staying on his diet until he was assigned to be my Coach.

A Coach and his Cadet are required to have their mid-shift meals on the beat, not at the Coach's home. Normally, without me he would have gone home for his meal.

Our relationship took a sharp downward turn when we were having our meal. Coach Vic had a salad and a cup of coffee. Me, the guy from the Academy's skinny table, ordered a stack of buttermilk pancakes with eggs and bacon.

Coach Vic wouldn't talk to me during our meal; he just glared at me. If I felt at times he was riding me to hard, then at the next meal, I would order practically everything on the menu and finish it with pie and ice cream to get back at him.

*   *   *

My Coach started my training by telling me he would drive and I would observe how he handled accident situations, pursuits, and identifying traffic violators. After a few days, he would let me drive and see how I worked out. I was extremely disappointed—I assumed I would start off driving and he would guide me along. To be told it may be a few more days before I was able to drive was unsettling. Instead, I had to sit back observe, and be patient.

For the first two or three hours, Coach Vic drove around the beat showing me the area, and the hot spots where most of the accidents occurred. We never stopped any violators. I wondered what we were doing other then wasting gas. After lunch, the Coach and I walked out of the restaurant and he said, "Hold up a minute," I turned to him, he tossed the car keys to me, and said he was too tired to drive anymore and for me to take over. He was just screwing with me. It was show time! Finally!

All of a sudden I lost my comfort zone and was wondering what the hell do I do now. We jumped in the patrol car, and he said, "Let's go." I knew this would not be easy because I had just forgotten everything I learned at the Academy.

*   *   *

I started driving too carefully, you know, not wanting to screw up or have an accident. I was driving so slowly on patrol, it was driving Coach Vic crazy. He would scream at me, "What the hell! Are you too scared to drive fast? For crying out loud, be a risk taker." If he only knew that during my teenage years I drove like a maniac. I did learn driving like a maniac did not qualify me to be a professional driver.

I got braver and picked up my speed to the posted limit. I hadn't realized I was driving that slowly. Still, my Coach was on my case. He would say, in a loud, unkind way, "If I have to reach over there and put my foot on the gas pedal, I might as well be driving. Please be a bit more aggressive. How can you determine if someone is speeding in front of you, if you don't drive over the posted limit a bit?"

You would think this was a simple thing to do. Actually, it was hard driving over the limit when for so many years, I had been taught to drive legally and not over the posted limit. But the rules had changed. I picked up my speed, and after a couple of hours I began to feel more comfortable behind the wheel.

*   *   *

In the first few days I learned how other traffic reacted to a patrol car. For example, if I were following behind someone, he would slow down and become too careful in his driving. I realized I could scare the shit out of anyone just by following him. Although this bothered me a bit, and I hoped everyone would just ignore my patrol car and me, but that wasn't going to happen. I realize it is human nature to worry when a police car is following you, even for me.

In a convoluted way, other motorists were watching me as I was watching them. I felt

pressured to be more careful, and to watch
my speed when on routine patrol, to use my
turn signals when required, and not follow
too closely. I understood the traffic laws
applied to everyone including me; however,
there was an exception. Police officers may
violate these laws while in the performance of
their duties. Otherwise, how would we be able
to pace a car for speeding, or respond quickly
to an injury accident?

*   *   *

We finally reached that point of the week
where Coach Vic had his days off. In this
case "our" days off fell on a Wednesday and
Thursday. I put on my uniform and headed home,
about sixty miles away. Before leaving I was
reminded again not to stop any violators on
the way there. Even though I knew this, I
still felt uncomfortable being in a Trooper's
uniform and patrol car by myself, as though I
was masquerading on Halloween.

It was scary knowing everyone who might see
me would believe I was "real" and on routine
patrol. I was beginning to wonder whether
or not I should have taken my personal car
instead, but it was too late; I was on the
road heading home.

It was so foggy out; I couldn't see more than
a hundred feet in front of the patrol car.
Everyone on the freeway was being careful and
driving slower than normal. The posted speed
limit is 60 mph, and yet traffic was running
around 35 to 40 mph. I wondered how could
anyone get in trouble at this speed. I was

pleased no one was passing me, so I didn't have to worry about ignoring speeders. The trip home would be a piece of cake, and I only had thirty miles left to go. No sooner did I think this, than I saw an accident in front of me.

At this point on the freeway I was in the middle lane of the three southbound lanes. Due to the lack of visibility I didn't recognize the accident until I was almost upon it. In the right lane was a sedan wedged in underneath a flatbed trailer that had apparently come off a tractor rig. The right lane was blocked.

Momentarily, I was like every other rubbernecking driver on the road, looking over to the right, thinking what a hell of an accident. It really looked bad. Oh shit, I remembered, I'm in a marked patrol car in uniform. I had to snap out of my tourist mode, because everyone saw me in the patrol car and were probably wondering why I hadn't stopped.

Everything happened so fast, I had already passed the accident scene, so I pulled over onto the right shoulder and backed up to the accident. I couldn't go around to the back of the trailer to turn on my emergency lights—it would be too dangerous because of the thick fog. I knew before I even got out of the car I would need an ambulance, but my radio didn't work, so I wasn't sure how that was going to work out. I grabbed the first aid kit out of the trunk and ran back to the wrecked sedan.

The occupants were still in the wrecked car, and people were beginning to gather around it.

One passerby asked how he could help, and I told him my radio was defective and would he please find a telephone, report the accident and ask them to dispatch an ambulance. The Good Samaritan took off.

For the moment I felt a sense of relief knowing help would be on its way.

I approached the male driver first and noticed he was injured, but not seriously. I looked across the front seat at the female passenger who was bleeding profusely from a head injury. I asked one of the bystanders to take one of my blankets and cover up the driver so he wouldn't go into severe shock, and then headed around to the other side of the car to check out the female passenger.

The car was wedged tightly underneath the trailer, and had come to rest right at the beginning of the windshield. At impact, the passenger, who was not wearing a seat belt, slammed forward into the windshield. The glass had pretty much shredded her front forehead and scalp. This type of injury produces a lot of bleeding and her appearance did reflect a great loss of blood.

With help, I was able to remove her from the car and lay her down on this slight incline of the embankment. We covered her up with blankets, and I immediately applied several two-inch compresses on her head. I told her she was going to be just fine and not to worry. I asked someone to stay with her while I ran back to the patrol car and grabbed a few flares to set up behind the accident, to prevent anyone from driving into our accident scene. Eventually the local Trooper arrived to conduct the investigation.

The truck driver pulling the trailer was not aware his trailer had come loose. The guy had traveled on for a mile or so until a witness flagged him down. He eventually returned to the scene of the accident. The injured woman survived with only a few scars.

As for the trauma of the uninitiated, I was okay. The investigating Trooper told me I had done everything properly, and complimented me for a job well done. Other then the personal embarrassment of passing by the accident, I survived my first unexpected test.

*   *   *

After returning from my two days off, I was back on patrol. Once in the driver's seat, my first concern was to drive in a safe and prudent manner. I was concentrating so hard on my driving, I forgot I was also supposed to spot traffic violators. I was acting like a tourist. Thank God, I wasn't chewing gum.

For the first two or three hours my Coach would say, "Didn't you see that?" or aren't you going to stop that guy?" It was a matter of not seeing anything because I was too nervous. After awhile I finally found one obvious speeder driving ten miles over the speed limit. I turned on the emergency equipment and used the siren to pull the violator over. The car immediately pulled off to the shoulder and stopped. The driver had stopped so fast I almost rear-ended him.

Coach Vic mentioned maybe using the siren was a bit of overkill. "I could see where the driver saw your red lights, so why use the siren?" he asked. I was dumb enough to say, "I thought we were to use the siren on all stops." "Hell no," he said. "We use the siren only when there isn't any acknowledgement. There's no sense in scaring the hell out of everyone around us on every stop we make. Be patient with each violator to see how he reacts."

I strutted up to the car looking really great wearing my Trooper's hat, gun, and stuff, really proud to be a State Trooper doing his job. The driver turned out to be a female. She asked what she had done wrong. When I saw tears welling up in her eyes, I realized this was not going to go well.

I informed her she had been speeding, and she broke down, crying—I mean, heavy tears, bawling uncontrollably. I was at a total loss for words. I didn't know what to say or do. I just stood there trying to figure what to do next.

Suddenly I noticed Coach Vic standing next to me, scaring the hell out of me. He asked, "What the hell is going on here?" I tried to explain, but the woman was sobbing louder now. Coach Vic turned to her and said, "Shut up, lady—this is not the end of the world." She quit. He turned to me and said, "Go back to the car and write her up, and quit fooling around." Lesson learned. Be firm, stay the course.

*   *   *

The most important part of a Coaching trip is to give the Trooper Cadets as much exposure as possible to dealing with traffic violators. The more you stop, the more you learn. Taking into account days off, in a two-week period a Trooper Cadet may only have eight to ten working days to gain much needed experience. This leads me into another story involving another one of my classmates.

This classmate was assigned to a Coach who was considered to be one of the top-producing Troopers in the state. It would be considered normal for a Trooper to stop an average of ten to fifteen violators a shift. This particular Trooper was stopping an average of thirty to forty cars a day. He never took coffee breaks or time off for lunch. He was dedicated to working a solid eight-hour day.

His assigned Trooper Cadet started off slowly. He did not stop one violator the first two workdays. The Coach was a bit frustrated and asked, "Why aren't you stopping any cars. I know you're seeing the same violations I am, happening right in front of us, so why not stop these people and talk to them?" The Trooper Cadet said he felt that if the traffic violation was not serious enough for a ticket, why waste everyone's time by stopping them. He wanted to concentrate only on the really bad violators.

Unfortunately, they hadn't witnessed any really bad violators for the first few days. His Coach almost went crazy. He tried to work with this Cadet's unusual philosophy but after a couple more days of only stopping a handful of violators, decided to end the Coaching trip. He told the Trooper Cadet to report back to the Academy immediately. Once the Cadet reached the Academy, he was fired.

*   *   *

At the end of the two-week Coaching trip everyone returned to the Academy for refresher training. The Coaches had critiqued our performance and provided feedback on where we needed to improve.

In my case, my Coach suggested I needed to be firmer with traffic violators and more aggressive in my driving. The part about needing to be a more aggressive driver hurt my feelings. Other then that, all but two of us were recommended for graduation.

*   *   *

It was time to become a State Trooper. The whole class was in full uniform. We had our assigned patrol cars lined up in a row according to our personnel/badge number—low to high. Each patrol car's license plate number reflected our badge number. For example, if my badge number were 435, the license plate would read WSP 435.

The trunks of the cars were full of equipment, and the back seats stuffed with extra uniforms and personal clothing. We were led from the Academy to the State Capitol for the graduation ceremony. It was pretty impressive seeing twenty-five State Patrol cars in a row heading to Olympia. Our families and friends were already at the Capitol.

Upon our arrival we marched in and formed on the stairs in the rotunda. A State Supreme Court Justice swore us our oath of service, and then the Governor congratulated us and issued our commission papers. After the ceremony we all met at a local restaurant for a luncheon with our families, and afterward, headed to our new assignment.

Half my class went to cities all over eastern Washington, the rest were assigned to counties in the immediate Puget Sound region. I considered myself lucky to be working on the west side of the mountains because that's where the action was. I was assigned to the District office in Snohomish County. I couldn't wait to get started.

*   *   *

Shift Work

The State Patrol work schedule is fairly basic. Everyone works a nine-hour, with one hour off for lunch and two twenty-minute coffee breaks, just like any other state employee. There are, however, a few exceptions. For example, there can be four separate day shift schedules, and five or six different swing shifts, followed by a graveyard shift.

Each shift will last twenty-eight days. If I were working a day shift, after four weeks I would then rotate to a swing shift for four weeks, before switching to an evening shift. I knew I would be working a day shift every three months. One of the few day shifts had weekends off; the rest of the days off were in the middle of the week.

My favorite shift began at 6 a.m. because I enjoyed being the first one out on the road. The next favorite would be the 10 a.m. shift because I could sleep in. I liked the 6 p.m. shift, knowing this was the best time to get DWI's. If I got one after the bars closed at 2 a.m. I could process the drunk and make it home without having to put in any overtime.

In most parts of the state, we provided twenty-four-hour coverage every day of the week. The supervising staff had to take into account several things when scheduling their Troopers.

Most important was to have coverage all day by using three basic shifts; 6 a.m. to 3 p.m., 3 p.m. to midnight, and 10 p.m. to 6 a.m.

Other criteria considered was having the most Troopers possible working evenings on Friday and Saturday, when, more then likely, we'll find drunk drivers and injury accidents. A shortage of Troopers happened often, and could result in elimination of the graveyard shift.

The other hot times of day were the early morning and late afternoon traffic messes; the majority of traffic accidents happened when there was heavy traffic volume. This was when you'd find the most State Patrol cars on the road at any one time. If there were enough personnel, a few shifts would overlap each other, primarily to allow Troopers to go home after their shift, or to have a break for lunch.

When I first started, my Sergeant assigned me to work a day shift, knowing there would be ample coverage working the same shift, with other Troopers to assist me if I needed help. After a week or so I felt I was familiar enough with the local roads on my beat, so I informed my boss I could be trusted and left on my own. Stupid me.

This was when he assigned me to work the graveyard shift. What a bonus. Actually, it was not a bonus; no one wanted to work this damn shift. I would just have less chance of screwing up, with the lack of things to do. I had to remind myself that I needed to take baby steps first.

This shift as a rule was not a busy one. The taverns and bars closed at 2 a.m., and after that, it was absolutely dead out there until 6 a.m. There was no traffic to speak of for four lonely empty hours. I might have had a better chance of encountering a drunk driver working this shift, but that was about it until the traffic started back up again at 6 a.m.

My Sergeant was aware I had never worked a graveyard shift before, and would probably have difficulty staying awake. He told me, in a kind way, he would not tolerate me falling asleep behind the wheel of my patrol car and having an accident. The department had too much money invested in the patrol car. If I wanted to fall asleep while driving, then I had to do it in my own personal vehicle on my own time.

He did care, so his instructions to me before I started my first graveyard shift were, "If I ever start getting tired or sleepy, get out of the damn car, walk around it, and get some fresh air. If that doesn't work, get out and do some pushups, and if that doesn't work, then park the damned car and go to sleep. Please, don't have an accident."

I took his advice to heart and vowed I would never fall asleep while on duty. I had sworn an oath to uphold the law and I would do just that, plus I would not fall asleep.

As it turned out, the Sergeant wasn't too far off the mark. I had only been working five hours on my first graveyard shift when I hit the proverbial wall. I could not keep my eyes open. There was absolutely no traffic out and about. There was nothing for me to do; no accidents to investigate, nor any drunk drivers to arrest. I was toast. I knew I needed to pull over and stop, so I did. I got out of the car and walked around it.

Well, I thought, that was refreshing; I hopped back into the patrol car and went back on patrol. That is, for only two miles. My eyes wanted to shut again. I pulled over to the shoulder stopped, hopped out of the car and walked around it a couple of times and felt better. Off I went again.

This happened a couple more times, but I made it to the end of the shift without mishap. What a relief it was to make it home in one piece. I was already dreading the next shift. I thought if I took a nap before going to work, this would allow me to stay awake throughout the shift. At least it was worth a try.

The following day I hit the road at 10 p.m., refreshed. Super Trooper is ready, so bring it on. This feeling lasted until 4 a.m. For whatever reason, my eyeballs were not in sync with my attitude. They didn't care that I had a job to do. They just wanted to rest for a while. So, here I was again, walking around the damned car trying to avoid having an accident.

It was really bad this time. I actually got out of the patrol car, took off my gun belt, and did some pushups. All that did was make me more tired. I knew I was toast again. It was around 4:30 a.m. and I knew I had to get off the road and park the patrol car like my boss had said.

I felt had to find that perfect place where I could stop and rest and not have the patrol car too visible. I was concerned for my own safety, especially if I was asleep in the car, and someone wanted to do me harm.

I drove around for about half an hour, finally finding a closed service station where there was a car parked next to the building but far enough away so there was room for me to squeeze in the patrol car. I wouldn't be visible from the highway and with the other car right next to me, my doors couldn't be opened unless I pulled out of the space. Perfect.

I carefully backed into the spot with about a foot left on each side of the car. Ok, I'm thinking, this will work out just fine for me. I'll just take a quick thirty-minute nap and then get back to work until the end of the shift. I ran the seat back as far as would go, turned the radio volume up high so it would wake me if there was any emergency traffic, leaned back and fell asleep.

I heard a sound but couldn't quite make it out. The noise finally woke me, and I looked around, seeing it was the early morning traffic. I looked left into the office window of the service station and saw three guys standing there staring at me. Holy crap, I looked at my watch, it was 6:30 a.m. My shift ended thirty minutes ago. I pushed the seat forward, waved at the guys and drove off. I knew this would come back to haunt me.

I called Radio and asked if they had any traffic for me, and they didn't. I told them to sign me out of service, and headed home. At least I made it through the shift without getting into trouble, and no one ever complained about me sleeping at the service station.

*   *   *

This graveyard shift could be dangerous if I wasn't careful, so I needed to get my act together. It didn't take long for me to learn what worked best to keep me awake when working a graveyard shift. After getting home at 6 a.m., I forced myself to stay awake until around 9 a.m., and then slept until 3 p.m. After having dinner around 6 p.m., I would take a nap from 8 p.m. to 9 p.m.

*   *   *

Through the years I did just fine after my first embarrassing moment of getting caught sleeping while on duty. However, I do have one last episode to share. It happened during a severe winter when everything was frozen. The roads were icy and the snow was two feet high on the shoulders. The conditions were terrible. The temperatures were so low; hardly anyone in his right mind would be out driving. This was especially true during the hours of my graveyard shift.

So, here I was again with nothing to do. I patrolled my beat for disabled cars, but there were none. Even the drunks were smart enough to not be out and about. I was beginning to feel my eyelids getting heavy. Damn, I'm not going to have another problem staying awake, am I? I'm sure as hell not getting out of this warm car to do pushups. I'm thinking, I'm not going to embarrass myself like I did the time before.

I continued on patrol but I was on a mission now to find the perfect place to park if I felt I couldn't stay awake any longer. It would have to be a place where I would be centrally located on the beat, but not visible. Some place where someone could not sneak up on me. I finally found the perfect spot—an on-ramp to the freeway. This ramp had been built in the anticipation of the local population increasing. As it turned out, there never was an increase, so the ramp was not being used by anyone. I could see there weren't any tire tracks in the snow on the ramp so I felt it was safe enough to park there.

At around 5 a.m. I finally hit the wall. I had only one hour left to go before the shift ended, but I absolutely could not keep my eyes open so I headed to the on-ramp to park. I felt it would be safe enough knowing no one would see me there, especially at that time of morning.

I parked the patrol car at the top of the ramp, turned the radio volume up high, locked the doors, ran the seat back and immediately fell asleep. About forty-five minutes had passed when my subconscious registered a rumbling sound that eventually woke me up.

I couldn't figure out where the noise was coming from until I realized it was diesel engines I was hearing. It sounded like a train passing by. I looked around, saw nothing until I looked in my review mirror and saw three highway department sand trucks parked behind me with their motors running. All the drivers were sound asleep. I snuck away and went home.

*   *   *

My mind set was to approach each shift differently whether it was the morning, swing, or graveyard shift. Take, for example, the day shift beginning at 6 a.m. I knew I would be the only one on duty for the next hour or two. If there were going to be a traffic accident, it would happen during this first one-hour period.

When I stepped out of the house to start work I had to have my act together. In a way it was kind of exhilarating. Everything and everyone was dependent on my being ready to do my job. I liked the feeling. I couldn't wait to get going on the early shift. If the weather was bad, I knew there would be some sort of action. I just had to be patient and wait for it to happen.

If the first part of the early shift went without mishap, I just worked the traffic congestion. Eventually other Troopers would be signing in service at different times, and when they did, it took the pressure off me. The only negative to working an early shift was it worked best if I took my lunch break around 10 a.m. This really screwed things up for having to wait until the family had dinner, around 6 p.m. That was a long eight hours, especially if I was not allowed any donuts during that time gap.

*   *   *

The swing shift generally began late in the afternoon, and went until late in the evening. This shift was kind of a mixed bag. First, it began around the start of the heavy afternoon traffic rush. I had to anticipate there would be traffic accidents and wait for them to happen. Once we worked our way through rush hour, it was time to arrange to have my mid-shift meal, or a late dinner with the family.

Returning to work after dinner, it would normally be dark. This was the time when shit happened. I had to be more alert, and be more careful. Of the three shifts, this one would more than likely result in my putting in overtime. Fatalities and DWI's were the main reason for having to work beyond the end of a shift.

The late shift was the one that excited me most. I knew something exciting would happen, regardless of what day of the week it was. This was when the adrenalin flowed. There would be routine DWI's, an occasional reckless driver, kids racing, accidents of all kinds, and fights. This shift could feel like it lasted only ten minutes, because I'd be that busy. Many times I had gone without a meal because there just wasn't time to eat.

Even though people may think my job was abnormal because of the different shifts I had to work,

I'm here to tell you, I would have been bored to tears if I hadn't had the variety and the constant change in working hours.

My job was incredible, every day different, and no two alike. It didn't get any better than that.

Patrol Preparation

Every day, without exception, I had to be organized before I signed in service with Radio. I had to have a clear head, be alert and mentally prepared for what could become the worst day of my life. I had to approach every day the same way. If I became lax or inattentive, others or myself could be hurt.

After leaving the house I walked around the patrol car checking the tires to make sure they were properly inflated, and looked for something amiss or not normal. For example, a Trooper who lived about three blocks away from me spotted two sticks of dynamite underneath his patrol car when he did his walk around one morning. Believe it or not, the patrol car was a magnet for trouble when parked in front of our homes, day or night. I never relaxed my guard when the patrol car was at my house.

Once I pulled out into the street I was officially on duty. There was no driving to the office, no stopping to visit friends, no gassing up the car, no time for a cup of coffee. I immediately start looking for traffic violations. Troopers cannot ease into their workday because it can't be done.

It was not unusual to sign in service with Radio and have the dispatcher respond with accident information I had to respond to immediately. So, two minutes into my shift I was already driving fast with the siren and emergency lights on. No "Good morning Super Trooper, have a nice day."

*   *   *

When I first started patrolling the state highways I worried about everything—safety issues involving myself, the safety of others, equipment failure, crashing the patrol car, and on and on.

For the first few months on the job, the stress of trying to be perfect and not make a mistake took its toll. However, once I got into the routine of things, I began to relax. When I did, the headaches I had been plagued with ended.

*   *   *

The Academy Pursuit Course instructors taught me to drive with my hands positioned on the steering wheel in what's called the relaxed position; right hand at 12 o'clock and the left hand at the 9 o'clock position. If I had to drive fast, I would then reposition my hands to the 10 o'clock and 2 o'clock positions.

*   *   *

Probably the most stressful time was when Radio had a report of an injury accident. All available Troopers would let Radio know their current location, and if I was the closest one to the accident scene, the pressure was on me to get there as soon as possible. We never knew the seriousness of the injuries, because the policy for the communication officers was never to report how bad it was.

Even though a Radio operator may be aware an accident involved a fatality, this information would never be broadcasted. What purpose would it serve? If they were to provide this information it would add to the stress of the situation and indirectly cause a Trooper to drive faster and possibly place him and others in danger.

I will admit, as will all other Troopers, when there was a report of an injury accident, just the word "injury" gave me an adrenalin rush. Nothing else mattered until I arrived at the scene of the accident. Despite this feeling, I never looked forward to it, and fortunately, it did not happen more then five to ten times a month.

When I was aware there were injuries, I needed to process how far I had to travel to reach the scene, how many minutes it would take me, if I would encounter heavy traffic conditions, or if I would need to run with my red lights and siren on.

Most importantly, how fast would I be able to travel safely without endangering others? I could use the siren to clear traffic out of the way, but there were times this could be a hindrance. People do stupid things when they see a police car coming up behind them at a high rate of speed with the emergency equipment flashing and siren blaring.

When I was running hot like this, I didn't have a clue how other drivers would respond to my emergency run. I could only assume from experience the driver in front of me could react by pulling over to the shoulder to stop and allow me to go by. Or, he could slow down in my lane of travel, waiting to see what I really wanted him to do.

I'm sure there was other choices I'm forgetting, but it sure could be frustrating and very stressful making an emergency run. I wished it wasn't against patrol policy to give these ignorant souls the finger when not yielding to an emergency vehicle.

*   *   *

It took me awhile to realize there wasn't any way to completely prepare for each workday. The stress, the excitement, the unexpected, would happen regardless of how I felt or prepared for work. So I took one day at a time and lived for the moment.

First Assignment
(Probationary Year)

In the back of my mind, I knew the next twelve months would be the most telling of my life. The probationary period was just that, a period of time where I would be judged for my conduct and job performance. If I made bad decisions and did not perform well, I could be fired without cause. This bit of pressure kept me on my toes.

I was assigned to what might be considered an outpost location, working east Snohomish County all the way to the summit of Stevens Pass. I was the only Trooper working this fifty-mile stretch of state highway for a twenty-four hour period, seven days a week.

My patrol beat included most of Snohomish County and part of King County. Regardless of my shift schedule, I was on call twenty-four hours a day. I had to take and respond to emergency calls even on my days off.

Over the first year working this beat I was called out on an average of three times a month. In my day, we were not paid overtime, so the State of Washington was very fortunate to have this free additional service.

*   *   *

My routine would begin when I signed in service and left my residence. I ended the shift when I arrived back home and signed out of service with Radio. Radio documented my in and out of service times. The patrol car remained at my residence until I signed in service the following day. I was responsible for the car's upkeep and maintenance. I washed the car at home and normally changed the oil on my days off. If I were away on vacation, the patrol car would be stored at the detachment or district office for safekeeping, or for other Troopers to use during my absence.

*   *   *

After I was assigned to my first Detachment, I rented a home in a nice neighborhood. I was proud of my new job and position; however, I was surprised at the community's response once I moved in. I didn't realize the patrol car would be a giant flashing beacon twenty-four hours a day. Everyone saw it and knew when I was on duty or not. That aside, the town's population was around 900. Ten percent of the residents were either parolees from the State Reformatory in Monroe, or were related to an inmate at the Reformatory. Let my WSP education begin.

*   *   *

Eventually the neighbors learned my work schedule. Most residents saw the patrol car as a deterrent to transients and were happy for me to be living there. But, as always, there was a minority who saw the patrol car and me as a challenge, or an annoyance affecting their life style. Like I really cared. I preferred to be left alone. It would be nice too if everyone would like me, but my new job prevented this from happening.

If there was a local problem with young neighborhood kids, my neighbors automatically assumed I was responsible for handling this 'trouble.' In the beginning I was more than happy to do this. It took awhile to learn these little annoyances affected my family's quality of life. However, over time I became more selective about what I was willing to undertake, because the issues happened mostly while I was off duty or on my days off.

*   *   *

In the beginning being on call twenty-four hours a day was exciting. I was eager and ready to respond to anything—just call me, I'll go. I didn't want to get too far from the house in case Radio wanted to reach me, so I became my own prisoner.

As it turned out, it wasn't fun at all waiting for something that may never happen. It took three months before I worked my way through being over-zealous.

I did learn to have my uniform assembled and hanging on a clothing rack, gun belt on the dresser, so all I had to do was back up to it and hook it around my waist. I would slip into my shoes and put on my jacket as I walked out the door.

From the moment I hung up the phone I could be in the patrol car in ten minutes fully

uniformed, ready to go. If I had to, I could
shave in the car while enroute. Whenever the
phone rang after 11 p.m., I was instantly
awake. I knew I was going somewhere quickly.

*   *   *

My first patrol beat was considered a rough
and tough neighborhood primarily because of
the local logging industry. My Sergeant warned
me this would be a difficult beat to patrol.
He said he was constantly getting complaints
of speeding log trucks. He was sick and tired
of this and wanted me to go out and kick
some butt. I interpreted that to mean issue
tickets.

I was the new kid on the block, so I had to
be careful because the loggers are a very
independent ornery group of people. They work
hard and play hard. I was told if I were fair
but firm in my enforcement, I would eventually
earn the log truck driver's respect. Easier
said then done.

*   *   *

Speeding complaints were the common denominator
with logging trucks. My beat consisted of long
stretches of a two-lane state highway with
no turns or hillcrests. I knew it would be
nearly impossible to enforce any speed laws.
To succeed, I would have to be innovative and
sneaky.

I quickly learned log truck drivers take care
of one another, and they do that by talking to
each other using their CB radios. They radioed

each other constantly letting each other know where I was parked, patrolling, or having a coffee break.

The reason truck drivers drive fast is money. The more log runs they can make to the mill, the more money they will make. Normally a driver will make two runs a day. If he has the opportunity to drive as fast as he can, he could possibly squeeze in a third run. The incentive to earn more is there, no denying it. I don't want to deny them making extra money, but when they endanger everyone else on the highway trying to make it, I take issue.

Over my fifty-mile stretch of highway there could be ten to fifteen log trucks traveling in either direction at any one time. With their CB radio chatter, they had a picture of my beat at all times of the day. When they spotted me patrolling in a certain area, they would disclose my location to the other truck drivers. They essentially painted me with what we call a "halo."

The halo effect had everyone complying with traffic laws one mile in front of me and one mile behind me, thus the halo. The log trucks would slow down when they approached me from the rear, and would speed up after I had turned off and went in a different direction.

I had very little success for the first few months trying to prevent the log trucks from speeding. Maybe four or five times a month, I might catch a log driver with his guard down, and issue a ticket for speeding, but normally, they ruled the road. This was a game with them and I didn't like it. I needed to change the rules of engagement.

*   *   *

Living in a small town was a strike against me. Everyone knew if I was at home or working the road. I either was working a day shift or evening shift. Very simple to figure out where I was. With my Sergeant's blessing I decided to change my routine a bit. I knew the log truck drivers started their loaded runs to the mill around 4 a.m. to 5 a.m.

With that in mind I decided to set up with the radar on a stretch of highway where the trucks were notorious for speeding. Since it was still dark out at this hour so I knew I would be difficult to see.

I would only catch two or three speeding log trucks before the word got out on the CB radios, so I would shut down and go home for a couple of hours then go back out and finish up the rest of my day shift.

Over a period of three or four weeks with adjustments to my working hours, I must have bagged, I mean issued twenty citations to log truck drivers for speeding. Now when I say speeding, I mean 15 to 25 mph over the posted limit. Regardless, the word was out I was working different hours, so the drivers were more careful. It was to the point now where I had to try something different.

*   *   *

Just before I quit adjusting my early morning working hours, I was at a different location of highway, an area that hadn't been worked before, seeing what I might stir up. I wasn't expecting anything to happen, but I was curious. I set up at 4 a.m. on a straight stretch. I parked my patrol car on top of an embankment looking down on the highway, and saw two pairs of headlights coming down the road toward me.

It appeared one log truck was passing another log truck. They entered my radar beam at 80 mph in a 55 mph zone running side by side. I'll be damned. To see one running fast was believable, but not two of them at the same time. I waited for them to pass by before taking off after them. They didn't see me because I was still on the hillside. Off I went after them.

Before I could even catch up to them, they had rounded a curve still side by side. When they disappeared out of sight, I assumed one of the trucks would hit another car head-on, but it didn't happened. I caught up and stopped the two log trucks. The drivers were flabbergasted, they couldn't figure out where I had come from. From what I saw, they ran side by side for almost two miles. I cited them both for reckless driving.

*   *   *

I thought long and hard of a different approach to log truck enforcement, but couldn't come up with a better idea. I decided to quit worrying about the speeding trucks. I would, instead, enforce all violations whether a moving traffic violation, or an equipment violation. Log trucks are notorious for having equipment violations, so I would start with that. Actually, I have to give myself a pat on the back because this idea really proved to be the most successful.

Almost all log trucks have some sort of defective equipment, ranging from a burned out light bulb in a turn signal, a headlight out, defective wiper—stuff I wouldn't normally write an arrest citation for, but rather a warning ticket. I reasoned I was actually helping the drivers out by informing them of their truck's defective equipment. They may not thank me for this service, but I enjoyed helping them out.

I began stopping every log truck I could find that had some minor problem, or for any minor traffic infraction the driver might have committed. This was easy pickings because no one is perfect.

I was almost able to stop every log truck I saw. Not one got by me. I mentioned earlier how important it is for the drivers to get as many loads as possible to the mill. My stopping them for every little picky violation, that they called chicken shit stuff, really hampered their timing.

I felt the need to take extra time out of my busy day to explain how their minor transgressions could cause accidents, time being the key word here. If a taillight were not working, then I would walk around the rig and check all the other equipment. This little tour of mine took an excruciating amount of time to complete.

Any time I stopped a car for defective equipment it would only take five minutes to discuss the merit of making the repair to the driver. However, with log truck drivers I wanted to be more considerate by explaining why these particular laws existed, and the reasons we enforced them. This little dissertation of mine could last as long as twenty to twenty-five minutes, time they couldn't afford to waste.

After two months of working my special emphasis on equipment issues, a really pissed-off log truck driver approached me one day and asked why I was harassing him and the other drivers. I filled him in about the constant complaints the State Patrol was getting involving speeding log trucks.

"You know as well as I do, every log truck driver is speeding. If they don't slow down and do the speed limit, then I'm forced to concentrate on equipment violations whenever I notice them." The message was well received and we all became reasonably good friends after that, and there was a noticeable drop in log truck speeding complaints.

* * *

Another thing the Academy staff pounded into our heads was, whenever we stopped someone for a traffic violation, we have to decide on a course of action before exiting the patrol car. If we decided to issue an arrest citation, then we had to stay the course, and not waver from that decision; bottom line—not be influenced by other circumstances and change your mind.

I understood this philosophy and hadn't yet encountered a situation where I might have been tempted to change my mind, until one hot summer day. I had been working the road for about two months now and was still wet behind the ears, a babe in the woods so to speak.

I had been following a Ford convertible that had its top down, for a short distance and finally got a pace of 10 mph over the posted speed limit. Anyone I caught driving at least 10 mph over the posted limit automatically received a citation for speeding. In this case, there would be no exception; it was just a matter of informing the driver of his violation, writing the ticket, and being done with it.

The driver in this case was a female. Boy was she a female. She was beautiful and was wearing a loose fitting halter showing a great amount of cleavage. She also wore what I would call really short, shorts displaying the most beautiful set of legs I have ever seen. Her voice would melt butter on a cold day. She was the complete package.

Even though I felt in control of the situation, I was speechless. I kind of forgot why I stopped her. Finally, I gathered myself and explained. She was so sweet and friendly, was very apologetic for her transgression, and promised to slow down for the rest of her gorgeous life. My heart told me this was the truth.

Following procedure I asked for her driver's license and told her I would go back to my patrol car to record this information, and then let her be on her way if she promised once again to slow down. She crossed her beautiful heart and said she would.

When I got back in the patrol car I looked at her driver's license for the first time and saw it had been expired for over a year. This was not good news for her, and it embarrassed me for saying she wasn't going to get a ticket; I knew had to draw the line somewhere. I finally got the blood flowing back to my head and realized I must do my job. I wrote her a ticket for the expired license, and went back to her car to have her sign the ticket.

I explained to the young lady that I had decided to give her break on the speed but was issuing a ticket for the expired license. She responded, "What, you're giving me a fucking ticket? Why you shithead, you goddamn fucking asshole, I hope you die in hell, thanks a fucking lot." She signed the ticket and drove off. After I got over my shock, I better understood why the decision must be made before leaving the patrol car. Lesson learned.

*   *   *

I'm a die-hard University of Washington football fan, and during the fall it seemed I was always working a day shift on game day. At the time, our patrol cars did not have AM/FM radios so I bought a portable radio and duct-taped it to the dash of my patrol car.

Even with the antenna sticking out the passenger window, reception was terrible. The only time I would get a decent signal was when I was traveling either west or south. Fortunately my beat had two state highways; the primary highway traveled east and west. The other, a secondary state highway, ran north and south. They intersected with each other on the western boundary of my patrol area.

I thought this would be a piece of cake; all I had to do to listen to the game without interruption was to patrol in those directions with the best reception. At the start of the game I began my patrol from the east end of the beat traveling west. When I reached the west end of the beat I headed south. Of course I would stop violators on the way, but they would be quick stops.

If there was a commercial break, or a time out, or at halftime, I would turn around and head in the opposite direction as fast as I could reasonably go, then turn around and head back when the game re-started. It was a very long unusual patrol method I used on Saturdays, but it worked for me, and I was visibly working. Fortunately for everyone, the season only lasted three months.

*   *   *

One Saturday while working a day shift in the fall I received a report of a car-deer accident with minor injuries involved. I was surprised at the location as it was in a heavily populated area. I raced to the scene and as I approached and slowed down I observed a car parked on the shoulder with front-end damage and a couple standing by the side of the car.

I could see the deceased deer lying in the ditch near the car.

This couple turned out to be husband and wife. I could see where the man was injured with a cut lip, and bruises about his face. The knuckles on his fists were cut and bleeding. Suddenly I'm wondering why he had these types of injuries, when it was the car that hit the deer, and there was only front-end damage. I was not sure how a car hitting a deer could have caused this.

Before I could ask how the accident happened, the wife said her husband was just in a fight. I asked whom he was fighting because there wasn't anyone else around. She said, after hitting the deer, both of them pulled the dead animal off the road and had flagged someone down to go and report the accident to the State Patrol.

Meanwhile, while waiting for a Trooper to show up, another car pulled up in front of the couple's car and a guy got out and went to check on the deer. He said out loud it looked like the deer meat was okay, because the deer died from a head injury. At this point he started dragging the animal back to his pickup. My accident victim asked him where in the hell he was going with the deer. The other guy said he was taking it home to butcher it to save the meat.

My guy says, "No way in hell." He needed the deer left here so the State Patrol could verify the accident was unavoidable, and this information would help his claim for damages with his insurance company. The other guy said, "Bullshit," he was taking it anyway. My guy took issue with this and they got into a fistfight. My guy won. The other guy left the scene before my arrival, without the deer.

* * *

One winter I was assigned to work Stevens Pass. One of my responsibilities was to park near the chain-up sign whenever it was posted, requiring chains on all cars and trucks attempting to cross the pass. In theory, the appearance of my patrol car parked at the sign should have been enough encouragement for drivers to chain up as required. However, when I was not parked there as a deterrent, there were drivers who ignored the chain requirement. This was when accidents happened.

* * *

I was assigned to work the pass while the other Trooper, assigned to the pass full time, was on his days off. I was told to keep a lid on everything and just patrol around looking important.

It was virtually impossible to stop anyone anyway when the road conditions were compact snow and ice. There were no shoulders to pull anyone over because of the snow banks created by the snowplows. For me this was a relaxing time.

One day while parked at the chain-up sign, a motorist pulled up alongside me, rolled his window down and asked if he could chain up the front wheels instead of the rear ones since his car had front wheel drive. "Of course you can," I told him, and he drove off to my front and proceeded to chain up. I was distracted by something so I never noticed him chaining up nor did I notice him leave.

About forty-five minutes later I received a report of a one-car rollover accident about two miles up the pass from where I was. I took off and a few minutes later found this guy standing by himself on the shoulder pointing down over the embankment, probably meaning that was where his car was. Sure enough, as I got out of the car I could see his car upside down in a creek bed.

At this moment I recognized this guy as the one who asked me earlier if he could chain up the front wheels of his car. I asked him what happened. He wouldn't look me in the eye because he was too embarrassed about what had happened.

He finally told me, he was so excited about going up to ski he forgot to chain up the front wheels, and instead chained the rear ones by habit. Being a trained investigator, it was easy to realize the car had no traction without chains on the front wheels, and that sometimes skiers are not very smart.

*   *   *

Another time I was assigned to work the pass for two days. Instead of using my patrol car, I used the other Trooper's patrol car because it had an additional radio, primarily to communicate with the highway department's snow removal crews who had their own radio set up. This second radio enabled me to connect with the snow removal crews in case of an emergency. The Highway Department's base station was at the summit of the pass and that was where the crew was housed during the winter.

I was parked near the posted chain-up sign when a motorist stopped and told me he needed to get to the summit to contact his friend and deliver an important message, and would I allow him to pass without installing chains. I said, "Are you kidding me, chains are required, doesn't that mean anything to you?" Now mind you this guy had skis mounted on the top of his car. I assumed he was just trying to avoid having to chain up his car. Does the word lazy come to mind?

This guy was not going to give up. Next he told me he was an experienced driver in these sorts of road conditions and had never had a problem in the past. Using my firm Trooper voice I informed him the sign was posted for a reason and I would strictly enforce those who violated it, and for him to quit arguing and chain up.

Mr. Obnoxious tried to bluff me by saying the message he needed to deliver was now of an emergency nature. Of course I didn't believe him. I held firm and told him to just chain up and go deliver his important message. He asked, "Why can't you take me up to the summit?" I told him, "I'm assigned to stay here to enforce the chain sign. I am not a taxi service."

My new best friend was undaunted and was not going to give up and asked, "Well then, why can't you use one of your radios to relay my message?"

I told him the WSP radio was to be used for emergency traffic only, and his problem didn't qualify. He said, "You have two radios why can't you use the other one?" I told the guy this radio was also for emergency traffic only. It belonged to the highway department and I could only use it if there was a traffic accident on the pass, not for relaying personal messages.

As soon as the words were out of my mouth, the cook at the summit office using this same radio, called down to the district office placing his order for food for the crew for the following week; "I need ten dozen eggs, eight loaves of bread, eight gallons of milk, twenty pounds of hamburger . . ." After hearing this, the guy just stared at me for a minute then left. What could I say, if the crew didn't have food, they would die.

*   *   *

My academy class, regardless of where everyone was assigned, stayed in touch. By nature we were a competitive group and were constantly asking each other what we have experienced, how many drunk drivers have we arrested, or have there been any high-speed chases.

One particular category that concerned us was the experience of investigating a traffic fatality, or any incident involving a death. We all knew eventually we'd be exposed to

death. It was the nature of our job. How we
responded or reacted to this exposure was the
big question. We all worried about it until it
happened. It could not be avoided.

In a later chapter I will discuss traffic
fatalities, however my first encounter with
death happened a couple of months after I
started working the beat. I was on routine
patrol on a sunny afternoon. Traffic was light
everyone was traveling legally. It was such
a slow day; boredom was taking its toll on
me. There were always days like this, and I
was beginning to understand that I just had
to learn to relax, and go with the flow. This
time I was having trouble staying awake.

Radio woke me to report an abandoned vehicle
parked off the state highway on a familiar
dirt road. The road lead down to a favorite
parking spot for fishermen. I'm assuming this
was someone fishing, but I had to check it out
anyway, so I headed in that direction. I was
the closest patrol, so I let the dispatcher
know I would handle the call.

I reached the location and exited off the
highway, working my way down the dirt road for
about a quarter of a mile, until I noticed the
car in question. I was surprised we even got
a call on this, because from the highway you
would never have noticed the car, considering
where it was parked. Also, where was the person
who called it in? This didn't smell right, so
I was on point now, being more careful.

I stopped the patrol car about twenty feet
away and get out. The abandoned car was facing

me. I didn't see anyone inside, so I walked around the car to see what was behind it. When I got to the rear of the car I saw a black flex hose running from the rear exhaust pipe into the back window on the opposite side of the car. The window was closed to the point where the pipe entered. The car's motor was not running.

I knew this was not going to end well. I rushed up to the car until I could see inside, and there was a male lying down lengthwise in the front seat. The doors were locked so I found a large rock and broke out the driver's window, reached in and unlocked the door. There was a strong odor of exhaust coming from inside. I checked for a pulse but there wasn't one. The body was cold and stiff as a board. The man had been deceased for a while.

I had an ambulance dispatched to take him away. I checked his car and found a suicide note on the front floorboard. I sent the note with the body. The only thing really left to do was to have the car impounded. I had now been exposed to my first suicide investigation. Not the last one by far, but very unnerving.

*   *   *

Being a State Trooper living in a small town did come with baggage. First, a patrol car in the driveway stood out like a sore thumb. When the kids saw the car in the driveway they assumed I was not on duty so they passed by my house racing, very frustrating.

Vandalism to the patrol car can be a problem, so I tried to be vigilant. The local Police Chief's patrol car was disabled because someone had put sugar in the gas tank, destroying the car's engine. So, I went out and bought two locking gas caps—not only for the patrol car, but also for my personal car.

*   *   *

One part of the job I enjoyed was working an emphasis patrol. The supervisor gathered as many of us as he could, then concentrated this gaggle of Troopers to work a five-mile stretch of highway. The intent was to stop every motorist who had committed an infraction no matter how minor it might be—a defective brake light, failing to signal, or even driving five miles over the posted limit.

The appearance of several Troopers working together in such a concentrated area made a statement with the motoring public and the local community. The general public didn't have a clue what we were doing, but it was impressive seeing us chasing and stopping cars all over the place. Friends have told me it was as though there were Troopers coming out of the woodwork. They were everywhere.

I have to admit it was a pretty impressive display of force. We scared the hell out of everyone. For us, it really wasn't difficult finding something wrong with someone's driving, or possibly something wrong with a car's equipment. Most of our stops did not result in a citation—maybe a warning ticket—but that was about the extent of our enforcement. Most drivers I've contacted during an emphasis patrol asked what was going on. I explained what we were doing, and they thought it was a great idea, and we should do it more often.

Every once in a while we encountered an expired or suspended driver's license, a car with defective equipment that had to be impounded, or, once in a blue moon, a DWI.

*   *   *

I was called out around 4 a.m. one morning to investigate a one-car roll over accident. The report mentioned the injured party had left the scene and the tow truck operator was standing by. In most one-car accidents late at night, if the driver is not standing by waiting, he is probably intoxicated, or trying to avoid getting a ticket.

Upon my arrival at the scene I could see the car lying upside down in a ditch. There wasn't much for me to do but wait while the tow truck driver pulled the car out of the ditch and righted it. Meanwhile I decided to take measurements of the skid marks. Obviously this driver was going too fast and lost control. Considering the time of morning, I figured the driver probably had too much to drink, but I wouldn't be able to prove it.

While taking the measurements I happened to notice money floating in the ditch that was filled with water from a recent rain. I turned on my flashlight to look further up the ditch and saw where there must have been ten to fifteen twenty dollar bills floating around.

I just assumed they belonged to the driver of this accident, and went to collect them.

They were everywhere, in the ditch, up on the shoulder, and on the road. The tow truck guy helped me collect the bills. We gathered up $280 worth of twenty-dollar bills. I put them in an envelope and the tow guy and I each initialed the envelope and the amount collected. I left the envelope with the tow person as part of the inventory of the contents of the car I had impounded for safekeeping.

A few days later a complaint was filed against me for stealing the driver's money. My Sergeant told the complainant that we had the money in evidence at the tow company and it could be claimed there. The complainant said there were some missing bills. He was told that we collected what was found.

The Sergeant asked if it was possible he had spent some of it, maybe on liquor? The complainant thought about it, and agreed that might have been the case. The driver withdrew his complaint against me.

One month later I stopped a driver I suspected was driving while intoxicated. I had him perform the physical tests, which he failed. I placed him under arrest and put him in the back of the patrol car, then went forward to inventory the car before it was impounded for safe keeping.

While conducting an inventory of the car's contents I noticed an envelope on the car's dashboard. It was stamped and ready to be mailed to the State Patrol district office where I worked. I asked my prisoner if he wanted me to mail his letter. He said, "Oh, I almost forgot, it's a thank you letter for this Trooper who helped me find money that I lost in a ditch when I rolled my car."

"Hey, I said, that's very nice of you. Thank you for your honesty, because I'm that Trooper." "Oh wow, really?" he responded. I asked him if he wanted me to mail the letter for him since it was already stamped. "Never mind" he said, "I'll mail it when I get out of jail." I never received the letter. My Sergeant said I should have taken the letter myself and mailed it.

*   *   *

One evening working a swing shift, I had a police officer from a local police department ride with me. It was good practice to have other police officers ride with me to form a good working relationship, and indirectly, as a recruiting tool for the State Patrol, looking for quality applicants.

As we traveled down one long dark stretch of highway, we hadn't seen any traffic for the last couple of miles, when we suddenly passed a pedestrian walking down the centerline. We barely missed this person by two feet—a woman wearing dark clothing. I had my headlights on low beam, so I didn't see her until it was nearly too late. This scared the hell out of both of us.

I immediately turned on my emergency lights, hit the brakes hard, did a U-turn and went back to this woman. As I pulled up behind her, she continued walking down the centerline, totally ignoring my red flashing lights.

Maybe walking is too strong of a word—staggering would best describe her gait. I pulled up alongside her, driving at her pace and asked where she was going. She never acknowledged the patrol car or me. She just kept walking. She was drunk as a skunk.

The officer riding with me said he knew the woman and that she was noted for having a drinking problem. Since she wasn't going to talk to me, or quit walking, I pulled ahead and parked the patrol car on the shoulder. Both of us got out of the car and waited for her. The woman stopped on the centerline when she approached us.

She told us she was just fine, and to leave her alone. I informed her she was a hazard to traffic, obviously drunk, and I was placing her under arrest for public intoxication. She told me she was not going to be arrested, so I began to escort her to the patrol car. She resisted by pulling away.

I should mention this woman was about 5'1" and weighed around 250 pounds, give or take a couple of pancakes. It was like dealing with a walking bowling ball. My partner and I grabbed both arms and crab walked her to the patrol car. She kicked at us and dragged her feet all the way.

She kept calling us sons-of-bitches, and telling us to leave her alone. We finally walked her over to the back door to put her in the back seat. No way was she going to get in quietly. Not only was she quite strong—trying to wedge her shape into the car was almost impossible. We struggled for a few minutes with her to no avail. I was trying to figure out a way to get her to come along quietly without having to mace her.

My partner, the city police officer, kept calling the woman by her first name, and telling her to give it up and get in the car. "No way in hell," she said. "I'm not going to jail." He grabbed her by one of her nipples and pinched down and twisted. Apparently there's a lot of pain when you pinch a nipple like he did and she became very cooperative, and quickly got into the back seat without mishap.

I was happy the woman was finally in the car, but I was also thinking this new come-a-long maneuver I just witnessed would not pass the smell test with my Sergeant. I felt this method of arrest would certainly result in a complaint. Regardless, I had her in the car now and asked the Sheriff's Office to dispatch a female matron to escort this woman to the jail, which they did. I felt an enormous relief when we got her out of my patrol car.

After we released the prisoner to the matron, my rider asked me if I had any uniforms in for cleaning. "No I don't, why do you ask?"

"Well," he said, "this woman works at the local dry cleaner and once she sobers up, heaven help anyone who has a uniform in there for cleaning." The dry cleaner he was referring

to was a local one where most of the local
Troopers took their uniforms for cleaning and
repair.

About a week later I was attending our monthly
detachment Trooper's meeting and noticed
one of the guys was really pissed off about
something. The Sergeant asked him what was
wrong. The Trooper said he just got his new
uniform trousers back yesterday after having
them hemmed. When he put them on this morning,
one leg was four inches too long and the other
side four inches too short.

Uh-oh, I forgot to tell everyone about the woman
I had arrested. I felt really badly about this
and told everyone what had happened with my
recent arrest. Everyone laughed except for this
one Trooper. Once word reached the ownership
of the laundry, the woman got fired.

*   *   *

Around ten months into my probationary year
I was cruising along feeling pretty good
about myself, like I hadn't really screwed
up yet. It looked like I was going to make it
off probation and be a full-fledged tenured
Trooper. That is, until around 9 a.m. when
Radio reported an incident involving a school
bus and directed me to contact the driver at a
shopping mall parking lot where he was standing
by. It seemed weird, but I headed over to the
mall. I arrived at the mall parking lot a few
minutes later and saw a public school bus full
of kids, and the driver standing outside. I
pulled up and parked. I approached the driver
and asked what the problem was. He informed me

he had a disruptive student on the bus that had been starting fights with the other kids.

The driver said he told the kid to sit down and be quiet, but he wouldn't, so, the driver decided to stop the bus and have the kid removed. Would I take him off the bus? Of course I would and I went into the bus where the driver pointed out a redheaded kid.

I motioned for the boy to follow me off the bus, which he did. I didn't say anything to him other then for him to hop in the back seat of my patrol car. I told the bus driver I would handle the situation and for him to go ahead and finish with his route.

Once in the patrol car I turned to the kid and asked what his problem was? He told me he got upset with one of the other boys on the bus who was giving him a bad time, so he was trying to knock his block off. I told him that's not the way to handle anger management issues, and for him to give me his student identification card.

I looked at the ID card to write down his name in my notebook. Oh shit! I looked at the name again and the kid's address turned around and looked at the kid, and suddenly a red flag popped up. Damn it, this has to be my Sergeant's son. I asked the kid where his dad worked. He was not feeling so good, his head was hanging down, and he mumbled that his dad worked for the State Patrol. Double Damn.

It should be known I feared my detachment Sergeant. He had a reputation for being a hard nosed and only saw things in black or white, with no gray, no deviation from the facts. I could never relax around him. Whenever he was around, I kept a very low quiet profile. No sense stirring up the beast in him. Did I mention I only had two months left to go on my probation?

I could tell the kid was really scared now, and he asked if I could just take him home and he would promise to be really good from now on. He apologized for his conduct and said it would never happen again. I thought, if I were his dad I would want to know about this. The question was, how to handle it.

I called Radio and asked if my supervisor was in service. They said yes, he was at the office. I asked that he contact me at my location ASAP. The Sergeant got on the radio and asked me the reason for the contact. I really didn't want to say why over the radio, so I said I needed assistance with a violator. Ok, he responded, he would be enroute. The son was scared shitless.

The Sergeant showed up and was about to ask me what the problem was when he saw his son sitting in the backseat of my patrol car. He yanked the door open and dragged his son out. "What the hell are you doing in one of my patrol cars," he yelled. The kid mumbled something. The dad said, "Get your butt home, now." They only lived about a mile away from where we were. The kid took off running.

The Sergeant turned to me and asked what his son had done wrong. I told him and he thanked me for my discretion, said he would take care of the problem, and promised it would never happen again. A couple of weeks later the son sent me a letter apologizing for his conduct and thanking me for not arresting him. Believe it or not, this little monster eventually became a Trooper.

*   *   *

I was taking a coffee break with another Trooper at a local hotdog stand. We were sipping Cokes at a picnic table when a car entered the graveled parking lot at a pretty good clip, and came to a sliding stop in front of our two patrol cars. The driver jumped out of the car and ran towards us yelling that his wife was having a baby, and he needed help.

We both jumped up and ran over to his car. Sure enough, his wife was in the back seat yelling that she was going to have the baby, now. This was going to be a first for the two of us. Since my partner's patrol car was the closest, we decided to move her to his car. My partner tossed me his keys and told me to drive and he'd get in the back seat with the pregnant woman.

I had the distraught husband hop in the front seat with me and we went to the hospital with the red light and siren on. I called Radio and had them inform the emergency room we'd be there in about three minutes.

The premature baby arrived in the patrol car. A week later I learned the child died soon after.

*   *   *

At this point, I'll jump forward a couple of years, when I requested a transfer to be closer to my hometown. I was sent to the Olympia detachment where I purchased my first home. My first exposure to being the new resident neighborhood cop involved a teenager who lived half a block away.

My house was located at the top of a "T" intersection. The bottom of the "T" was where the kid resided. He had just received his driver's license and was a terror on wheels. The complaints I received had him speeding, spinning his wheels, cutting donuts in intersections, failing to yield and running stop signs. All this happened within the first two or three weeks of him getting his license.

I would leave my beat on occasion, and drive through the neighborhood on the chance I might catch him doing something wrong, but my timing was always off. Neighbors would call me later and say they saw me drive around, but as soon as I left, the kid was back screwing around. I was at my wit's end. I was getting pissed. I had to find a way of stopping this little monster.

I approached his parents one day and told them about the complaints I had received from our neighbors. I assumed, since they both worked, they probably were not aware of their son's conduct. I recommended they get a handle on this kid, or he was going to wind up hurting someone. I explained what the consequences might be if I were to get involved, and that this could prove costly for them.

I didn't have a very good feeling after leaving the parents. It was like talking to a wall. They heard me but they weren't listening.

Only two days later I received another complaint about the kid. Enough is enough. I was going to nail this kid and it would not be a pleasant experience for him or his parents. I would feel better, but they wouldn't.

I lived in a house that had three garages. In one garage I just stored stuff. I normally parked my patrol car in front of the third garage. I had decided to re-organize my garages, and cleared out one side so I could later park the patrol car inside.

On my first day off, I backed the patrol car unnoticed into the extra bay. I hoped with the patrol car out of sight, the little monster would think I was away working.

This was in the middle of the week. The kid was in school and I figured he would be out of school and home by 3 p.m. Even though this was one of my regular days off, I put on the uniform after I had lunch, and went to the garage, got into the patrol car with a book, and waited. The top of the garage door had windows so I could see the bottom of the "T" where the kid lived. I didn't have to wait too long.

The school bus dropped several kids off in front of my house, including the monster. I saw him glance in my direction to see if the patrol car was there, and I knew, I had suckered him. I patiently waited while holding the garage door remote in my hand. The kid came out of his house about ten minutes later, hopped into his piece of junk and peeled rubber out of the driveway. I told myself to hold off, there would be more, so I waited a bit longer.

Sure enough he came sliding around through a turn as fast he could go. He came to a stop, revved up the motor and took off again, spinning the tires. Show time. I opened the garage door, hit the red lights and took off. He hadn't seen me yet. He had turned a corner to the right and was accelerating. I was right on his butt.

We are in a 25 mph zone and he was already up to 35 mph and going faster. At this moment he crapped his pants—he had seen me with the lights on.

The kid pulled over and stopped. Before I could say anything he asked me where I came from. I told him I just happened to be driving through the neighborhood and noticed him driving recklessly, and how this turned out to be my lucky day.

I informed him I had the responsibility to give him his first lesson in respect for his neighbors, parents, and the obligation to drive legally. I told him what the charges would be. First, speeding and spinning your wheels, meaning he didn't have total control of the car, and spinning in a circle at the last intersection.

Whenever I have three or more charges like this, I lump them together and issue a ticket for Reckless Driving. "You can't do that," he says. I sensed he had an attitude problem, so I told him to pay close attention and learn how the legal process works.

I placed him under arrest, handcuffed him and placed him in the back seat of the patrol car. I then had his car impounded and towed away. Normally I would leave the car if it were this close to the kid's house. However, I wanted to make a point with the parents, and the consequences of their lack of parenting skills. The cost of the tow would awaken them. After the tow truck left I transported the monster and incarcerated him in the juvenile center. He could only be released to his parents.

It must have taken two or three days for word of the arrest to filter its way through the neighborhood. I never looked for any thank you notes, or phone calls for doing my job. However, in this case, I did appreciate the several plates of cookies left at my front door. I love cookies.

Quotas/Profiling

If I haven't heard it a hundred times, I've heard it an annoying thousand times. We Troopers have a quota to adhere to in how many speeding tickets we must write up in a shift. This is the only reason we write so many—because of our "quota" system. How gullible can the public be? As it stands, we never receive credit for doing our job enforcing the speed limit, the one violation most attributed to causing accidents.

*   *   *

To even consider trying to fulfill a quota is damned near impossible. Let me explain how my time is spent with each violator I come into contact with.

I saw thousands of cars every day. The majority are doing something wrong. I mean hundreds of them were making small, inconsequential mistakes. I knew for a fact if I followed a driver over any distance, that person would make a mistake, whether a bad one or a simple one—it would happen. We all had a few bad driving habits. There were no perfect drivers, including myself.

I knew I couldn't stop hundreds of cars in one shift, let alone in a week's time. I processed what I saw, and concerned myself only with those people who made a serious enough mistake that could cause an accident, or would involve them in one. If I were to stop everyone I witnessed committing a violation, on a good day, time permitting, I might have been able to reach out to thirty drivers.

The number of contacts I made during a shift depended on circumstances over which I had no control. Stopping a violator took a few minutes, depending on whether the driver immediately responded to the red lights and pulled over, if traffic was not a hindrance.

Once we were stopped, it took two or three minutes for me to see if the car was stolen or wanted for anything, before I felt safe enough to exit my patrol car and approach the violator's car.

I contacted the driver and explained the violation, and asked to see the driver's license and the car's registration. This took another few minutes depending on the driver's ability to find his registration. If all went well, I released the driver with a verbal warning. The time taken was fifteen minutes.

If anything out of the ordinary were to happen—the driver didn't pull over right away, the registration was missing, or the driver's license was expired—these things added time to the contact. If it was necessary to issue a warning ticket or an arrest citation, more time was required before releasing the driver. The reality was, if I contacted ten to twelve violators a day, I felt I did a good day's work.

When I was not contacting violators, most of my time was spent assisting disabled motorists, or having to appear in court.

*   *   *

I'm officially telling the reader there has never been, nor will there ever be a quota system. It just doesn't make sense for any police department to implement such a stupid idea. The Troopers are not graded on how many cars they stop. Hell, they can stop as many cars as they wish.

I figure, of the twelve violators I stopped during a shift, three or four got an arrest citation; two or three, written warning tickets, and the rest were released with a verbal warning. There were days I issued ten arrest citations, and days when none were issued. In all the time I worked the road, my Sergeant never asked how many tickets I issued. His policy allowed Troopers to write as many tickets as they wanted to, but to always make sure they were quality arrests.

*   *   *

The United States Supreme Court ruled police officers could not use profiling as a tool to enforce the law. For example, if I observed two cars that appeared suspicious and decided to single out the one that was being driven by a minority, hoping to find something wrong that could lead to an arrest, this would have been considered profiling.

In my line of work, there never was a need to profile for criminal activity. In our business if I saw a violation, I stopped the driver. If I saw a suspicious car being driven by a minority, and I couldn't find a legal reason to stop it, I didn't, as frustrating as that might have been.

If I saw a driver acting suspiciously and felt a need to check the car out, I followed the car until I noticed a violation so I could legally pull the car over. It could be for as simple a reason as a defective brake light, or burned out license plate light, or the failure to signal a lane change. Why profile when it was not necessary?

Once I found a reason to stop the car, I informed the driver why they had been stopped. During our conversation I always looked inside the car for contraband or evidence of a crime. If the driver appeared nervous, I would bluntly ask if they had done something wrong.

Almost every time they would answer, "No, everything is ok." "Well, if you haven't done anything wrong, and I do believe you," I would ask, "then you wouldn't mind if I took a look in your car's trunk, would you?" I don't know why, but most drivers allowed me to search further. They always said, "Go ahead and look." I could now search by consent.

*   *   *

One of my fellow Troopers fell in behind a fairly new Dodge pickup truck, with California license plates, being driven by a Latino wearing a cowboy hat. Seeing this, and noticing decals of Brahma bulls posted on the windows, were signs the driver might be a possible member of the Sinaloa Cowboy's gang out of central Mexico. This was a very ruthless gang noted for transporting narcotics into our country. They favored Dodge pickups.

The driver was doing fine, very legal in the operation of his pickup. The truck was so new there weren't any equipment deficiencies to find. The Trooper followed the car for two or three miles and was about to give up and go in another direction, when suddenly the driver went three miles an hour over the posted speed limit. Well, damn, the Trooper's thinking, we can't have this driver disrespecting our traffic laws. He hit his red lights and pulled the pickup over.

As he walked up to the truck, the Trooper noticed gasoline dripping on the ground near where the gas tank should be. He bent down, looked underneath and saw the gas coming from a crack in the seam of the gas tank. This shouldn't be happening with a newer rig like this, but there was something else that didn't look right. There was a second gas tank.

The driver didn't speak English, or choose not to. Since the Trooper was not going to get an explanation for why there was a second tank, the Trooper impounded the truck, because it was leaking gas and was a hazard.

Since the driver committed a traffic offense, it wasn't necessary to profile the driver. The driver was cited and released and dropped off at the local bus station.

Afterward the Trooper obtained a search warrant on the premise the second gas tank was not factory installed and might contain narcotics contraband. They discovered fifty kilos of cocaine shrink—wrapped inside the second gas tank. The street value of the narcotic was nearly $500,000.

Judicial System

A Trooper was taught to gather as much evidence as possible. If the facts revealed a person had violated the law, he was arrested. There were no extenuating circumstances allowed, this is a black or white business. Every arrest I made was personal. If I did my job correctly, every person I arrested was guilty of that charge; otherwise I would never have charged the person.

If a driver were to contest one of my citations, he would be required to appear before a Magistrate, whether a City Court Judge, a Justice of the Peace, District Court Judge, or Superior Court Judge, depending on the seriousness of the charge.

*   *   *

When I started my career as a line Trooper, the first two or three judges I was required to work with were Justices-of-the-Peace (JP's). If I remember correctly, these officials were appointed or elected to the position. As far as I know, anyone could be a JP. There were no specific qualifications to become a Judge. All one could hope for was that this person would apply common sense to their judicial responsibilities.

The JP's handled almost all of the minor traffic violations and other misdemeanors. Serious misdemeanor violations were forwarded adjudicated by the Superior Court.

*   *   *

My outpost beat was overseen by the local Justice-of-the-Peace of the city I lived in and was my first exposure to working with any court. I assumed all Judges were the same, and followed the same rules. I later learned the JP system had a very relaxed way of resolving traffic and minor criminal cases. I was shocked at how relaxed the proceedings could be. I guess I had watched too many Perry Mason TV shows, and expected more structure and court decorum.

The Judges did not follow what I would call normal court procedures. Out in the boondocks, judicial rulings reflected the local communities' sense of justice. My first court experience reminded me of the old Wild West and Judge Roy Bean.

The first JP I worked with was a very nice man who owned a restaurant. He held court sessions in the back banquet room. When conducting court, for privacy between the main restaurant and his courtroom, he pulled the accordion-style doors closed. During a court session you could hear people ordering and eating in the next room. It was a distraction to me, and must have been to the defendants.

This judge would eventually become a good friend of mine. He respected my position in the community, and my professionalism, and felt I was trustworthy and truthful. I could do no wrong in his eyes.

This is an example of how crazy it could get in his court. On one occasion I issued a ticket to a driver who had passed another car on a bridge that had limited visibility, and was posted as a no—passing zone. To make matters worse, he began his pass at the beginning of a hill crest, even though he could not see ahead.

I was stuck in a long line of cars following the violator, and when I saw him begin his pass, I knew I was going to witness a fatality. However, he was lucky, since there was no oncoming traffic.

It took me several miles to pass the line of cars and catch up with the violator. When I finally was able to pull him over, he was shocked he was getting stopped. He thought he was driving legally. I explained he was being stopped for what happened several miles back. I explained he was had following too close, passed on the bridge that was posted a no-passing zone, and then, passed on a hillcrest without any visibility of oncoming traffic.

He responded he had been following a car that was driving too slowly and was impeding traffic; why hadn't I stopped that car? To make matters worse, the impeding car drove by us. My violator blew his stack, saying, "There he goes now, stop him." "I will," I said, "as soon as I finish up with you."

The driver's story was that when he saw there wasn't any traffic on the bridge, this was his first opportunity to pass the other car. He didn't see the no-passing sign, or the double yellow no-passing lines on the road. I knew he wasn't blind, otherwise he wouldn't be driving. He simply chose to ignore the traffic restrictions.

He told me it was because of the slow driver, and that I should not arrest him. I said, "No way, you are the dangerous one on the road, not the other driver." I cited him for Reckless Driving. He was not a happy person and said he would contest the ticket in court. I told him to consider himself lucky I didn't impound his car.

Unbelievably this guy did contest the citation. He scheduled a court date and I had to appear to testify. My friend the Judge (JP) opened the proceedings by having the defendant and me raise our hands and promise to tell the truth, the whole truth, and nothing but the truth. We did.

The Judge turned to the defendant and asked how he would plead, Guilty or Not Guilty. The defendant said, "not guilty." The Judge said, "That's fine. I find you guilty, and I'll now hear testimony from the Trooper."

Folks, this is not the way a trial is supposed to run. I was so surprised by the JP rendering a decision before I had a chance to testify, it rattled me. The defendant was in shock as well, and while he was trying to figure out what had happened, I got over my surprise and testified to the circumstances of the arrest. The defendant left the court mumbling to himself. This is what I call old western-style justice.

*   *   *

This same Judge was a firm believer in helping drunk drivers mend their ways. He felt if he could keep a DWI from future drunk driving arrests, he would become a better citizen.

If a person was found guilty of driving while intoxicated, the JP would render the normal fine of a few hundred dollars, but, instead of ordering jail time with the fine, he offered an alternative: the defendants could avoid jail if they submitted to a program of Antabuse for a given period of time.

Antabuse is a drug used to treat chronic alcoholism. When alcohol is consumed while taking this drug, vomiting will occur. If this doesn't stop you from drinking, what will? In all the years I've appeared in court on drunk driver cases, I never heard of any other Judge offering this alternative. I don't know whether it was successful or not.

*   *   *

My crew cut was getting too long so it was time for me to get a haircut. There wasn't a barbershop in my town so I had to drive about eight miles away. I hopped in my personal car and left for the barbershop. On my way, I saw a car, about half a mile away, coming toward me, when it began to drift over into my lane.

I was surprised, but not worried. It would eventually return to its own lane.

This car couldn't have been traveling more than 35 mph in a 50 mph zone, so I had time to flash my headlights on and off to alert the other driver he was in the wrong lane, but he kept coming directly at me. Oh shit, I thought, I was running out of time and room. I headed to the shoulder to get out of the way.

As I drove onto the shoulder, the oncoming car still hadn't moved into its own lane. The car was still coming right at me. In a matter of a couple of seconds, the car was tracking me and heading towards the shoulder. As a last resort, I went off the shoulder, down into the ditch. I was lucky the shoulder dipped down gradually into a flat area, so I knew if I kept my wheels straight as I drove off the road, I wouldn't rollover.

As I headed downward, I glanced back at the oncoming car when it passed by me. A little old woman was driving. She didn't even look at me, she just continued on by, eventually getting back into her own lane as if nothing happened. I recognized her and the car from town. Since I was too busy trying to avoid an accident, I couldn't shoot her.

It took me a few minutes to get out of the ditch and back up on the road. I was lucky not to have any damage to my car. Even though I was pissed off, I decided I needed to calm down so I continued on to get my haircut. I thought I would file a complaint against her when I got back to town.

After the haircut I went to see the JP in his restaurant and told him I wanted to file a complaint against this woman. I knew who she was since she lived only three blocks from me. I also planned to submit her for re-examination for her driver's license. If I had anything to do with this, she would never drive again—not if I could prevent it.

The Judge told me he knew I was upset, and to please calm down. He knew this woman for years, and felt very sorry for her, so he wanted me to let him talk to her first and see if he couldn't get her off the road without charging her. The Judge added that she only drove around town slowly and she couldn't really hurt anyone. This did not sit well with me, since my problem had happened outside the city. But, I had no choice in the matter, so I consented.

About two weeks later, still stewing over the Judge's interference, I heard this old woman had just had an accident. I quickly found out she was at home when it happened. She had asked her ninety year-old husband to help her back out of their driveway. As he stood behind the car guiding her, she backed over him breaking both his legs.

Hearing this, I went to find the Judge and asked him what he was going to do about this woman now? He felt really badly, saying he screwed up by not being firmer with her. Later that same day, the Judge went to the woman's house and took her license away. Ah, instant justice. I did submit her for re-examination for her driver's license. The license was later suspended.

*   *   *

Two of my Detachment teammates were working during a heavy snowstorm on a stretch of highway where there were several accidents. Most involved cars that had slid off the road into the ditch. Most of them were not damaged. All they needed was to be pulled from the ditch. The accidents were so close to each other; the Troopers could walk back and forth to each without having to move their patrol cars.

Near the road was a large house with a row of trees in front providing sort of a buffer between it and the highway. On this day, two teenage boys were hiding behind the barrier of the trees throwing snowballs at a Trooper. There wasn't much he could do other than dodge the snowballs. He was too busy investigating the accidents, and could not afford to be distracted by the kids.

When everything calmed down and the road was clear of accidents, the two Troopers left the area. The Trooper who was the object of the snowballs being thrown, drove to the next major intersection, and turned right. Passing a grocery store near the intersection, he glanced over at the store and saw the two kids who had been throwing the snowballs. As the Trooper passed them, one of the boys flashed him the finger.

Enough is enough. The Trooper was now pissed. He drove around the store and came back to where the two kids were standing. He got out of his patrol car and approached the boy who gave him the finger, and said, "You are under arrest for displaying an obscene gesture, and are going to the county jail." It was payback time.

Two weeks later the Trooper received a message from Radio for him to contact the local District Court Judge. Once at the court, the Judge took him back to his office and asked for him to explain why this charge had been issued to the teenager. The Trooper explained the history behind the charge involving the snowballs. The judge said, "I feel sorry for what happened to you, but let's be clear about this, there isn't any law on the books that covers this charge. That aside, I will dismiss the charge, but will have a talk with the boy. Let me take care of this, okay?"

A bit later the Trooper learned the judge had the boy appear in his private chamber and explained to him the consequences of his actions. He was told this charge could become a permanent part of his record, and would follow him his whole life. So, instead of rendering a fine, he was going to dismiss the charge and put the boy on probation for six months. The boy was ecstatic and promised to be good.

In hindsight, the Trooper was embarrassed he'd gotten caught up in the moment. He probably would have been better off throwing snowballs back at the kids.

Weather Conditions

Weather plays a large role when patrolling the highways in Washington State. Our state has three predominate seasons. The longest season is the rainy one, which can last as long as twelve months. Then we'll have two bring brief periods of sun, and maybe two or three weeks of snow and ice.

*   *   *

When the snow and ice conditions were at their worst, I got excited, and couldn't wait to go to work. It was a given accidents would happen. With these type of conditions, I knew when I signed in service I'd probably be dispatched to an accident waiting for an investigator. If I were not sent to an accident scene, I'd just drive around patiently and wait for Radio to kick out accident reports. I was never wanting.

It was not that I want people to have traffic accidents; they happened regardless, and this was when I was able to do my best to help those who needed it.

There were times when so many accidents happened, the other Troopers and I couldn't keep up. On a few occasions, I would be enroute to one accident and pass others that were less serious, that is, cars in the ditch, but with no damage. All they needed was a tow truck, which I would have Radio dispatch. With the help of the radio dispatchers, we tried to prioritize which accidents needed our attention: injury accidents always received first priority. For those people I passed by, I'm sorry, but help was on the way.

*   *   *

I was on a patrol in the middle of July working a day shift. The temperature was in the middle 70's. I was feeling good; traffic was flowing smoothly and legally. Suddenly, Radio reported a multiple car injury accident a few miles away in the direction I was traveling. I let Radio know I was two minutes away and would be enroute.

The location of this accident was on a four-mile straight stretch of freeway with no obstructions. I was at a loss how there could have been a multiple car accident at this particular stretch of highway.

As I approached the scene I could see where a dark cloud must have just passed over the freeway going from my left to the right. I was surprised, since there weren't any other clouds about, just one giant, very dark cloud. Otherwise the sky was clear.

As I got closer to the scene I drove into what appeared to be three inches of snow, then realized it was hail. The hail was deep, forcing me to slow down quickly, and I could feel the patrol car begin to aquaplane. Just two hundred yards ahead I saw ten to fifteen cars scattered all over the freeway. This section of road had two lanes going in both directions, separated by a 100-foot wide grassy median.

There were two cars facing north in the southbound inside lanes, five in the median facing in all different direction, four more in front of me stopped in the northbound lanes, and two down over the right shoulder, one of which was upside down.

All of the cars showed serious, but not disabling, damage. There were people congregated around the upside down car, so I assumed there were injured people in that one. There were drivers and passengers scattered all about the scene.

This was an absolute mess; the freeway was blocked in one direction and partially restricted in the oncoming lanes. I asked Radio for assistance.

What was really weird was the hail was almost completely melted by the time I had come to a stop. The length of the road that got hit with this downpour must have been about a thousand feet. Who would have believed any of this could happen in the middle of July?

From statements of those involved, the whole pack of cars was tooling along at the posted speed limit of 70 mph. They all said they could see ahead where there might be rain from the dark cloud passing over the freeway, but no reason for concern.

Then everyone entered this small patch of hail on the road and began sliding all over the place. One driver said it was like driving bumper cars at the Puyallup Fair, everyone banging into one another. It was difficult to even determine who hit whom during this crazy scattering of cars. I was at the scene so quickly that everyone was still in a daze wandering around. I parked the patrol car crossways in the northbound lanes to block off the scene.

After getting out of the patrol car I asked around to see if there were any serious injuries other then those in the upside down car. Most appeared okay, with a few minor bumps and bruises. I was told there was a woman pinned in the upside down car.

I worked my way down the embankment to the car and bent down to see how badly injured she was. She was a middle-aged woman who was not pinned but had serious back pain and couldn't move her extremities. As I spoke with her, the ambulance crew arrived.

The woman was in bad shape. Time was an issue and we needed to get her to a hospital immediately. We were quite a distance from the closest hospital, and it was going to take some time to extricate the woman from the car, so to save time I had Radio ask for the U.S. Army's Dust Off helicopter to be dispatched. I'll discuss the use of a military helicopter in a later chapter.

The helo arrived within twenty minutes. We had already removed the woman from the car and had her on a stretcher. She was quickly strapped inside the helo and it left. I later learned she had a broken back, but did survive without complications.

Once she was removed from the scene, and with the help of a couple of tow trucks, we got all the cars back up on the road's shoulder. With the northbound lanes now clear, I released the backed-up traffic. It took me nearly two more hours to complete my investigation. Never again did I witness an accident similar to this one. I'm sure the insurance companies enjoyed working things out.

*   *   *

Probably one of my five scariest moments working the road happened while I was responding to an injury accident that was a good distance away—about fifteen miles. There were six or seven inches of snow on the road. The temperature had risen a few degrees, so now most of the snow was beginning to turn to slush. At the time I had a Cadet riding with me, so I was in a teaching mode. I thought, this would be a great opportunity for me to instruct the Cadet how to properly respond to an accident while driving on a slushy road surface.

Because of time and distance issues, I felt it necessary to push a little bit harder since the accident scene was far away, so I increased my speed. I had a running commentary with the Cadet on why I was driving faster, and why it was best to stay in the tracks of previous traffic. It did not make sense to drive in the other lane that had compact snow and slush.

So, I stayed in the tracks of previous traffic in front of me at this higher speed. Eventually I overtook another car that was obviously being more careful than me and traveling much slower.

I didn't have my emergency lights on, for fear that if I did encounter traffic the drivers might panic, and try to get out of my way by moving over to the shoulder. Turning on my lights would probably cause another accident, so, no lights. I explained all this to the Cadet. Since the accident I was responding to had injuries, I got a bit impatient and decided to pass the slow mover.

I knew this might not be one of my best ideas, but was sure that if I were careful and relied on my many years of experience, everything would turn out just fine. I slowly edged my way to the inside lane where there were no tire tracks, hoping I would find traction and be able to complete the pass.

As I slowly moved to the left lane, I could feel the patrol car wanting to aquaplane in the slush. I held the steering wheel firmly. Once I worked my way to the inside lane, I slowly turned the steering wheel to the right to straighten out the patrol car. It was at this exact moment I realized how stupid and inexperienced I really was.

The patrol car did not straighten out but continued to go straight toward the inside shoulder, sliding in that direction on the slush. Oh shit! Out of the corner of my eye, I could see the Cadet bracing against the dashboard for the pending accident. At this point the road began a gradual turn to the right. To the left is a drop off, about fifty feet down to the oncoming lanes. This was not going to end well.

The rear end of my patrol car began to break loose and I felt it starting to slide to the left. I didn't help the Cadet's composure when I yelled "Oh shit!" All I could do was wait and pray. Then, one of the luckiest moments of my life happened. My car's speed dropped low enough so the tires finally achieved traction, and we came to a stop on the inside shoulder. Whew!

I acted as if nothing happened and started back up, continuing to the accident scene as if everything was normal. We Troopers are thought to be perfect and we have to maintain that image with the Cadets. Regardless, I believe this Cadet had to change his shorts when he got home.

*   *   *

One day, while parked at the chain-up sign, a car blew by me, without chains, heading up the pass. As it passed I could see a male driver and a female passenger in the car. They didn't even look at the patrol car. The car had Canadian license plates, so that might have explained everything. The Canadians are crazy drivers.

I was dumbfounded the driver ignored the chain sign, so I took off after him. The driver had a pretty good lead on me before I got up to speed. With chains on I was pretty much limited to a maximum speed of 60 mph. Any faster, the chains would blow off and damage the patrol car.

I finally got my speed up to around 60 mph, but I was not gaining on the car. I couldn't believe this guy was able to drive this well without chains. The mountain pass was a two-lane road with a lot of curves. There was a steep drop off into a canyon on the left side, and snow piled up on the right shoulder in snowdrifts as high as eight feet. There was no room for error for either of us. We were both pushing our luck and I began to think, I should just give it up, but that's just not my nature.

I eventually closed the gap between us to about 100 yards but couldn't get any closer because of my speed limitation. We were approaching a big sweeping curve to the right with a 400-foot drop off the left side.

I was sure this driver didn't know I was behind him so I tried to warn him to slow down, otherwise his car might turn into an airplane and fly off the cliff.

I turned on my overhead lights hoping he'd notice me and slow down. As I waited for a reaction, I saw inside the car where the woman passenger turned around and looked back at me. She must have noticed the lights because she quickly turned back and spoke to the driver. Mr. Stupid didn't even look in his review mirror; instead he physically turned around to look back at me.

Suddenly there was an explosion of white. All I could see was a large cloud of powdery snow in front of me. It was like a solid fog bank with zero visibility. I couldn't see through or beyond it. I slammed on my brakes and came to a sliding halt. I had no idea what had happened. After the powdery snow settled down, I could see where the other car had swerved right into the snow bank. The only things showing were his taillights and the rear bumper.

The car's occupants turned out to be okay, and there was only minor damage to their car. I asked the driver why he hadn't chained up. He said he was used to driving in the snow back up in Canada so he didn't feel the need to. I asked him to explain to me why he was stuck in the snow embankment, just to illustrate a point. All he did was scratch his head and think about it.

His passenger told me, she had told her dummy husband to put chains on but he wouldn't listen. I was tempted to cite him for Negligent Driving for driving at the speed he was going, especially without chains. Instead, I issued a ticket for not chaining up.

*   *   *

You know how everyone says weird things happen whenever there's a full moon? From a law enforcement perspective, we believed whenever there was a full moon, the crazies came out. It was as if all the drivers decided to do as they damn well pleased. If I was working an evening shift during a full moon, it was a given I would come across a drunk driver, or

even something worse, like a fatality accident.
I considered myself forewarned when there was
a full moon.

*   *   *

Half way up Stevens Pass, the highway department
had mounted a 105 mm Howitzer cannon. The
purpose of the cannon was to lob a shell up
to a higher elevation to break the snow lose,
forcing an avalanche. This may sound strange but
the process was called "Avalanche Prevention"
to purposely start a slide when there wasn't
any traffic.

Beforehand, the highway department stopped the
traffic to make sure no one got caught in the
slide as the snow cascades down and over the
highway. After the avalanche, the snow was
removed from the road.

I wanted to witness the firing of the cannon.
I parked just past where it was mounted so
I could see the muzzle flash when it fired.
When it happened, the concussion from the
firing dislodged snow from the trees above me,
covering my patrol car to the point where I
couldn't see out.

Fortunately it was only a dusting of about half
an inch deep. All I had to do was turn on my
wipers to clear the snow from my windshield. I
did get to see the flash before the concussion
reached the car. Exciting.

Enough background. One winter day, it was time
for avalanche control. The highway department
snow removal crews stopped the traffic before

firing the cannon. In one of the stopped string of cars was an FBI agent traveling over the pass. When the cannon fired, his car was covered with a dusting just like I experienced. However, this agent thought he was trapped in a snow slide.

He was concerned others might not know where he was covered up, so he took out his weapon and fired several rounds through the roof of his car to let others know where he was trapped. In addition to having hearing issues, the embarrassment of the event would never end once his story appeared in the local newspapers.

*   *   *

There was one hill that was the steepest on my beat. It was about a mile in length. Whenever the weather turned bad, I could always count on accidents happening somewhere on the hill. One day after a severe snowstorm had passed through the area, this hill had become caked with compact snow and ice. All traffic trying to make it up the hill had come to a standstill for the lack of traction.

I was in the backup, mid-way down the hill. Even though I had studded tires on the patrol car, I could have gone into the oncoming lanes and worked my way forward to see if the sand trucks were addressing the problem. However, I decided it wasn't worth the risk, and to wait my turn along with everyone else.

Other drivers, standing around, asked what was happening. I got out of the patrol car and bonded with them by filling them in, killing time by telling them my favorite jokes. All of a sudden, one of the drivers yelled out, "Watch out, a car is coming right at us." I turned around and looked up the hill, and sure enough a car was coming, spinning down the hill.

It was the only car in the oncoming lanes and was spinning 360 degrees, time after time. We all jumped behind our cars in case it was coming in our direction; however, the car stayed in its own two downhill lanes. This feat was incredible because from top to bottom I would guess it spun around ten to twelve times without hitting a thing. The car continued after it reached the bottom of the hill as if nothing happened. I'm sure the driver had to change his or her underwear.

Most Annoying Violators

To operate a motor vehicle is a privilege, not a right or entitlement. To be allowed to drive, a person must first show he or she has the skills to operate a car, and a comprehensive understanding of the traffic laws. My job exist because a percentage of drivers are rude, inconsiderate, and only care about themselves.

For those others who drive safely and sanely, nothing can make them madder than seeing others driving erratically and irresponsibly. I'm no different; I get upset as well when I see these inconsiderate boobs. What is really cool is I can actually do something about it. Being a State Trooper does allow me to rid myself of any anxiety I might have.

Obviously, I'm concerned with removing drunk and reckless drivers from our highways, however, there are other violations drivers committed, whether intentionally or inadvertently, that annoy me greatly. I would like to take the time to rank them in the order of what is most upsetting.

Impeding Traffic—From my point of view this violation is the most difficult to apprehend or stop. Normally it involves a driver driving at a lower speed then what's posted, for example, driving 40 mph when the posted speed limit is 50 mph. If the offending driver is on a two-lane highway with hills and curves, it's almost impossible to get past this person.

Traffic accumulates behind this driver with no recourse but to tag along until they can pass. All one can do is hope the driver's journey is a short one. The law does require if you have five or more cars backed up behind you, you must yield and pull over and allow them to pass.

My experience is that one out of a hundred will be considerate enough to do this. For me it's very difficult to stop an impeding driver. For example, if the person impeding is approaching me, and I see cars stacked up behind his car, there's nothing I can do, until all of the traffic has passed by.

Only then can I turn around and chase after the person. When I catch up to the long string of traffic, it is best not to turn on my siren and red lights to pass, because this can cause more harm then good. I just have to wait for the opportunity to work my way safely forward, until I reach this soon to be very unhappy driver.

I realize I've been put on notice by all the other drivers that I had better do something about this slow driver, or else. This is not going to be easy—it never is. This whole process of trying to reach an impeding car might take several miles. There was many times where the impeder turned off before I could reach him.

This can be an absolute no-win situation for me, and for the other drivers following behind.

There have been a few violators I've stopped who weren't even aware there were cars backed up behind them. Senior citizens are probably the most frequent violators for impeding. They should just be a bit more careful, that's all.

The irony of this particular violation is that the fine for impeding is probably the least expensive of all tickets, yet it creates more hatred and discontent then most other violations.

Failure to Yield Right of Way—I probably should have rated this violation number one. It is a very irritating traffic violation. I've seen drivers pull out in front of another car from a stop sign or driveway failing to yield, but the worst and most dangerous offenders, in my opinion, are those people entering a limited access freeway, and failing to yield to the traffic already on that highway. Please remember, every entrance to a freeway has a posted YIELD sign. The traffic on the freeway HAS THE RIGHT OF WAY.

Just one simple fail to yield violation can have so many ramifications that it would boggle your mind. The simple rule to yield means the driver intending to enter the freeway is required to make sure the lane is clear before entering. If there is traffic, then you must yield to it, letting it pass by until there's an opening to safely enter the freeway. This is a very simple rule to follow.

I can only guess why drivers don't yield. They must feel they're entitled to enter, often charging out on to the freeway, totally ignoring the yield sign. A high percentage won't even grant you the courtesy of signaling their intention to merge. I almost forgot, this too is a requirement. When attempting to enter the freeway, you must signal your intention to enter. It's a courtesy or at least a warning the driver is entering, watch out.

I'm just beginning to touch upon this failing to yield problem. For merging drivers who don't yield, and force their way into heavy traffic between two cars, the second car is now forced to slow down to make room. If this driver doesn't, then two cars will be following too closely. Everyone is a loser if traffic slows rapidly or stops. If it does, we'd have two rear-end accidents. When I see this happen I cite the offending merging driver with Negligent Driving.

Good safe drivers worry about these rude merging drivers, and become defensive, to maintain their space in a line of heavy traffic. So, they follow the car to their front too closely to prevent the merging boobs from forcing their way in line.

These drivers have now put themselves at risk by following too closely. Of course this isn't defensive driving, but that's the way people react. They defend their place in line.

Failure to Signal—This law is not asking much. All that is required is for the driver to indicate his or her intention to make a turn, make a lane change, or to pass another car. It requires very little physical effort. The driver must use their left hand to push up or down on the turn signal lever to show they are changing direction. Can it be any simpler?

Most drivers I stop for this violation admit they were just lazy. Others forgot to do it, or were too busy talking to passengers, or listening to the radio.

If I happened to notice a motorist not signaling when making lane changes, I would follow this car for a short distance to see how many times they fail to signal when required.

Strangely, they will signal when they see a State Patrol car behind them. When I turn on my overhead lights to stop them, they now remember to signal when being pulled over.

Following too Closely—There shall be a separation between cars of 20 feet for every ten miles an hour of speed. For example, if you are traveling at 60 mph on the freeway behind another car, you should not be any closer then 120 feet. I realize this is not realistic considering how everyone drives today. I would venture a guess that fifty percent of all accidents are attributable to people following too closely.

As I mentioned earlier, drivers get caught up following other cars too closely because of other drivers making unsafe lane changes. Since almost everyone follows too closely, I have to pick and choose from the worst. I can't get all of them.

*   *   *

To better illustrate how dangerous following too closely can be, there is a special patrol car used by instructors at the Academy to illustrate to the Trooper Cadets the distance a car will travel once the brakes are applied. The exercise shows how far a car will travel from the moment danger is sensed to actually hitting the brake pedal, to beginning to stop, at the speed of 20 mph. In that brief moment, the car will travel a minimum of twenty feet before the brakes are actually engaged. This distance equates to your reaction time, not braking.

Using the example above, a car traveling at 60 mph will travel an additional 80 feet before the brakes are even engaged, because of the reaction time of the driver. I hope I've made some sense out of this.

Let me do math that might make more sense. You have to figure, a car is twenty feet in length. At 60 mph, you should have 120 feet, or six car lengths, between you and the car to your front. Taking into account the reaction time I mentioned earlier, add three more car lengths to your following distance.

Unfortunately, this distance is not realistic according to the driving habits of most drivers.

I have investigated hundreds of accidents that could have been avoided if the drivers had been more attentive, and had proper separation between their car and the one to their front.

* * *

Every once in a while, I'll have access to an unmarked patrol car to use while on routine patrol, kind of a break in the routine for me. The Sergeant's patrol car is unmarked and comes in a variety of colors, while my patrol car is white with the WSP markings on the side. For the rank of Captain and above, patrol cars come in different colors as well, but more importantly; have no WSP license plates, and no special antennas, which are a give-away.

There are many savvy drivers who disregard traffic laws when they know we're not near by. They are always looking for the white State Patrol cars. When they see us, they are more careful. This is why, on occasion, I like to use one of the unmarked patrol cars, primarily to get these cheaters—to mess with their comfort zone, stir things up a bit.

One experience that happens most often is when I'm in the inside lane on the freeway, traveling at the speed limit, and another motorist comes up really fast from behind and begins tailgating me, basically letting me know to get the hell out of the way. Did this ever happen to you? Since I'm driving at the speed limit I'm not too concerned about impeding traffic so I continue.

The other driver may blink his or her high beams at me as a sign they want me to pull over to let him by, or he might get a bit closer to show his impatience. I decide, oh what the heck, if he is in that much of a hurry why not let him by.

I pull over to the right lane the first chance I get. The following car bombs by and as it does, the driver gives me the finger to show his frustration. This is the really cool part of the story, because as the driver's flipping me off, he notices I'm wearing a blue uniform with the gold State Patrol patch on my shoulder. Now it's time for him to change his shorts and get a ticket.

*   *   *

Many times, these impatient drivers don't notice I'm a Trooper as they pass by, getting their speed up to ten to twenty miles an hour over the posted limit before I finally decide to draw the line, and stop them. A few drivers are dumbfounded and ask where I was hiding or where did I come from.

I tell them to look back and see what kind of car I'm driving. They quickly get the message and now have the privilege to make a generous contribution to the General Fund for the State of Washington.

*   *   *

In Seattle and parts of King County, the freeway system is rated as one of the top ten worst gridlock messes in the country. In a way I take pride in our state being in the top ten, but as a State Trooper, it's a giant headache resulting in thousands of traffic accidents every year. There are times motorists are lucky to do 10 mph in a 60 mph zone. When the traffic bogs down, tempers flare, and road rage can surface.

To alleviate some of this congestion, the highway department has designated one lane as a High Occupancy Vehicle (HOV) lane. To qualify to be in this lane a car must have two occupants. Since most drivers choose not to car pool, they must drive in the remaining lanes.

Gridlock can happen at the slightest provocation. It can begin when a small fender bender accident happens, with the involved cars parked on the side shoulder. The road isn't blocked; it's just that the other drivers must slow down to see what's going on. Even a parked State Patrol car on the side of the road without its emergency equipment on, may cause drivers to slow down and wonder what the heck the Trooper's doing. In a matter of minutes the whole freeway can become bogged down.

There are drivers who cannot tolerate gridlock, or are impatient enough to disregard the rules and enter into the HOV lane to avoid the backup, even though they don't have the required extra passenger.

The HOV hotline receives hundreds of complaints every day from motorists reporting violators of this lane. For State Troopers, this type of violation is difficult to address. Often there isn't enough shoulder to park my patrol car to monitor the HOV lane traffic for violators.

If I were to spot one, it can become very dangerous to try to stop the violator once I reach him, especially if there isn't an inside shoulder. Trying to get the violator to pull over all the way to the right shoulder through four lanes of travel is not easy.

I personally have received more complaints of HOV violators than any other type of violation. Most drivers I've stopped for this violation are late to work. There are a small percentage of drivers so pissed off with the gridlock problem they don't care if they are caught. Then there are a few who attempt to disguise their transgression. They are hard to detect, but we do catch them eventually.

*   *   *

I did arrest one driver with an inflatable doll in the right rear seat. He almost got away with it, but I thought it unusual the second person was sitting in the back instead of the right front seat. I didn't notice any head movement, and this passenger was sitting too rigidly. I took a gamble and pulled the driver over to verify he was legally allowed in the HOV lane.

The driver was cool; he told me he had been using the doll for several months. His biggest problem was keeping the doll inflated. There were times air would leak out and the doll would collapse while he was in the HOV lane. This guy thought he was being clever by putting a doll in the back seat. I'm sure he'll try it again, but more than likely place the doll in the front seat the next time.

*   *   *

The all time winner for ingenuity was a pregnant woman stopped by one of my friends. She didn't argue with the Trooper but decided to fight the ticket in court. Her story was so unique it appeared in all the major newspapers around the country.

In the District Court trial she testified she was seven months pregnant with child at the time of her arrest. She said since she was full term her baby qualified as the second occupant of her car and therefore she qualified to be in the HOV lane. The Judge seriously thought it over, agreed with her unusual argument and found her not guilty of the HOV violation. However, he did find her guilty for not having her second passenger wear a seat belt.

*   *   *

I always try to interact with violators in an attempt to establish a dialog to emphasize the importance of safe driving habits. Most drivers agree and understand they have made a mistake, and will improve.

That aside, whether I have decided to issue a ticket, or even give a simple verbal warning, unusual personalities at times surface in spite of my good intentions. It becomes difficult for me to find a way for both the motorist and myself to walk away with a positive feeling.

Of all the people I have come into contact with through traffic enforcement, there are certain professions I can anticipate will create an argument. It will be a verbal exercise where the violator will try to convince me I have made an egregious error in stopping him, and that it would be a mistake to issue him a citation.

Those professional people who most often take issue with me are doctors, lawyers, and teachers. These people are obviously well educated, and can be just a bit more aggressive verbally. I have listed them according to my frustration level in past dealings involving them.

Doctors—Doctors are always in a hurry. Most of them I have stopped for speeding. It seems they are responding to some sort of an emergency, and I should not delay them any further. Even though they may be in a hurry and time is of essence, they take the time to argue their point about why they were speeding.

I patiently listen to them, letting them vent, then after a few minutes I mention I thought they had an emergency and we are wasting their time. I add they could have been on their way several minutes ago, and yet, I haven't issued a ticket yet, so I guess we'll be here a bit longer.

Several times I have stopped drivers who led me to believe they were physicians or hinted they were surgeons, but instead, through further questioning were actually professors, pharmacists, or Doctors of Waste Management Principles, not actual medical doctors. They take the gamble that doctors might get a free pass for speeding.

Lawyers—Most of my close lawyer friends might disagree with me, but they love to talk. I believe they love to hear themselves talk. The ones I have encountered on the road are quite elegant in their presentation to me about how familiar they are with the law. Mostly with general criminal or civil law, but, surprisingly, not with traffic laws and regulations.

Most of those Lawyers I have stopped do not argue with me, but rather threaten to take the matter to court to fight the ticket. Not one ever did. For whatever reason the threat of having to go to court was supposed to scare me. I'm sorry, but that is part of my job, going to court.

There have been a few instances when I have stopped lawyers for drunk driving who I have encountered in previous court cases—where they have represented DWI clients I had arrested. These few know I'm good at what I do, so very few ever contested their arrest. They have the opportunity for their cases to be adjudicated in other ways without the embarrassment of a trial.

Teachers—I save this profession for last. Teachers have probably caused me the most grief. They are notorious for arguing because they feel they are never wrong. How dare I tell them what was wrong with their driving? It gets worse when I tell them they are receiving a ticket for their violation.

When they realize they are actually going to get a ticket, there will be a lengthy conversation about how I will morally regret this later. When I realize I can't reason with them, I just want to write the damn ticket and let them be on their merry way.

From my experience I believe teachers are so used to teaching their students right from wrong, that it is foreign to them to be told they have done something wrong. However, this is just an educated guess.

Investigating Traffic Accidents

The most important part of a Trooper's job is traffic law enforcement as mandated by our state legislature: to enforce traffic laws to reduce and prevent traffic accidents. However, after a brief learning period, there is as much emphasis placed upon the need to conduct thorough traffic accident investigations.

I realize I'll never know if my enforcement of traffic laws actually helped reduce traffic accidents, but I know this; I damned well better be good at accident investigation. It is incredible how many people depend upon the complete, accurate investigation of a traffic accident.

If a driver is found to be at fault for causing an accident, a citation more than likely may be issued. If the accident involves severe injuries or a fatality, then criminal charges may be filed. Either situation will require supportive evidence showing how the accident happened and how the driver erred.

The court system may become involved at the conclusion of an investigation; however, there are many other interested parties requiring information; insurance adjusters representing the insured, the state highway department, medic units, hospitals, passengers, and witnesses.

I could not afford to make mistakes. From the moment I arrived at the scene of an accident until the moment I cleared it, I could not relax one moment, leave any clue unnoticed, leave a skid mark not measured, or a photograph not taken. Justice and restitution are the name of the game.

*   *   *

Upon arriving at the scene of an accident, I quickly assess if the road is blocked, and if so, what it will take to unblock it? If the car damage is severe enough to be inoperable, then I need Radio to dispatch a tow truck quickly. I cannot afford to have the road blocked for too long, because traffic will begin backing up, and other accidents may result.

The next order of business is to determine who the drivers are, if they are injured, or are aware of any others that might have injuries. If so, I must quickly check the extent of each injury and determine whether or not I can handle the first aid issues, or need a medic unit or ambulance to be dispatched. Only after the injured have been taken care of, can I begin the accident investigation.

I start by contacting the involved drivers and collecting their driver's licenses, and vehicle registrations. Once I have that information in hand, I can relax for a moment because no one is going anywhere until I'm finished with the drivers. I now have the time to seek out witnesses, if there are any. Witnesses may stay for a while, but if you don't look for them right a way, they'll take off. If I find one, I'll write down his contact information and get a brief statement on how the accident happened, then release him.

Once I have the drivers on hold and have already checked for witnesses, I record any physical evidence that might show how the accident happened. The evidence will help collaborate the driver and witness's statements.

If an accident involves two cars, there will be dust and debris at the point of impact. Even with the cars removed, I can always determine where they struck each other from the debris on the road. If the damage is severe enough, the cars will gouge out the pavement, or oil or other liquids will spill.

I must determine if there are any telling signs of the drivers attempting to avoid the accident. Did they swerve to get out of the way, and did anyone apply their brakes leaving skid marks? It's quite easy to reconstruct an accident with the driver and witness's statements; however, having the physical evidence in hand is sometimes the best information.

All the information I have gathered is recorded in my officer's notebook (our bible), and on the investigator's accident report. This document is kept on file at our district office and with the State Department of Licensing.

The last thing I need to take care of is assisting the drivers' exchange their respective information for their own accident reports.

*   *   *

No two accidents are alike: like snowflakes, each one is different. That's why my job is so interesting. It can be a one car, two cars, or a 22-car accident. The more the merrier. It's a challenge to figure out what precipitated the accident, why it couldn't have been avoided, and how the drivers responded in this moment of impending doom; did they panic, were they in the wrong, or just not being attentive, or—and I hate having to write this—wrong time, wrong place.

There have been many times in two-car accidents when both drivers were at fault. Obviously one driver caused the accident, but the other driver could possibly have avoided it. When this happens, the second driver is guilty of contributory negligence, even though that person didn't originally cause the accident. The insurance companies really like it when their insured may have been wrong, but the other driver may have to pay for their own damaged car.

*   *   *

Every driver has his or her version of how an accident happened. Most are in agreement about who is at fault, however, on occasion there will be disagreement. When this happens, impartial witnesses and physical evidence will be the deciding factor. It's interesting to listen to a driver tell me what happened when the physical evidence shows otherwise, and I will explain why.

One of the more popular arguments I have heard is the driver was not speeding, and yet the skid marks they laid down on the pavement contradict their statement. To assist Troopers in determining speed from skid marks, there is a formula inside the Officer's Notebook that takes into account weather-related road conditions, and type of surface, such as gravel, dirt, or sand.

The chart helps in determining the minimum speed of a car prior to impact. I often show the chart to doubting drivers and they concede the possibility they might have been going a little too fast prior to impact.

It's not unusual for a driver to have forgotten what had happened, simply for the reason he is in shock. Regardless, I have tried to reason with him, explaining what the evidence showed, and how I interpreted the accident. If I decide to issue a citation to a driver, it is important he know why he is getting a ticket. I do not want him surprised when he gets one in the mail a week later.

*   *   *

Once dispatched to a traffic accident, there were no excuses for me not reaching the scene unless I screwed up, which I eventually did. I was enroute to a one-car injury accident where the road conditions were ice and snow. I had such a great distance to cover, I pushed it a bit too hard and lost control on the ice and slid off into a ditch. There wasn't any damage to my patrol car, but I was stuck and would need a tow to get out.

I was out in the middle of nowhere, so I anticipated the tow truck wouldn't arrive for at least half an hour. All I could do was sit in the patrol car and wave at the people as they drove by. Very embarrassing.

There were a few drivers who had stopped and asked if I needed any help. I then wondered about all the other cars that had passed by, and why they didn't stop and ask if I needed help. I decided to remove them from my Christmas list.

So much time had passed, the people who were involved in the injury accident eventually drove by. They must have given up waiting for me. I could see one passenger wearing bandages on his head. Everyone in the car just glared at me as they passed. I was so embarrassed about this; I promised myself I would never ever overdrive the road conditions again.

* * *

When I needed to confirm a car's speed from skid marks, I would refer to my skid mark scale to determine the minimum speed, but not the actual speed. If this minimum speed is greater than the posted speed limit, then the driver is automatically going to be cited for speeding.

One difficult question often not answered is, what is the actual speed, not the minimum speed? For example, skid marks reveal a car was traveling at a minimum speed of 58 mph prior to the accident, in a posted 55 mph zone. And yet, there's severe frontend damage to the car. How much faster would the car have to be going to sustain that much damage?

The courts will take this into account: what always worked best for me was to show pictures of the damaged cars to illustrate my contention the speed was greater then I could prove from the chart.

Only an engineer can determine the true speed by analyzing the metallurgical stress experienced when the metal was damaged. We retain their expertise only when we have charged a driver for negligent homicide traffic cases.

*   *   *

I never paid attention to motorcycles until I joined the State Patrol. They actually scare me. There is no protection if you hit something. If you fall over, your body's not going to like it. Bugs sting when they hit your body and they coat your teeth, and your cheeks blow open to receive more road contraband. I figure I can enjoy those same experiences by driving with my head stuck out my car window while driving down the road.

During my probationary period the state legislature was in the process of enacting a new law requiring operators of motorcycles to wear helmets with a face shield, or at the minimum, to have a windscreen on the motorcycle. Also, whenever the motorcycle was in operation, the headlight must be turned on.

Despite this common-sense approach to reducing the injuries and fatalities associated with motorcycle accidents, there was tremendous resistance to these changes, mostly from the motorcyclist community who were up in arms over this pending law. It denied them the right to enjoy the air flowing through their hair, and in my opinion, hitting solid objects.

Turning on the headlight I felt was the most important part of the law. Most of the motorcycle accidents I investigated were caused by the driver of a car failing to notice the motorcycle, because of the small silhouette the motorcycle presents.

With the headlight on, car drivers would hopefully notice the motorcycles. As for wearing a helmet, if you are dumb enough to ride a motorcycle, you should be required to wear one to protect your stupid head. Well, I got that off my chest without too much damage.

*   *   *

I investigated two separate motorcycle accidents within my first six months of duty. In both instances a car turned left in front of the motorcycle. In both cases the motorcycle rider hit the car broadside then catapulted over the handlebars and crashed upside down into the car's windshield. Both operators experienced severed spinal cords from the broken glass in the windshield. Both are quadriplegics.

In those two investigations, I was able to determine both motorcycles' front headlights were not turned on. If they had been, I firmly believe both accidents might have been avoided. I am a staunch supporter of the new helmet &

headlight law, and when it became a law I strictly enforced it.

*   *   *

One of the injury accidents I responded to involved two cars that had hit head on. As I approached the scene, the roadway was blocked and I could see both cars had sustained extensive damage. As I got out of the patrol car, a witness ran up to me and said there was a badly injured girl lying on the shoulder who probably needed an ambulance right away. I grabbed my first aid kit out of the trunk and ran over to the young woman.

She was in obvious shock, so I asked one of the witnesses to run back to my patrol car, get the packet of blankets and bring them over so we could cover the girl. I could see where the girl's right leg was almost severed at mid-thigh.

Both ends of the bones were exposed, and she was in the process of bleeding out. Someone handed me his or her belt so I was able to quickly tie it around the upper part of her leg, making a tourniquet to stop the bleeding. I had this person hold the tourniquet in place so I could return to the patrol car to get my leg air splint.

With the help of others, I quickly but gently slid the splint up the leg through the severed area to the crotch, removed the tourniquet, then zippered the splint up. I bent down and blew into the splint to inflate it. When it was inflated, the bleeding stopped and the leg was stabilized. The girl was unconscious but stable.

I assumed the leg was lost, but at least she was alive. About this time, the ambulance arrived and we loaded the girl and they went to the hospital. I completed my investigation and cleared the scene.

Two weeks later, I heard back from the hospital. They told me the doctors were able to save the girl's leg. I was surprised, because when we were applying the splint, all I could see holding the leg together was a long stretch of skin. To save an extremity was something new for us Troopers in the 1960's. For the first time in a long while, I felt I had done something good.

*   *   *

There was a period of time—about four months—when my detachment investigated a series of serious accidents involving older Volkswagens, where the gas tank was installed in the front portion of the car, right in front of the passenger compartment.

Two of these accidents were head-on collisions, and were severe enough for the gas tank to rupture, splashing gas back into the passenger compartment, igniting, and burning both drivers, and resulting in their deaths.

The first accident was unusual in itself, but when the second happened a short time later, with the same result, the media jumped all over it. It was later learned the unusual location of the gas tank was only found in older models. The newer models had been redesigned to avoid this from happening again.

About a month after the last fatality, I was dispatched to an injury accident. As I arrived at the scene, I could see one of the cars with serious front-end damage. It happened to be one of those VW's with the gas tank in front.

As I approached the car I smelled a very strong odor of gasoline. I saw it spilling on the ground from the front end of the car, and it had pooled underneath the car. It was like a time bomb waiting to ignite. To make matters worse, the driver was pinned in the car. He wasn't injured but it was obvious we would need the fire department's jaws-of-life to extricate him. I had Radio dispatch the fire department.

While waiting for the fire truck, I talked to the driver who was in a mild form of shock and white as a sheet. His clothes were drenched in gasoline. The driver was crying and praying and all I could do was console him. He told me he was aware of the two previous car fires and never thought the same thing would happen to him in his older car.

The fire department arrived, and quickly sprayed foam on the driver and around the car where the gas had spilled. With the situation now stabilized the fire department personnel easily removed the driver. I can't believe to this day that the car didn't catch fire on impact.

John Young

*   *   *

The first Trooper Cadet ever assigned to me for his coaching trip was a really nice young guy. I was told he was highly thought of by the training staff, and if he passed the grade while on this coaching assignment, he would more than likely be assigned to our detachment.

At the time, we had two vacancies, and the Sergeant was guaranteed to get at least one Cadet from this graduating class, possibly two. I was told to make sure this newbie would work well within our detachment and with the other Troopers.

The coaching trip went well without any hiccups. We had coffee at one time or another with all the other Troopers in the detachment. Everyone liked this new kid. He was not aware he might be assigned to our detachment. Everything went well, and I released him to the academy with high marks. We were all looking forward to his return once he graduated.

Sure enough, two weeks later, he reported to the District and was assigned to our Detachment. He was just as excited as we were. We thought he would easily fit in, because he knew the area now, and the other Troopers liked him.

As it turned out, in the beginning, I wasn't able to connect with him because we worked different shifts. I didn't see him that often, but kept a close watch to see how he was progressing and to make myself available if he had any questions.

One evening, about four months later, a tow truck owner was returning to his storage yard when he came upon a two car head-on accident. It must have happened seconds before he arrived. There was still dust and smoke in the air, and no one was moving inside the cars.

The tow truck guy quickly got on his CB radio and had his office call the State Patrol to report the accident and to dispatch an ambulance, as there were obviously going to be serious injuries involved.

Two Troopers responded, took care of the injured and completed the accident investigation. For the tow truck driver, it was a scary experience, seeing and hearing the injured cry out for help when he was by himself. It was the first time anything like this had happened to him in twenty-five years of the towing business.

A few days after the accident the tow driver called me at home and asked if I would stop by his tow yard the next time I signed in service. I thought the call unusual in itself, because he knew how we valued our time off without the job interfering. The next time I was in service, I drove to his tow yard and met with him.

I asked what the problem was. He said he felt the State Patrol might have a problem and he wasn't sure how to report it. He trusted me enough to hear his story. I told him, "Ok, it can't be all that bad, what's bothering you." He asked me, "Do you recall the injury accident the other night that I witnessed?" I said, "I kind of remember, what about it?"

175

He told me that right after he called in the accident on his CB radio, he turned on his overhead emergency tow truck lights, and was going to get out of his tow truck to place some flares to warn other traffic. As he opened the door he saw a State Patrol car approach from the other side of the accident, and stop for a few seconds.

The tow driver thought, thank heavens there's a Trooper here now, I don't have to worry about what to do next. He continued, "As I was getting out of my truck, I looked at the patrol car when suddenly it turned around and drove away in the opposite direction.

He couldn't believe what he saw. The truck owner said he was kind of in shock, but then thought maybe it wasn't a patrol car. Maybe he just imagined it, wanting to see a patrol car because he was scared. However, he forgot about it once the two other Troopers showed up to investigate the accident.

Over the next couple of days the more he thought about it, the more he was convinced it was a Trooper's car that turned away, and it was a blue patrol car. At the time we had both white and blue patrol cars. I asked him to keep this quiet and let me do some digging and see what I could find out, before we started accusing someone of something that might not have happened.

I quickly checked the work schedule for that night to see who was working that shift. There were three Troopers working that night, two of which drove white patrol cars and they were the ones at the accident scene. The third Trooper had a blue patrol car, and it turned out to be my recent Cadet, who was the new guy in our detachment. I was in shock. This couldn't be true.

I immediately passed this information on to my Sergeant. I told my boss I would be absolutely shocked if it were this new Trooper. He had done a great job when I coached him. I never experienced any issues when we investigated traffic accidents, although we never encountered any serious injury accidents. The Sergeant decided to re-enact a similar situation to see if the allegation might be true, before letting the other Troopers know.

The Sergeant put together a scenario that involved another Trooper. The traffic was light one evening, with nothing going on. Around mid-shift, the second Trooper happened to see the new Trooper and was pretty certain the new guy didn't see him, so he called Radio on a separate frequency using a preset code, to put out a false report of an injury accident near the present location of the new guy.

Taking into account the direction the new guy was traveling, the accident location would be less than a mile from where he was working. There was no way to avoid responding to it. To avoid doing so, the Trooper would have to turn around in a private driveway and go in the opposite direction.

Radio kicked out the report of a multiple car injury accident with the road blocked. The older Trooper acknowledged his location a few

miles away. This meant the only other Trooper
on duty was the new guy who was now half a
mile away from the scene of the accident.
Since he was the closest, he was responsible
for the investigation. Everyone waited for his
response.

The new guy turned around and went in the
opposite direction. He never did acknowledge
with Radio that he received the accident
information. The other Trooper witnessed the
turn-around so he called radio to advise them
to cancel the accident report, which they did.
He then went to the Sergeant's home and filled
him in on what had happened. The Sergeant was
upset. He put on his uniform, went to the
office, and had Radio advise the new Trooper
to report to the District office.

The Sergeant explained the original complaint
about avoiding an injury accident a few days
earlier. He also noted his recent non-response
to an accident reported an hour earlier on
this evening's shift. The Trooper readily
admitted his transgressions and felt bad about
it. He confessed he just couldn't stand the
sight of blood. He dreaded going to work every
day knowing he might have to investigate an
accident with people bleeding.

The Sergeant told him this was a very serious
violation of policy and it would be best if he
resigned his commission rather then be fired.
The new Trooper turned in his gear and patrol
car that evening, and was driven home by the
Sergeant.

*   *   *

Fog combined with freezing temperatures is an evil combination. With the heavy moisture in the air, and the temperature below 32 degrees, ice on the road becomes an issue. Probably the worst circumstance I can foresee is when ice forms on bridges first.

This is exactly what happened early one morning during the commute near Seattle. The temperature dropped into the low 20's; with fog so thick you couldn't see more than 200 hundred feet. One bridge on the interstate freeway had a solid coat of ice. One of my partners was dispatched to the scene of a multiple car accident on the bridge.

Before the Trooper arrived at the scene, the motorists already involved in the accident were standing around their cars waiting for help to arrive. Everyone was a little skittish because cars were still sliding around when they drove onto the bridge in the fog. The accident victims could hear the sound of other cars getting hit, and sure enough, coming out of the fog was a bus sliding out of control towards them.

One of the drivers standing at the side of the bridge thought the bus was heading for him, so he jumped over the railing to get out of the way. The jumper thought there was a dirt shoulder on the other side of the railing.

Unfortunately he jumped over the railing at the exact center of the bridge. There wasn't any shoulder. It was a forty-foot drop to the Duwamish River below. The guy missed the river and landed on the shore breaking both legs. If he had landed in the river with these temperatures, he might have drowned instead.

It took my friend a few minutes to realize from witnesses that this guy had jumped off the bridge. When he did, he radioed to have Seattle Police check for the victim down below. They found him and had sent him to the local hospital.

Fatality Accidents

Every once in awhile, when someone learns I'm a State Trooper, they say they could never do a job like mine. They just couldn't handle all the blood and guts we are exposed to. I guess I never thought about it in that light, however, I did like the challenge of handling adversity, and if the gore of a traffic accident is part of the job, so be it. Traffic fatalities are part of that job.

*   *   *

The responsibility of investigating a fatality accident is not finished at the end of the day. We must process the photographs taken, and double-check the measurements. Trust me when I say this; we measure absolutely everything that can be measured, leaving nothing to chance.

There are the countless forms and reports to be completed: witnesses and their statements followed up on, re-examining the vehicles in question, and acquiring coroner and hospital records. Additionally, the cars involved are generally impounded, and the contents inventoried.

Once all the information has been compiled into a neat stack of paper, or into three-ring binders, the case is presented to the prosecutor, who then determines what, if any, charges will be filed in the case. Normally he or she will follow our recommendation.

If the at-fault driver is deceased, then our records will only be applicable if civil liability is in question. The highway department may want restitution for damage to state property, such as guardrails, lampposts, etc. Other injured parties may want reimbursement for their injuries. Last but not least, the insurance carriers have to be reckoned with. These companies often have to determine whether or not their client is liable, and if so, make restitution.

If the at-fault driver is living, then he will be charged for his transgression, the normal charge being Negligent Homicide while in the operation of a motor vehicle, a felony that could result in jail time.

In the beginning, I did have concerns about whether I could handle working with a dead body. But over time, I learned I would be so busy rendering first aid, taking care of the survivors, and investigating the accident, I wouldn't have the time to worry about seeing the injured or deceased. Plain and simple, regardless of the hardships, it was a job I enjoyed doing. The following stories are descriptive and may be somewhat gruesome, but they did happen and still continue to happen every day.

*   *   *

The minute I received my commission, I knew there would be a day of reckoning. It would just be a matter of time before I had to investigate a fatality accident. I did not worry about arresting drunk drivers, or chasing violators at high speeds. But I did worry about not wanting to screw up when faced with a fatality investigation, or one with very serious injuries. I was thinking, let it happen fast so I can quit worrying about it. As it turned out, life isn't always fair.

I had been working for four months and was beginning to wonder whether or not I would ever investigate a fatality. The Detachment had investigated two fatalities since I reported in, however, they happened on my days off. I know this sounds morbid, but I just wanted the exposure to investigating any serious incident involving a death, whether it was a traffic accident or not. I didn't know it, but the shit was about to hit the proverbial fan in a couple of weeks.

*   *   *

I spent my two days off out of town and was returning home. It was late in the afternoon, and I was tired. I couldn't wait to go to work the next day, because I was still new enough to miss the action.

I was approaching the city limits of my town, when I noticed the flashing red lights up ahead. I could see one State Patrol car, an ambulance and two tow trucks. One of the two lanes was blocked with two cars facing each other, both with extensive front-end damage. Obviously the cars had hit head-on at a high rate of speed.

As I worked my way through the backed-up traffic, I could see that the Trooper was from my Detachment. When I reached the scene I pulled over onto the shoulder and yelled over to the Trooper, asking if he needed any help, and he did.

The traffic congestion was terrible, so I figured I would help direct traffic around the scene, to free the Trooper to complete his investigation. I wasn't aware that this was a fatality accident because the Coroner had already removed the victim and left the scene.

Once I had the traffic flowing normally, I had free time, so I walked over, looked inside the car and saw a lot of blood in the front seat and all over the dashboard. Other then that, nothing seemed out of the ordinary. This is when I learned this car's driver was fatally injured.

I did notice thousands of pennies all over the back seat and floorboard. I felt a sense of frustration that this accident happened a half mile from my home, and I was not the investigating officer.

I could see the Trooper was almost finished with his investigation, so I told him if he didn't need any further help, I would head home. He asked if I would do him one last favor; inventory the penny collection scattered about in the victim's car. It would help him out tremendously, and allow him to get home for dinner. Sure, why not, I told him, I had nothing better to do.

I opened the driver's door, folded the back of the front seat forward so I could get in the back seat, being careful not to get any blood on me. There was a small cardboard box in the back, so I used that to collect the pennies. This was beginning to take longer then I thought, there had been more than a thousand. As I worked my way through this mess, I looked forward through the front windshield to see if the traffic was still flowing by okay.

This is when I noticed the driver's visor was down, flat, like it was horizontal or level with the ground. Resting on top of the visor, I was soon to learn, was the top of the victim's head; the top of his skull with brains leaking out. Holy shit! I got myself out of the backseat in record time. Screw the pennies.

The investigating Trooper saw me making this fast exit and called out asking what was wrong. It took me a minute or two to collect my wits, but I finally filled him in on what I had just seen. His response was, "That explains everything, I wondered what happened to this guy's missing head parts. I guess I should have checked inside the car, but forgot to." "No shit," I told him. "I'm out of here. You inventory your own damn pennies." I didn't sleep well that night.

In the reconstruction of the accident, apparently at the moment of impact, the visor had been in the perfect, horizontal/flat position and it acted as a blade. When the body of the driver slammed forward, the perfectly aligned visor severed off the top of his head.

The top part would never have been noticed if
I hadn't been in the back seat gathering the
stupid pennies.

*   *   *

Traffic fatalities continued to happen in my
area, but it was other Troopers who were the
investigators. I was either off duty, or too
far away to respond in time to be the lead
investigator. This all changed one evening
right before the end of my shift at 2 a.m.

I was the last one on duty for my part of
the county. It had been a quiet evening with
nothing unusual happening. I was looking
forward to going home and getting some sleep.
I was beginning to head in that direction, when
Radio reported a multiple car injury accident
about five miles away from my location on a
state highway near Maltby. I let Radio know I
would be enroute and should be there in three
or four minutes. I hit the siren and turned on
the emergency lights.

While enroute, Radio advised me the roadway
was blocked and that an ambulance had been
dispatched. This was a relief, knowing I would
have some help on the way and they would get
there not too long after me.

As I approached the scene I could see one car,
pulling a small camping trailer, was stopped
in the eastbound lane, facing east. The left
side of the trailer appeared to have been
opened with a can opener. It was sliced open
the full length of the trailer, about two feet
above the wheel well.

A second car was facing west in the westbound lane with extensive front-end damage. The third car was just west of the other two cars, and was on the shoulder perpendicular to the centerline. It, too, had extensive front-end damage, and both cars appeared to be totaled.

There were a few people milling around the scene but most were standing by the third car. As I pulled up to the scene, I could see one body on the shoulder near the third car, and what appeared to be two more in that car. I grabbed my first aid kit out of the trunk and ran over to the body on the shoulder, where people were kneeling, checking the person's injuries. As I walked up, I asked if anyone else was injured. A witness told me there appeared to be two other seriously hurt people in the third car. I decided to check the one on the ground first.

Since I didn't see a driver behind the wheel of the third car, I assumed this person was the driver. He was a young male in his twenties with no apparent injuries. I didn't see any signs of blood. I reached down to check his pulse. His body was warm to the touch. I couldn't find a pulse with his carotid artery, so I switched to the other side of his neck—still no pulse.

I began to wonder if I was not doing this right. I checked for a radial pulse, still nothing. I was really shaken. I felt I was wasting my time because I was worried about the other two occupants of the third car. It bothered me to leave this young man because I hadn't seen any obvious injuries, but with no sign of a pulse, I felt the pressure to keep moving, to check on the others. If they were okay, I'd quickly come back to this victim.

I ran over to the car where people were standing by, looking in the car to see what was wrong with the occupants. I saw a young, probably mid-twenties female in the front seat, and a young boy about twelve years old in the back seat. Both were unconscious and didn't show any signs of visible injuries. I yelled at both of them to see if I could get a response. Nothing.

I forced the driver's door open and got partially inside to check the female's pulse. I couldn't find one on her, no matter where I checked. She felt warm to the touch just like the guy lying on the shoulder. I keep thinking I must be doing something wrong since I couldn't get a pulse from either one.

I reached over the seat into the back and shook the boy. No response. I checked him for a pulse and didn't get one. For crying out loud, I thought, what in the hell am I doing wrong. At this same moment, I realized the ambulance crew had arrived, and were working on the guy on the ground.

The medic yelled that the one they were working on was deceased, and asked if I needed any help. Hearing that question forced me to realize I probably had a triple fatality on my hands. I asked the ambulance crew to come over to the car to verify the two occupants were deceased, and to validate what I suspected was the truth.

It hit me like a ton of bricks. The reason I was not getting a pulse on anyone was because they were dead. All three occupants of this third car were not wearing seatbelts. The Coroner later told me all three suffered broken necks from the impact. Because I had arrived so soon after the accident, the bodies were still warm when I checked for pulses.

I had Radio inform my Sergeant of the seriousness of the accident, to dispatch the Coroner and a photographer, and for additional officers to assist me with traffic control. I knew I was going to be there for a few hours.

After I took my measurements, interviewed the witnesses and other drivers and passengers, I was able to put together how the accident happened. The car with two couples in it, pulling a camping trailer was driving eastbound. A second car traveling westbound approached them from the east. The third car with the deceased occupants had been following behind the car pulling the trailer. I believe all three cars were doing the posted speed limit prior to the accident.

No one was able to tell me, nor will I know why, but the driver of the third car pulled out from behind the car towing the trailer, to pass. In the next second or two it hit the second oncoming car head-on. The impact was so great the two cars in essence catapulted in the air and spun around. As one of the cars was spun around, its fender sliced open the camping trailer as it passed by. Everything happened at 60 mph. Surprisingly, the occupants of the first and second car were not injured at all.

It took me several hours to piece everything together, arrange for transportation for everyone, clear the scene, and go home. I finished my shift six hours after it was to have ended.

This accident bothered me for a couple of months before I began to let go of it. I was slowly but surely becoming seasoned. Not a pleasant thing to experience, but I was indirectly being toughened up for the next one.

*   *   *

It was a Friday night around midnight. Things were kind of slow, but it was drunk time, so I was especially vigilant for DWI drivers. That's when Radio reported a suspected drunk driver northbound from Snohomish heading in the direction of Everett.

I let Radio and the other Troopers know I was a couple of miles in front of the suspected DWI's path so I would handle the call. All I had to do was pull over to a side road and wait. If the car were really heading in my direction, it would just be a matter of two or three minutes before it reached me.

Sure enough, the car approached and fit the description reported earlier. I waited for it to pass by, and when it did, it turned left onto a long trestle that crossed over a slough leading into Everett.

The bridge is a two-lane highway, with no shoulders, about a mile in length leading into the city. The car was traveling at a pretty good speed, and slid a bit as it turned onto the bridge. When it finally got on the bridge, it accelerated at a good clip. Wow, I thought, I had better get my butt in gear so I don't lose him—so I took off after him.

Once on the bridge I tried to get my speed up as fast as I could to close the distance between us. It was only when I reached 100 mph that I realized I wasn't gaining on the car, but it wasn't pulling away from me either. Since I couldn't overtake him, I had Radio inform the city police of my runner, and to ask them to intercept the car when it exited off the trestle.

There was no other traffic on the trestle at the moment, but I was worried about the last little jog in the road as the bridge crossed over a river into the city. I needed to get this driver to lower his speed, since the car might not be able to negotiate this curve at its present speed. So I turned on my overhead emergency lights with the anticipation the driver would acknowledge me and slow down.

The car's speed didn't diminish, so I kept accelerating. My speed was up to 110 mph. We were nearing the bridge high rise. This worried me because I was certain the car couldn't negotiate the curve entering the bridge. Just as I thought this, I saw an oncoming car crossing over the high rise of the bridge. I was really worried because this DWI had been in and out of both lanes and we were covering a hell lot of real estate real fast. There were no shoulders for escape.

In a split second everything in front of me went dark; no lights from either car, no street lights, nothing but the light from my headlights. The car I was after had disappeared. I was still traveling at over 100 mph.

I yelled out for the other oncoming car to turn on its damn lights. I might have used the "F" word. Suddenly I entered a cloud of dust and debris filtering down in front of me. I then realized these two cars had hit head-on and were blocking the road. Damn, there was no room for me to avoid the accident. All I could do was lock up the brakes.

Try making a panic stop at 110 mph. It took what seemed like a lifetime for my patrol car to slow down. There was absolutely no doubt in my mind I was toast. All I could hope for was the damage wouldn't be too great when I hit the two cars. Fortunately my patrol car had the ABS anti-lock braking system, allowing the car to brake straight forward, and not slide off to the left or right.

This turned out to be one of the luckiest moments of my life. I came to a complete stop about ten feet away from the car I was following. Most of the dust had filtered down and my headlights revealed the oncoming car sideways in its lane with major damage. The car in front of me was also sideways facing right. I knew there was only one occupant in this car, and that driver, a male, was now pinned in the backseat. Before I got out of my car, I knew he wasn't alive. I let radio know what had happened and requested they dispatch an ambulance and send assistance.

The car I was following was the closest to me so I went there first. The driver had been forced back into the back seat because the engine was now in the front seat. He had suffered major trauma to his head and chest and was not breathing. There were no signs of life. He was killed instantly.

I went over to the other car to check on those occupants. I found both the driver and passenger were wearing seatbelts, and both were still belted in. They were not seriously injured, but they were in shock. They were also pinned in their car because the front doors collapsed and would not open. I assured them help was on the way. I went back to the patrol car and retrieved my blankets to cover up the injured. By this time another Trooper showed up at the scene to help out.

In the course of my investigation I determined the point of impact to be approximately four feet into the oncoming lane. The DWI had drifted over the centerline and hit the oncoming car headlight to headlight. The DWI driver's speedometer was stuck at 98 mph. There were no skid marks. The other driver had no warning whatsoever.

The Coroner eventually showed up and removed the deceased, and the other victims left in an ambulance. All I could do was take measurements and wait for the photographer to show up. Until he did, traffic was at a stand still and backed up for a mile. Two tow trucks were on standby waiting to remove the two cars.

During our wait, quite a few people had gotten out of their cars and walked up to the accident scene to see what had happened. The other Trooper and I were busy keeping everyone back while we completed the investigation so they would not contaminate the scene. Most of them were respectful of the situation, but I did notice two women, one with her arm around another who was sobbing uncontrollably.

I went over to the two and asked if they might be witnesses. One said her sobbing friend thought the driver I was chasing might be her husband. I asked her why she thought that. She said her friend recognized the car and they saw a shoe about twenty feet away from the car that looked like one her husband wore. This shoe had been knocked off by the impact.

I didn't feel this was the time, nor the place to inform them the driver was deceased. His body had already been removed, so I said all occupants had been removed and taken to the local hospital. Once I had the road clear, they could continue to the hospital to check the status of her husband.

After I cleared the scene, I headed to the hospital to gather the rest of the information for my report from the other victims. I already had the deceased's information. While there, one of the attending nurses told me the deceased's wife was in the waiting room and wanted to talk to me. I went out to the waiting room and met a woman who was different from the one at the accident scene.

I was totally confused at this point. Before saying anything, I asked for some identification. She produced information showing she had the same last name and lived at the same address as the deceased. I then recalled seeing her name on the registration as co-owner of the car. Since she was the surviving spouse I began filling her in on how the accident happened, when the other woman and her friend from the accident scene walked in. This was going to be interesting.

Before I could ask anyone any questions about what the hell was going on, the women saw one another. The sobbing one, from the accident scene, suddenly quit crying, turned around and walked out the door with her friend. I later learned this woman was the driver's mistress.

*   *   *

Over a short period of time I was beginning to feel I'd had my share of fatality investigations, and it was now someone else's turn to cover one.

The next one happened late one night around 11 p.m. I was in bed asleep when the phone rang. I was on twenty-four-hour call, so I knew I was being called out for something. It was Radio, informing me of a one-car possible injury accident on a state highway near Index, about fifteen miles from where I lived. I put on my uniform and was out of the house and in the patrol car in less then ten minutes.

There was little or no traffic on the road at that hour, so I could drive a bit faster without concern. Radio informed me witnesses at the scene were now reporting there were injuries, so an ambulance had been dispatched. I reached the scene a few minutes later. I did not see any damaged cars on the road, only the witness's cars. Most of the people were standing on the shoulder looking down over an embankment on the north side of the road. As I arrived, so did the local tow truck

As I walked to the shoulder area, bystanders were bringing up four small children from a wrecked car down below. The kids appeared to be okay, but with bruises and scrapes. There was no place to put them other then laying them down on the shoulder, so I had the tow truck driver get my stretcher out of the patrol car and placed the most seriously injured kid on it. He also grabbed my two packs of blankets. Each kit held three wool blankets, and with the help of others we covered the four kids to prevent them from going into shock. While overseeing this I was also looking down at the damaged car.

What I saw was a four-door sedan lying on its right side but not touching the ground because it was wrapped around a large tree. The tree was across the front seat area caving in the roof. The car must have flown off the road, and as it went over the embankment, wrapped itself around the tree. It was about three or four feet above the ground, and two or three feet away from the embankment, stuck to this tree.

I now remember, I had only seen children so far and no adults. Looking at the driver's compartment I assumed the driver was still in the car. I needed to get down and check inside to see if anyone was still in the car. It was possible the driver could have been ejected from the car upon impact.

I needed to first check inside the car before doing anything else. This would require jumping about three feet off the embankment onto the left side of the car that's now parallel to the ground. I removed my gun belt and handed it to the tow truck driver to lock in the trunk of my patrol car. I then jumped.

I crawled across the body of the car, lay down and looked inside through the driver's door. The window was missing. The tree had crushed the top of the car down to the front seat. I could see that the driver was female, but was obviously crushed with the top caved in on her. I reached in to check for vital signs, but there weren't any.

I could also see below the driver, a leg and hand of another person in the front seat. I assumed this person was deceased as well considering the collapsed roof. I turned around and took a look inside the back door, and could see a young boy pinned in the backseat. I had enough room to reach down through the broken window to reach the kid's arm and found it cold to the touch. There was no pulse. I pushed him and yelled at him but there wasn't any response.

While in this position I thought I detected movement below the boy and wondered whether there was another passenger in the back seat. I jumped from the car and slid down the embankment until I was underneath the car and could look up into the back seat. I did see a small girl but couldn't reach her to see if she was alive or dead. She didn't respond to my yelling. While in this position I looked forward into the front seat as best as I could, considering the tree was blocking my view, but I did see another adult female. I hadn't any access to her but it was apparent the tree crushed her.

The car's damage was so severe I knew we couldn't remove any of the occupants until the car was pulled off the tree and placed up on top of the road. Even then I knew we would need a welding torch to cut the car open. I yelled to the tow truck driver to go ahead and remove the wreck.

I climbed up the embankment, and went to see how the four kids were doing. I was concerned about shock becoming an issue, especially since the ambulance hadn't arrived yet. As I reached the top I saw the four kids without blankets on them. I asked what the hell happened to the blankets, why weren't they covered up?

A witness told me they were covered, then a few minutes ago a passing car pulled up to the scene and a passenger jumped out, ran over to the kids, pulled the blankets off the kids and drove off. I said, "You must be kidding?" The bystanders were so dumfounded no one got the license number of the car.

I found this to be absolutely, incredibly, unbelievable. There were no other blankets so I took off my patrol coat and covered up the kid on the stretcher, while others did the same for the other three. The ambulance arrived a short time later and took the kids off to the hospital for treatment. I promised myself if I ever learned who stole the blankets I would render some old town instant justice. They were scum.

The tow truck finally got the car hooked up and began to slowly pull it off the tree and up the embankment. Once the car was up on the shoulder I could see the remaining occupants had suffered extreme trauma. They all had died instantly. The car was so severely crushed it would take a cutting torch to remove the bodies.

Sunrise was almost upon us, and traffic would be increasing, so it was decided to put the crushed car on a flatbed trailer, cover it with a tarp, and tow it to the towing outfit's storage yard where we would have more privacy. There, we could cut the car open and extricate the victims. That is where the Coroner met us. With the top cut off, the bodies were removed and taken to the local mortuary.

Later I learned from the victim's relatives this was a family of two sisters and their six children. They were returning from a day visit to Wenatchee. The really sad part was one of the sisters was visiting from California and it was her two children who were killed.

Without witnesses, I had to rely on the physical evidence at the scene of the accident. After examining the road, debris, skid marks, and the car itself, I was of the opinion the car was traveling just a bit over the speed limit when it entered a sharp curve to the left. The driver might have been inattentive and allowed the car to drift onto the right shoulder as she entered the curve.

Once she realized she was going off the road, she over-corrected by steering hard to the left causing her car to cross into the oncoming lane onto the south shoulder. She needed to correct back to the right.

The eastbound shoulder had worn away from the asphalt; so much so, there was a four-inch drop from the road surface. With the car now on the opposite shoulder the woman corrected back to the right to get back into her own lane. This is when the car's left front steering rod broke, apparently from the stress of hitting the gap from the shoulder to the pavement.

As the car headed back to the right, the driver must have tried to correct left to stay in her own lane; however, with the broken steering rod, the car couldn't turn back, and went over and down the embankment, striking the tree. This family outing turned into a terrible tragedy. To make matters worse, some scum-sucking asshole stole the blankets from those four poor kids.

*   *   *

When I signed in service one evening shift, Radio informed me there had been a previous fatality accident a short distance from the boundary of my beat. It was a "for your information" only in case anyone asked about it. The investigation had been completed prior to my reporting for duty.

Through the early course of my shift I was curious about where the accident happened, so I thought I would drive to it and take a look. As I drove by, I saw the investigating Trooper was still at the scene walking around up on an embankment. He was by himself. I wondered if something was wrong so I stopped. I got out of my patrol car and walked up the embankment to meet him and asked why he was still out there. I thought the investigation had finished a few hours ago.

He said he still had some unfinished business to tend to before he could clear the scene. Well okay, let me help, I told him. He told me to go ahead and take off, it would be only be a matter of a few minutes and he would be finished. Strange. I watched him walk away and wander around and through the brush looking for something. I said, "For crying out loud, let me help." He gave in and told me what he was looking for.

The accident had involved a fatality where the car left the road and rolled over several times. The driver was killed when he was ejected from the car. He wasn't wearing any seat belt at the time. The Trooper told me, as the body exited the car, the head was decapitated, and he hadn't found it yet.

"Jesus, you have to be kidding, right?"

Before he could answer, he said, "Never mind I found it." I quickly walked over to where he was standing and I saw it in the middle of a crop of medium size boulders. The head was upright, with the eyes open looking right at us. If we hadn't had our flashlights on we would never have seen it. It was absolutely eerie and creepy.

This Trooper had to remain at the scene until he found it, even if it meant staying until daylight. There was no way he could allow some unsuspecting passing motorist see this head. It could cause someone to have a heart attack, because I almost had one.

*   *   *

Late one night there was a report of a two-car injury accident just across the county line from my patrol area. I was not responsible for that county's accidents, but in this instance I was only about a mile away from the accident scene, so I responded to at least take care of the injured until a Trooper from that area arrived to finish up with the investigation.

It took me just a minute or two to reach the scene. I could see two cars with major extensive damage in the middle of an intersection. As I jumped out of my patrol car a bystander approached me and said one of the passengers was dead. Swell! I let Radio know this accident would require the Sergeant to be present, as required by policy.

Looking at the two cars' damage told the story. One had hit the other broadside at a great speed. I went over to the car with front-end damage and found the male driver to have sustained minor injures. He was lucky because he had been wearing his seatbelt.

Since he was all right for the moment, I quickly went over to check the other car out. That car had major damage to the left side. This was the car that everyone was huddled around.

The driver was out of his car, tending to his female passenger who was in the backseat on the damaged side of the car. Apparently there were other passengers in this car, as they were all standing close by crying.

I pushed everyone away to check the female passenger. I tried several different locations for a pulse, but there was none. It appeared the left side of her body sustained a crushing blow from the impact and she was killed instantly. I checked around, and all the other involved people appeared to be all right. The only thing I could do now was wait for the investigating Trooper to arrive and take over.

After the injured and deceased had been removed, I assisted the other Trooper with the investigation by interviewing the drivers and witnesses, and taking measurements. What we learned was the car with the deceased was traveling northbound in the inside lane racing with another car that was in the right lane. It was estimated from the damage and skid marks, the car was traveling at least 80 mph at the time of impact, in a 50 mph zone.

While the two cars were racing, a third car had come down a hill from the left, or west, approaching the traffic light that was red for this driver. As it turned out, this driver was intoxicated, failed to stop for the light, and entered the intersection at approximately 35 to 40 mph, hitting the racing car broadside, killing the passenger in the backseat. The other unidentified racing car did not stop and left the scene.

There were more then enough witnesses to verify the two cars were racing, while another witness could testify to the traffic light being in the red mode for the DWI driver. A toxicology report verified this driver was inebriated. The accumulated statements and physical evidence was so overwhelming the County Prosecutor was convinced he had enough information to file felony Negligent Homicide charges against both drivers.

This would be the first time in state history when both drivers in an accident were charged with a felony. It was the opinion of the Prosecutor that if one driver had not been racing there might never have been an accident, whether or not the second driver was intoxicated.

The late-arriving Trooper was responsible for presenting the evidence, and I was required to testify regarding my involvement. The trial proved to be very interesting and did receive a ton of publicity. Both drivers were found guilty of Negligent Homicide.

*   *   *

When I first started as a Trooper I was not aware I would, at times, be responsible for notifying the next of kin that a relative had been killed in an automobile accident. This was a shock since the subject had never been raised during my Academy training.

Oddly, this was not discussed at any time once I started working the road. For whatever reason my fellow seasoned Troopers thought I already knew this could happen, so it was never mentioned.

In my first fatality investigation, all the victims were from out of state, and it took the Coroner a couple of days to identify who the relatives were, so he made the notification.

In my second fatality investigation, I was forced into the role still not knowing what was ahead of me after I finished my investigation. Before my arrival at the scene, the victim had already been removed by ambulance personnel and taken to the local hospital. After I completed my investigation and cleared the scene, I went to the hospital to learn who the victim was.

When I arrived at the hospital, the staff informed me the victim was dead on arrival. They handed me the person's identification for my accident report.

The deceased was from the town where the hospital was located, so I asked if the staff had informed the family. They said they hadn't had time, and besides that, it was my responsibility, not theirs. I said, "You have to be kidding, I've never done this before." "Well," the nurse responded, "now's the time to start." She was not a very nice person.

It was around 2 a.m. and in a few hours I thought the accident information could be on the local radio station, so I had better get going. It wouldn't be right for family to learn of this death by listening to the local news during breakfast. I got my courage up and drove to the victim's home.

It was close to 3 a.m. when I approached the house. All the interior lights were off. I was nervous as hell and I couldn't stop shaking. I knocked on the front door. I had to knock a couple more times before lights began turning on inside. Finally this older woman, I believe the mother of the victim, opened the front door. Her eyes first saw my uniform, then looked up at me, then to the driveway and saw my patrol car.

I immediately saw the fear in her eyes and she yelled out her husband's name and began to sob. I didn't know what to do or say, so I waited for the husband to show up. When he did, he said, "Oh shit, what has happened?" I figured there was no way of soft selling this, so I told him their son had been killed in a traffic accident a few miles away from their home.

The mother fainted and collapsed to the floor. I helped the husband lift her to the couch and waited for her to come around. I filled them in about what I knew and where the body was, asked if there was anything I could do to help them, encouraged them to give me a call, and left. I did not tell them their son was probably intoxicated at the time of the accident, it wouldn't have mattered anyway.

This new experience kind of rattled me. I called my Sergeant the next day and told him what had happened and asked if this was normal. He was somewhat apologetic for not having filled me in on other responsibilities we have when investigating fatalities.

He recommended next time to try and find a nurse or clergy to accompany me when delivering this message. He added, "You can never tell how a person will respond to devastating news like this. If you can't find someone to accompany you, go next door to see if there's a neighbor close to the victim's family who can help out." Oh great, I can scare the shit out of the other family, before scaring the one I'm to contact. Two for one.

Two or three years later it was decided by a higher authority that the Coroner would be the person responsible for delivering the death message. Thankfully I only had to do it two or three more times.

*   *   *

Late one evening I was directed to assist another Trooper who was investigating a fatality accident on the eastside of Stevens Pass near Rayrock. As I understood the situation he had been at the scene for a few hours and needed relief.

On the way there, I wondered why he needed relief, and why the scene had not been cleared after all this time. As I approached the scene I got caught up in a long string of traffic that was stopped, probably because of the accident scene.

It took me a few minutes to work my way up to the scene, and I was dumbfounded at what I saw. There was a giant boulder, about the size of a large SUV, resting in the middle of a four-door sedan. What I mean to say is I could see the rear bumper and the front bumper only. The rock had apparently fallen off a cliff and landed right in the middle of this car squashing it flat. The boulder was larger then the car.

The investigating Trooper walked over to tell me the boulder was so large, he had to ask the highway department to dispatch a crane big enough to remove it. The problem was, this specialized equipment was so heavy and cumbersome, it would take a few hours for it to reach the scene of this accident. It was still an hour or so away. That's why he needed relief. He needed to hit the restroom and find something to eat. He had already been at the scene for four hours.

He said he felt there were two occupants in the car, only because he could see a foot here and a hand there, but other then that nothing. Radio reported the car's registration came back to an elderly couple as being the owners. No one would really know for certain whom the occupants were until the boulder was removed. With that he went off to find a restaurant.

I could see removing the boulder was not going to be easy, with the bodies still in the wreckage. For the time being, all I could do now was redirect traffic around the scene until the crane arrived. Eventually the other Trooper returned to the scene and relieved me, allowing me to return to my beat. Once the rock was removed they found the elderly couple in the car.

*   *   *

During the morning rush hour as I was signing in service, Radio dispatched me to the scene of a fatality accident. The investigating Trooper was already at the scene and was requesting assistance because of the uniqueness of the accident. At the time I was coaching a Cadet from the Academy and this was a great opportunity for him. We hurried to the scene. I told the Cadet to follow me until I knew where we were needed.

The accident only involved one car. The driver was heading south from Everett on the freeway in the inside lane, when he apparently had a heart attack. A witness said he saw the driver slump over the steering wheel and his car swerved left onto the inside shoulder, struck and flipped over the guard rail, tumbling down a fifty foot embankment.

The car came to rest upside down in the northbound lanes. The investigating Trooper was down below with the car, while I was up on the embankment. He called me on the radio telling me the body had already been removed. Would I, from my position, follow the path of the car down the embankment and see if any personal belongings belonging to the driver might have fallen out as the car flipped several times on its way down to the bottom.

The Cadet and I hopped over the guardrail and began our descent down. We saw pieces of metal and other parts of the car all the way down. While working our way down we keep seeing small particles of gray matter. The Cadet kept asking me what that stuff was, but I didn't have the heart to tell him. I decided to tell him later what the "stuff" was, when things got back to normal.

When we reached the bottom where the car was resting upside down, I introduced myself to the Coroner, who was at the scene, since this was my first meeting with him after he was elected to the position. He told me what he knew and how the person might have died. Basically the driver was not wearing a seatbelt at the time of the accident and was ejected while his car was flipping end over end down the embankment.

The Cadet interrupted and asked the Coroner what this gray stuff was we saw coming down the embankment. The Coroner said "That's just brain matter that spilled out from this guy's head when it was crushed as the car rolled over on him." I turned to the Cadet and said, "It's a good thing you didn't pick that stuff up." He vomited.

*   *   *

Cop humor is a form of humor used among us to keep our sanity and to relieve stress. At times we can be a bit too caustic, but over the years it becomes difficult to refrain. It becomes a way of life, and we sometimes offend others, including our friends and family. This story is an example of where one of us tested civility.

There was a one-car roll over accident in which the driver was killed instantly. The car was upside down in the middle of the road with the male driver in the car hanging upside down because he was still belted in. The deceased could not be removed until the Coroner arrived to officially declare the person dead. All the investigating Trooper could do was standby and wait for his arrival. Until then, he covered the car up with a blanket so passing motorists couldn't see the body.

During this long wait another Trooper signed in service, and was advised by Radio of the continuing investigation of a fatality and where it happened. So, with no other traffic obligations, this Trooper decided to drive over to the fatality accident scene and check it out.

Upon arriving at the scene the new Trooper was filled in on what had happened, and it was mentioned the deceased was still strapped in by his seat belt. Being somewhat curious the second Trooper walked over to victim's car and picked up the blanket to look inside the car. He picked up the victim's arm and pointed at it and yelled over to the first Trooper, "Hey, look it's a Timex. It just goes to prove, 'it takes a lickin but keeps on tickin,'" a reference to an old watch commercial.

*   *   *

It must have been 4 a.m. when Radio advised of a one-car injury accident at the most southern part of my beat, south of Clearview near the King County line. Considering where I was at the moment, I figured it would take me at least ten to fifteen minutes to reach the scene. I was the only one on duty so I should be the first one there, even before the ambulance crew.

As I pulled up to the scene, there was one car on the right shoulder, which I assumed was a witness. The accident car was smashed up against a concrete pillar head-on. This pillar was exactly in the center of the median, being the sole support of an overpass.

I didn't see any skid marks leading up to the accident scene. The driver of the other car approached me as I was getting out of the patrol car to tell me he was the one that discovered this accident and had called it in to the State Patrol. He believed the driver of the car was dead.

I approached the car and saw the driver was still in the front seat. When his car impacted with the pillar he impacted into the steering wheel, ripping open his chest and abdominal area. Most of his intestines were exposed outside of the body. He was killed instantly. I had Radio notify the Coroner to proceed to the scene.

This was a pretty gruesome accident with guts and blood all over the inside the car. Regardless, I needed to identify the driver and collect the car's information for my report.

When I entered through the passenger door I saw a slip of paper on the front seat. It turned out to be a suicide note written by the driver. With this note and how the accident happened, I assumed he intentionally drove into the pillar. That explained why there weren't any skid marks leading up to the scene.

I couldn't say how long ago this accident had happened. The body was cold to the touch, so it could have happened long before my arrival. That aside, it took the Coroner about an hour to reach the scene.

When he did arrive I walked with him up to the fatal car, and informed him of the suicide note. As we reached the car he immediately began his examination of the deceased. As he was doing this I happened to notice this large balloon like thing in the chest cavity. It was about the size of volleyball.

Pointing at this bulge, I asked the Coroner, "What the heck is that?" He turned and looked, took a ballpoint pen out of his jacket and popped it like a balloon. When it popped it splattered blood everywhere, and on my uniform.

He said it was the guy's bladder and they sometimes inflate like that. I thought I was going to lose my cookies, but I toughed it out.

*   *   *

Knowing I had to work a late day shift of 10 a.m. to 7 p.m., I took the liberty of partying the night before in the belief I could sleep in the following morning. At 7 a.m. the phone began ringing and wouldn't quit. I found the phone and was ready to throw it against the wall, but thought maybe I should answer.

Radio was calling to report a two-car injury accident. "Why in the hell are you calling me?" I asked. "I don't go to work till ten." Radio said the two other Troopers; one working the 6 a.m. shift and the other assigned to the 8 a.m. shift had called in sick. I was the only one left to respond to the accident. Shit. I hauled my butt out of bed, got in uniform and took off to the accident scene about six miles away.

While enroute to the scene, Radio advised the roadway was blocked, and the Coroner had been dispatched. If this were going to be a fatality investigation, I'd damn well need some help. I advised Radio to get one of the other supposedly sick Troopers out of bed to respond to this accident scene and assist me.

As I pulled up to the scene of the accident I saw two mangled cars with extensive front-end damage. The cars were sideways in the road blocking the two eastbound lanes of the freeway. People were crowding around one car, so I assumed this one had the more seriously injured occupants.

I checked this car first and found a male driver, who had not been wearing a seatbelt, apparently impaled himself on the steering wheel and had died instantly.

The female passenger also had not been wearing a seatbelt and slammed into the dashboard. She had died instantly from a crushing blow to the thoracic region. The lone occupant of the second car, the driver, had already been removed by bystanders and was not seriously injured. I let Radio know we needed an ambulance for the other driver.

Eventually both of the early shift Troopers showed up, worse for wear, but they were a great help. What we learned was the older couple must have been confused when entering the freeway and accidently entered the eastbound lanes instead of the westbound lanes, and had driven for half mile before encountering this second car traveling west.

Since the accident happened on a curve, the other driver had very little warning to avoid the accident.

—

I assisted with a traffic fatality on the Narrows Bridge between Gig Harbor and Tacoma. An older pickup with a canopy covering the bed of the truck was beginning to enter onto the bridge, which was experiencing strong winds crossing from the south to the north (left). The canopy was attached to the bed of the truck with four small screws and bolts.

Once the pickup got on the bridge, the strong cross wind struck the side of the pickup, ripping off the canopy. The canopy flew across three lanes of traffic and struck a sedan that was traveling east. The canopy hit in the corner of the windshield in front of the female driver, caving in that portion of the car killing the woman instantly. Her car continued on veering left into the on-coming lanes going forward striking the south side bridge railing.

The car continued on grinding along the railing until it came to a stop a hundred yards later. The driver of the pickup had continued on as if he wasn't aware of his missing canopy. There wasn't any information on the canopy to identify the owner, so no charges were filed. A very sad accident.

Halo Effect

I made earlier mention of the "Halo Effect" that surrounds a patrol car when we're on patrol. It's a frustrating effect we face everyday, but we learn to live with it and adapt accordingly. The only way it can be avoided is to patrol in unmarked patrol cars.

Do you remember the last time you were driving down the freeway minding your own business, but maybe running a few miles an hour over the speed limit, when suddenly you realize you are overtaking a State Patrol car in front of you.

Obviously the first thing you'll do is slow down to the legal limit. No sense asking for trouble. Now you must drive at the annoying speed limit until this damn patrol car exits off the freeway.

Here's another example—you're tooling along over the speed limit when you happen to notice a marked State Patrol car in your review mirror, coming up behind you. Your first concern is the Trooper pacing you, or someone else in front of you? Who knows, but to play it super safe, you get your speed down to the posted limit.

Now you wait to see what happens next. I know it's kind of scary not knowing if you're being

217

watched, but until the moment the Trooper passes you, or exits off the freeway, you drive legally.

In either instance, once the Trooper is not in front of, or behind you, all bets are off. People go back to their normal driving habits and become a bit more careless again. This is what we called the "Halo Effect." Everyone is being good a mile in front of us and a mile behind us. Our patrol cars stick out like sore thumbs, so this indirectly forces everyone to drive safely and legally.

From my perspective when I'm driving an all white patrol car with a blue and red light bar on top, a push bar on the front-end, and State Patrol markings on the side, everyone around me will be the best drivers I'll see all day. That is until I exit the freeway or stop someone, then the halo disappears and there are no more rules to follow.

I experienced the Halo Effect every day I worked. There were times when I got so frustrated with everyone being goody two-shoes, I would pull over into the far right lane and drop my speed down 5 or 10 mph. This really screwed everyone up. They wouldn't know whether to pass me or not, or slow down. Eventually the traffic would get so stacked up behind me, I'd exit the freeway to free up the backup, but at least I got rid of some frustration.

I know that once I take the exit ramp, there will be a few motorists who'll begin picking up their speeds. Out of that group will be a bright shining star that'll break loose from the pack and really take off.

As I slowly take the exit ramp, I watch for that one impatient driver. If there is one, I'll hesitate just a bit then cross over the overpass and enter back onto the freeway and set my speed at ten mph over the limit to see if anyone is pulling away from me. This technique works almost every time.

*   *   *

I have two other choices of how to patrol the freeways to offset the Halo Effect. I can patrol either by being aggressive or passive. If aggressive, I'll drive faster than the posted limit to monitor more traffic, and to overtake other cars while looking for licensing infractions—stuff I would miss if I had been moving slower.

Patrolling passively is when I drive slower allowing traffic to pass me. Either patrol method has merit, so which method I use depends upon my mood for that day

*   *   *

I have always worked for progressive supervisors. My first Sergeant encouraged me to use his patrol car when he was off duty or on his days off. The supervisor's patrol cars do not have WSP markings on them, other then their WSP license plate. They also come in different colors. Most motorists never notice them because of their lower profile. I would

use one every chance I got. Being able to
patrol with a less obvious patrol car is a
tremendous help in traffic law enforcement,
and a hell a lot of fun.

*   *   *

Use of Radar

Statistics have shown speed to be the major contributing factor to most traffic accidents. Everyone speeds at one time or another, its human nature. The more we speed, the more we become careless, and increase the chances of having a traffic accident.

Even though my State Trooper commission grants me full state police powers, our legislature has mandated the State Patrol's primary mission is to prevent traffic accidents. The way to fulfill this mission is to enforce the speed limits. Many times I've been called a speed cop, but I don't really care. It's my job, and it is imperative I be the best at it.

To enforce the speed limit laws, we have radar units and aircraft at our disposal. The aircraft are used most often during fair weather. To conduct a pace of a speeding car takes a certain amount of time, patience, and distance. Heavy traffic conditions can prevent any of the above from happening. Often the only way to effectively conduct speed enforcement is through the use of the radar set.

It's a very difficult task to conduct a speed emphasis patrol in a marked patrol car. Being this visible makes it almost impossible to catch drivers who are intentionally speeding. To save time and money, and for safety purposes, we most often use radar to identify the speeders. Indirectly, there is less danger to others and to us when we're stationary on the shoulder working the radar unit. Use of the radar also allows us to be more selective of whom we stop.

I used the radar unit whenever it was available, and as often as time permitted. There might be only one or two radar units in a Detachment, so I didn't get to use them that often. Since I could not conceal my marked patrol car when using the radar, I had other alternatives. One way was to park on the other side of a hillcrest, preventing the approaching drivers from seeing me until they crested the hill.

The radar beam will reach back about half a mile, so by the time the danger registers with the driver, I will already have recorded his speed. I would never work radar where the traffic might be traveling downhill.

I feel most drivers will be speeding. As a rule, most traffic passing through the radar will be anywhere from 5 mph to 15 mph over the posted limit. Since there are so many over the limit, I had to draw the line somewhere. I couldn't stop them all. So, I set my parameter at 10 mph over the limit. If anyone was traveling over 10 mph, I stopped them and issued citations. There were instances where this minimum limit was too low.

On any given day, the traffic can be traveling as a group well over the limit. When this happens I sometimes have to sit back and figure out where to begin stopping cars. I recall several times other Troopers and I had to set the minimum speed at 15 mph over the limit. Regardless of what speed the cars are running at, if I stop them they will be cited, no excuses.

There were times when we knew from experience traffic would be heavy and fast. One example would be fans traveling to Seattle for a Husky football game. Everyone would be in a hurry to get to the stadium before the kick off, so there were a lot of speeders hell bent to get there. I enjoyed working those days when the Huskies played the University of Oregon. I loved hunting Oregon Duck drivers.

*   *   *

Whenever there is an anticipated speeding issue or problem, a State Patrol Detachment will pool as many Troopers as it can to conduct a radar emphasis patrol. This is where one patrol car will have the radar and remain stationary in a unsuspected spot, while the other Troopers will be parked further down the road and will be the chase cars. The motoring public commonly refers to "unsuspected hiding spots" as "fishing holes."

No matter how the public might interpret this, we need to work these special spots on a regular basis. One "fishing hole" I'm most familiar with is a stretch of freeway north of Olympia where the road drops down slightly then begins a long sweeping curve to the left, then after a short distance begins another turn, to the right. Speed has been the common denominator of most traffic accidents that have happened in this area of the two curves.

The purpose of working the radar prior to this set of curves is to get everyone's speed down before entering them. Common sense should prevail here. Over time our concentrated radar speed enforcement at this "fishing hole" has reduced the accident rate to almost zero.

Unfortunately, we cannot relax and say the problem has been resolved. It is a continual problem and the Troopers will be using the radar at this one location forever, or until the design of the freeway changes.

*   *   *

Thinking back to the previous "fishing hole" I talked about, I remember a time when I decided to retrieve the radar unit from the Detachment office the night before my early day shift. This way, I saved time by already having the radar mounted and ready to go in my patrol car. If I had to go to the office and mount it there, I wouldn't get out on the beat for probably an hour.

My shift began at 6 a.m., and the traffic is as heavy at that hour as it is at 7 a.m. I figured the motorists believed we didn't really start work till 8 a.m., so, I wanted to surprise everyone and actually be at the "fishing hole'" at 6 a.m.

This particular morning, I thought I had planned for everything until the alarm went off. I got up and looked out the bedroom window to see what the weather was like. It was foggy and it was so thick I couldn't even see the house across the street from mine. I figured I would be wasting my time today trying to work the radar. Damn. Regardless, I was going to give it a try anyway.

I headed to the freeway to set up at the "fishing hole." The speed limit where I planned to work is 70 mph. Being still dark at this hour, the traffic would be traveling at the posted nighttime speed of 60 mph. With the fog as thick as it was, the prudent safe speed should be around 45 to 50 mph, not 60 mph. Remember, a driver must not exceed the reasonable safe speed.

Visibility was 200 feet. At 60 mph, there would not be enough distance for drivers to react to danger. They simply would not be able to stop in time. I assumed I wouldn't have any activity until the fog cleared and motorists become more venturesome.

Another problem I faced was if I did chase after a speeder, just starting up entering onto the freeway could in itself be dangerous for me and other drivers.

I planned to sit alongside the highway and scare the shit out of drivers when they popped out of the fog and saw my patrol car on the shoulder. That should slow them down. Anyone speeding in this stuff would have to be crazy.

I couldn't have been set up for more than five minutes when the radar started beeping indicating it had a reading in excess of the

10 mph over the speed limit. I had programmed the unit to alert me whenever there was a speed above the minimum of 10 mph over speed limit. This reading was 83 mph. I couldn't believe it. I looked in the rear view mirror to see what I snagged, but the car hadn't popped out of the fog yet. A second or two later it did, and the car was still traveling at 83 mph.

Screw the safety factor of worrying about pulling out in this fog; I was going after this imbecile. I immediately turned on my red lights and went after the car. By the time I did, he was already beginning to pull over to the inside shoulder, knowing he'd been had.

To be going this fast under these conditions, the driver must lack common sense, or be very stupid. I cited him for Negligent Driving. The driver admitted he didn't have an excuse for his high speed; he was simply late for work and didn't think it was all that dangerous with the fog as it was.

After I released the driver, I still couldn't get over how high this guy's speed was in this dense fog. I went back to my Gotcha hole and set up again. Christ, no sooner then I got set up, another guy comes doing 79 mph. I nailed that guy.

About this time other Troopers are signing in service, and I call them on the radio telling them what's happening and to come over to my location to work the radar with me. In the following two hours three Troopers issued thirteen citations, all for speed in excess of 75 mph in solid fog. Go figure.

*　　　*　　　*

There was one unique enforcement tactic we learned from the Oregon State Police. It involved having three radar units working in tandem. The units would be set up over a distance of two or three miles.

The prevailing thought was, if motorists made it through the first radar without getting stopped for speeding, the drivers may relax, feeling it was safe enough to go ahead and speed up. If that were to happen, the Oregon State Police had a second radar unit about a mile further down the road from the first one.

If speeding drivers were fortunate enough to make it through the second radar, they probably knew for certain they were home free, and off to the races they would go. Third time's the charm.

*　　　*　　　*

I was part of a team of ten Troopers assigned to work an emphasis patrol to confront the Canadians entering in and traveling through our state in celebration of their national Labor Day holiday weekend.

The Canadians are a fun-loving friendly people and they do enjoy partying. Unfortunately, a large percentage of their drivers are too free-spirited, and love to drive fast. When they enter our state, its like there are no traffic rules once they've left home.

It was decided we would not tolerate their total disregard of our traffic rules and regulations. So, we were going to work one long straight five-mile stretch of highway south of Mount Vernon, with multiple radar sets, and our State Patrol aircraft working overhead. This was going to be a fun event for us. I couldn't wait for the emphasis patrol to begin.

As anticipated, here come the Canadians on a Saturday morning without a concern for their own safety, or for other motorists. They just plowed through. If memory serves me we cited approximately 110 British Columbia drivers in two days. Four were cited for reckless driving because their speed was well over 100 mph. It was impressive seeing all these patrol cars with violators stopped, all day long.

*   *   *

There is one long stretch of freeway that intersected with a county road just north of Purdy. The intersection was controlled by a stop sign for the county road traffic. We experienced a high volume of injury accidents at this location, and most were caused by traffic from the county road failing to yield the right of way to the freeway traffic. Adding fuel to the fire, most of the freeway traffic was traveling above the posted speed limit. Quite a few of the accidents could have been avoided if we were able to conduct speed enforcement.

We were fortunate to not have experienced any fatalities up to this point. However, we had to be more proactive to avoid having further serious accidents, and the best way to do that was by enforcing the speed limit.

We had tried using the radar but to no avail. We just couldn't hide well enough with our marked patrol cars. We even tried using the Sergeant's unmarked patrol car, and that didn't work. We increased our patrol time traveling through the area, hoping this would be effective, however, accidents continued to happen. Our District office was continually plagued with complaints from people asking when we were going to do something about this problem.

Thinking about it out loud to my Sergeant, I asked if it was a requirement to have the radar mounted in a patrol car. Does it matter what kind of car we use for the radar? He didn't think so, but would check with his Lieutenant for his insight.

It was the collective opinion of everyone we could use any car as long as it was parked legally and not perceived to be a traffic hazard. They wondered why I raised this question, and did I have an idea we had not tried before.

My plan was to mount the radar unit in a private vehicle, not a state-owned car. They responded by telling me I could not use my own personal car, so that idea was out. "No, that's not what I was thinking; my idea involves my neighbor's car. I have already approached him to use one of his family cars that he hasn't been using. My friend said we could use it, but he wanted me to make sure he wouldn't be held liable if anything were to happen to his car."

Well now, the staff kind of liked this idea. What kind of car is it? I told them, "It's a yellow Chevrolet Vega, a small economy car that was brought over from the Philippines. It has body rust and dents all over it. It really is a piece of crap."

This car would be perfect for working radar. Even the owner was getting a kick out of this, and wanted a picture of the car with the radar in it. The only restriction placed upon us was that I was to be the designated driver, no one else.

The day finally arrived when we were able to bring together four Troopers as chase cars. The plan was, I would park the Vega just off the shoulder in the median where it would not be a hazard to other traffic. I would have the hood up as if it were an abandoned disabled car. The other Troopers would wait further down the road out of sight at the intersection. They wouldn't be able to see the traffic but when a speeder passed me, I would call the description of the car and its speed. They would pull up to the intersection and wait for the car to appear.

It worked like a charm. We must have issued fifteen citations in one hour. The frustrating part was I couldn't chase any of them. I had to sit and wait until the patrol cars returned after each stop to set up again for the next speeder. If I remember correctly, we did not stop anyone less then 15 mph over the posted limit. They were all at a much higher speed.

As successful as this experiment was, the department felt we were pushing the envelope a bit, and elected not to continue using the Vega even though we had permission to use it as often as we wanted.

*   *   *

To avoid speeding tickets from radar, a lot of people have radar detectors mounted in their cars, to get enough warning ahead of time to avoid getting a speeding ticket. The detection units are effective but owning one can be expensive.

If I stopped a car for speeding or for any other infraction, and I saw one of these units mounted in the car, the driver automatically got a ticket for the infraction. I am of the opinion the radar detector means the driver's intention is not to travel at a safe and legal speed, but rather to speed and not get caught.

For drivers to argue they use the detectors to monitor and help them maintain a safe speed is rubbish. I tell them they have a speed control device in their car, so use it.

*   *   *

Radar technology has improved with time. One of the newer versions of radar I never had access to was called moving radar, and we used it when patrolling two lane roads. The unit faces forward and will record the speeds of oncoming cars. To achieve an accurate reading, the operator of the patrol car must be always be maintaining a constant speed. Better yet, if a Trooper has access to an unmarked patrol

231

car, or a patrol car without a light bar, the moving radar is that much more effective.

*   *   *

Today's latest technology is a unit that sends out a laser beam rather then a radar beam. Using the laser makes it easier to identify individual speeders from as far away as 4,000 feet. This is just short of a mile. At this distance speeders will have been identified long before they know it, or before seeing the Trooper.

Speeders

It took me awhile to learn how to detect or sense when a driver is speeding. The sound of a moving car is one way. The relationship of a car moving rapidly through traffic, and experience and a bit of common sense gained over time are other ways. Pacing a speeder is an art in itself. I learned it takes time, distance, and being crafty when driving a marked patrol car.

I know I have to conduct a pace quickly before the driver spots me. Whatever the posted speed limit is, I will set my patrol car speed at 10 mph over that limit. For example, if the limit is 60 mph, I'll set my car's speed at 70 mph and hold it for a short distance. I need to know if the car I'm following is pulling away from me or not. If it is, I know I have cause to issue a citation for speeding.

If the car is still continuing to pull away from me at 70 mph, I'll increase my speed by 5 mph, and hold it for a short distance. If the car is still pulling away, I now have a solid pace at 75 mph plus, or 15 mph over the posted limit. Either way, I'll go forward and stop the driver and issue the ticket. If the car is running faster then 75 mph, then I need to rethink the situation. Should I still try to determine the exact maximum speed this driver is traveling, distance permitting, or do I stop the car before the situation becomes worse.

*   *   *

When drivers are caught speeding and are confronted with the error of their ways, they'll often say they didn't realize it, or, they may tell me they weren't speeding. For those drivers who admit they were speeding, or just weren't paying attention, I'll give them a break by recording a lesser speed, and indirectly a lesser fine.

I do explain to them, if they decide later to appear in court to contest the ticket, I will testify to their actual speed. In most cases the Judge will change the speeding charge to the actual speed I testified to, and the cost of the ticket will increase. Hearing this, drivers are most appreciative, and as a result I never have to appear in court on my days off.

*   *   *

There are times when I've come into contact with drivers with an attitude problem. In a way they can be difficult, but challenging. I know I'm in charge of the situation, and hopefully they'll soon learn this. If the question asked is, "Why in the hell am I stopping them?" I simply explain how I determined they had committed a traffic violation, and how I plan to resolve it.

If they still can't accept my critique of their driving, it's time for me to quit talking, issue the damn ticket and walk back to the patrol car. I have learned arguing gets me nowhere.

There have been a handful of drivers who wouldn't accept anything I say and were truly assholes. No matter how professional I'd try to be, the situation sometimes would get worse. I'm not proud to say I have dropped my guard and adjusted my attitude to that of the violator.

Instead of citing the driver for speeding, if that's the case, I will include other charges that I purposely overlooked. Obviously, doing this is like pouring more fuel on the fire, but in for a penny, in for a dollar. When this has happened, several of the hostile drivers realized they should have just shut up and accepted their medicine.

*   *   *

I must have issued two thousand speeding tickets while working the road. It was a way of life when I was assigned to the freeway. There were obviously other types of violations I issued tickets for, but the majority of them were for speeding. There is a routine to issuing speeding tickets. But some are not normal arrests.

One afternoon while working on the freeway I noticed a car in front of me weaving in and out of traffic. Experience told me this driver was going to take off at a pretty good rate of speed once he cleared the heavy traffic. Meanwhile, I slowly worked my way forward trying to close the gap between the two of us, so I could pace the car once it took off.

It didn't take much longer before the driver was finally able to break loose and take off at a good clip. The stretch of freeway we were on was straight, in an unpopulated area just south of Olympia—nothing but pasture and trees. When I finally got a pace on the car doing 10 mph over the posted limit, I pulled forward to stop it. The car had California plates and there appeared to be a family of four in the car.

As we approached the freeway overpass, I turned on my overhead lights to stop the car. I was hoping the driver would slow down and pull over to the right as we cleared the on-ramp from the overpass. The car was just passing underneath the overpass, when suddenly, a medium sized black bear ran out onto the freeway from a stand of trees from the right side, into the path of the speeder.

The driver immediately hit his brakes to avoid hitting the bear, but did clip it with the right front fender. At impact, the bear was spun around and when it came to a stop, was facing the direction it had just come from. The animal didn't appear to be injured and it went back into the woods. The driver of the car appeared kind of shook up, then realized I was behind him trying to stop him, so he pulled over and stopped.

As I walked up to the car, I saw the wife in the front seat and two small kids in the back, all shaking scared. I mentioned that he was speeding and he acknowledged he was speeding and was in a hurry to visit friends. This is when I got a bit frisky and said, "You know, if you hadn't been speeding, you might not have hit the bear." I told him, tongue in check, the reason we have lower speed limits in our state than in California is because we have wildlife running all over the place.

"So here's the deal," I tell him. "I'm not going to cite you for speeding because I believe you got the message without having a ticket. I'm also not going to arrest you for hunting bear without a license." For whatever reason, he never saw the humor in this, but did swear to obey the speed limit.

*   *   *

One afternoon I met with another Trooper from an adjacent county. We were parked on an on-ramp facing toward his county a few miles away. We were discussing his investigation of a recent fatality.

As traffic passed below he would flinch believing the car was speeding. The reason he was flinching was the speed limit where we were was set at 70 mph. In his patrol area the maximum freeway speed is 60 mph. So, if a car passed by us doing the speed limit, his experienced ear thought the car was speeding. After a few times with him on point, I told him when a car passed by over our limit of 70 mph, I would let him know. He began to relax, and we continued with our conversation.

A few minutes later a 1947 Buick sedan passed below going damned fast. I figured it was doing a minimum of 80 mph. I told my friend, "Now this car is going too fast, go get him." I jumped out of his patrol car and he took off after him. I walked back to my car got in and went to follow him to see how it worked out.

As I entered the freeway I expected to see the two of them stopped a couple of miles from where we had been parked. It should have been a quick simple pace. All one had to do was enter the freeway at 80 mph, and if the car was pulling away, it was a valid pace. In this case as I rounded a slight curve I didn't see them, they were nowhere in sight. What the hell!

I was concerned, so I accelerated to see if I could catch up with them to see if my partner needed help. About two miles later I finally saw them pulled over on the shoulder stopped. I pull up behind my friend's patrol car and saw him inside writing out a citation. I asked him what the hell happened.

Apparently as my friend started down the on-ramp, the Buick was well ahead and had passed out of sight. The unsuspecting driver wanted to test his new engine to see how good it would perform, so he had stomped on the gas pedal and got his speed up to 100 mph.

When my buddy entered the freeway and rounded the curve he expected to see the Buick, but it wasn't anywhere in sight. For a second he thought the car had run off the road into the brush. He quickly got his speed up and eventually spotted the Buick.

He finally paced the other driver at 110 mph. The driver was dumbfounded at being caught, but strangely satisfied he had gotten his speed up to 110 mph. He loved his newly installed engine. Instead of citing him for Reckless Driving, the Trooper cited him for a straight speed violation. This meant a higher fine but his driver's license wouldn't get suspended.

*   *   *

I hear supposedly smart people telling others never to own a red sports car. They say owning one is like owning a magnet to State Troopers. They say it's a known fact that Troopers will chase after red sports cars every time for speeding, because red stands out like a sore thumb and that's what Troopers look for. However, there is another theory to consider, that of the Troopers.

I'm officially announcing this red car theory is a bunch of crap. I will be the first one to admit I did chase after red sports cars; however, I also chased after blue ones, black, white, green, and even purple sports cars. On a few occasions I even chased after red sedans, blue trucks, yellow pickups, even Greyhound buses. How often do you think we see red sports cars? Maybe one out of every 5,000 cars? Get real. I have better things to do than waste my time looking for red sports cars.

*   *   *

One Friday morning I spotted a car traveling well in excess of the speed limit near Monroe, possibly heading towards Seattle for the weekend. I got a pace on it and pulled the car over.

I explained to the male driver how much he was over the posted limit, and that he would receive a ticket for speeding. After I said this, his wife sitting in the front seat started nagging on him; "You moron, I told you, you were going too fast. I told you to slow down, but noooo, you didn't pay any attention to me because you are so dumb. Where are we going to get the money for this ticket, Mr. Stupid? We might as well turn around and go back home."

Wow, the poor guy. I didn't want to hear anymore so I quickly went back to my patrol car to write out the ticket. I felt so sorry for this guy I wanted to let him go, or even reduce the fine, but I stayed the course and issued the ticket for the speed he was doing, primarily because he was too far over the limit.

When I returned to their car to have him sign the ticket, she was still nagging him. If I could have gotten away with it, I would have booked her for verbal assault. Giving him the ticket left me with a sour taste in my mouth. Thank heavens I wasn't married to this woman.

The following Sunday I was working heavy traffic as it headed out of Seattle when I spotted a car traveling over the speed limit. I got a pace on the car and pulled it over. The driver was a female and I explained the speeding infraction to her, and that she would receive a citation for this violation.

While I was writing out the ticket in the patrol car, I could see into her car and the male passenger appeared to be really happy. He was bouncing around, belly laughing so hard I could hear him.

I returned to the driver's door and explained to the woman the procedure for paying the ticket. All this time the male passenger was really yucking it up.

I couldn't hold back any longer, I had to ask this guy what was so funny. He asked me," Don't you remember this car?" "No, why should I," I asked?

He said, "You stopped me a couple days ago for speeding. Don't you remember this bitch nagging me for getting a speeding ticket?" Suddenly it came to me, it was pay back time for his wife.

Can you imagine what would have happened if I had let her go without a ticket? I felt really good after issuing this one ticket. What goes around comes around.

*   *   *

I had been working traffic late one evening on a two lane state highway east of Monroe. I was eastbound when I noticed a single headlight coming towards me. I assumed it was a motorcycle. Sure enough it was as it passed me at a high rate of speed. I immediately did a U-turn and went after him.

Considering the speed the cycle was running, I never thought I would catch up, but I gave it the old college try. I finally did catch him after running for two to three miles. I got a quick pace of 100 mph, and even at this speed, the motorcycle was slightly pulling away from me. I estimated his speed at 115 mph.

We were beginning to approach the city limits of Monroe about half a mile away. My first thought was to get this guy to slow down before we entered the city, so I turned on my overhead lights to let him know I was right behind him. At this point we were cresting a slight rise in the road before entering the city. After the hillcrest the speed limit dropped from 55 mph down to 35 mph as we entered the city. The distance from the 35 mph sign to the city limits was about 200 yards.

The motorcycle rider never slowed down, he crested the hill still traveling over a 100 mph. Fortunately for us, the traffic light at the bottom of the hillcrest was green in our favor. The intersection has a "Y," either you continue west on the state highway or angle left to enter the city. If you go left the speed limit drops down to 25 mph. The imbecile I was following decided to go left at 100 mph.

I knew there was no way in hell he was going to make it, so I backed off waiting for the accident to happen. As the motorcycle began to angle left it tipped over onto its side and slide for 200 feet before coming to a stop. The rider pretty much stayed with the bike all the way. I pulled up behind him and checked him for injuries. He was lucky enough to be wearing a leather outfit that protected him from any serious injury, skinned up a bit, but was able enough to sign a citation for Reckless Driving. He was very, very lucky he didn't kill himself.

*   *   *

You should know the State Patrol does not financially benefit from any of the tickets we issue. The money generated from a ticket is divided into various portions; a percentage goes to the administration of the District Courts, the Department of Licensing, Department of Transportation, and the State of Washington's general fund. The WSP does not get one penny, so the idea we are trying to fulfill a quota for our benefit is nonsense.

*   *   *

During the gas crunch quite a few years back, fuel was expensive and hard to come by. Gas stations closed early in the evening, making travel difficult for some motorists when traveling at night.

To conserve fuel, the State of Washington followed a federal mandate to reduce our maximum speed limit from 70 mph to 55 mph. Why the lower speed limit you ask? Well, a study proved the limit of visibility of your headlights is 55 mph during the hours of darkness. Plus, the optimum best gas mileage can be achieved somewhere in the range of 45 to 50 mph.

For us Troopers it was a nightmare for many reasons. The primary reason was the general public had major difficulty trying to reduce their speed of 70 mph to the new lower limit. Even I felt dropping down 15 mph was like going from the fast lane to a parking zone. It took quite a few months, educating the public to comply with the new limit, before we could reasonably begin to enforce the new law.

One interesting point resulting from this change was that in the past whenever I cited someone for speeding well over the posted limit of 70 mph, 95 percent of the drivers were male. With the new limit of 55 mph, I would guess 50 percent of the speeding drivers were now female. Equal rights prevailed.

Drunk Drivers (DWI/DUI)

Alcohol is a major contributor in fatality accidents. Even though our mission is to conduct traffic law enforcement to prevent traffic accidents, getting the drunk driver off the road was my personal goal. In my opinion a Trooper's worth is determined by how many DWI's he has removed from the road. I measured how successful I was at my job by how many DWI's I arrested each month.

*　　　*　　　*

When I first started as a Trooper, a drunk driver was always referred to as a DWI, meaning **D**riving **W**hile under the **I**nfluence of an alcoholic beverage. For a long time DWI was the common slang word for a drunk driver. As time passed we began to encounter more drivers under the influence of drugs and narcotics. So, there was a change in the verbiage from DWI to DUI, meaning, **D**riving **U**nder the **I**nfluence, instead of While Intoxicated. For the purpose of my stories I will use the term DWI.

*　　　*　　　*

It is not an easy task to find DWI's, place them under arrest, incarcerate them, and testify against them in court. First, it's a given that the best time to find a drunk driver is late in the evening, often on a Friday or Saturday

245

night. Knowing this, I always got charged up when assigned to an evening shift. Later on, I learned DWI's drive at all times of the day or night.

The best DWI hunting time is from 10 p.m. to 3 a.m. I assume some drivers begin drinking around 7 p.m., and will be toast by ten. That's when they start heading home, thinking they're okay. On the other hand, midnight seems to be the witching hour.

One of my truisms is, after the bars close their doors at 2 a.m., I will either find a DWI or I'll be sent to investigate an accident caused by a DWI.

My favorite shift is 6 p.m. to 3 a.m. This shift allows me to have a leisurely dinner around 8 p.m., and afterwards, go DWI hunting. I always work best on a full stomach. Working a late weekend shift will often result in putting in overtime because it takes time to arrest someone, conduct the Breathalyzer test, and book the driver in the county jail.

*   *   *

It is important to know the most common roads a DWI will travel. I began the process by first checking the location of the most popular taverns and cocktail lounges based on previous DWI arrest information. Then, from these establishments, which direction do the drunks most often drive? It's not appropriate to stake out the place, but rather to catch them on the highway a short distance away.

*   *   *

How much does it take to get drunk? A person's body weight does play a role. The larger the person, the longer it might take for them to show signs of intoxication. Regardless of size, you may ask, how many drinks does it take to be legally intoxicated?

The rule of thumb when comparing types of drinks according to alcohol content are, a shot of hard liquor is equal to a bottle of beer, or is equal to a glass of wine. Hard liquor normally has an alcohol content of 80 proof (40 percent), vs. a glass of wine at 14 percent, or a bottle of beer at 4 percent. The alcohol content differs but because of the size of the different drinks, they all balance out to being equal to one another.

As a rule of thumb, a cocktail, a beer, or a glass of wine consumed will add .015 percent of alcohol to one's body. It will take approximately one hour for this drink to be totally assimilated into the vascular system. The more drinks one consumes in an hour, the faster they will become intoxicated. In theory, you have to have five to six drinks in one hour to hit the threshold of .08 percent and be legally intoxicated. Many drunk drivers have told me they only had two drinks, or two beers. These drivers are either very bad at arithmetic, just plain stupid, or drunk.

All people react differently to alcohol. A few will act drunk after only one drink, like my mother-in-law. Others can drink a whole case of beer and not appear drunk, although they are definitely affected.

Another question might be, how can one drink all evening and still stay below the legal limit? Surprisingly, the body will assimilate or rid itself of one drink in one hour. So, if you have one drink per hour, then about an hour later you decide to have a second one, the first one should have dissipated. One drink an hour should keep you out of trouble. More then that, you'll probably become my problem.

*   *   *

If you have been drinking and are driving, I want to find you before you hurt yourself or others. Here's what I look for when hunting DWI's. If the weather is bad and raining, I look for the tire tracks left in the water on the road. If a driver is weaving, the tracks will show that. All I have to do is pick up my speed to see if I can overtake the car before losing it.

When monitoring oncoming traffic at night, I look to see if headlights weave or have jerky movement. I look in my rearview mirror as the car passes to see if it weaves. When I simply come up behind a car that's driving a little under the posted speed limit, a red flag is raised. The slow movers are an indication drivers are trying to be careful, so less speed means less chance of them getting in trouble.

A slow driver will make fewer mistakes, but if I follow them long enough, they'll screw up. It may be just a simple mistake, touching the centerline or fog line, not necessarily going over it. This means a driver is having difficulty staying in his or her own lane of travel.

If I follow them for a while, the mistakes will increase, especially when they need to make a turn or round a curve. Going straight is okay but when you need to steer around something, it can be hard if one has been drinking.

The more evidence I record of a person's impaired driving, the better the chance of a conviction. If a driver hits the line once, it can happen, hit it several times, then something is wrong and I will talk to the driver to see what the problem might be. Anything out of the ordinary will call for a look-see. Does the driver have jerky movement, weaving within his own lane, impeding traffic, going too slow, even speeding, all valid reasons for me to see if the driver is okay to drive.

★   ★   ★

Once I spot a car being driven by an inebriated driver, the prospect of pulling this car over is another experience in itself. I have encountered several DWI's who fail to recognize I'm trying to stop them; they just continue to drive, even after I use my siren. It's times like this when I'm the most careful. Trying to get them to pull over safely is another matter.

First, I must never get too close, when I hit the siren and turn on the overhead lights. There have been a few times when drivers have panicked and locked up their brakes right in the middle of the road. If there are multiple lanes, I can never predict which shoulder they will use to pull off. This can be a major problem in heavy traffic.

My first concern is when the driver has pulled over and stopped. Is the car still in gear? I never stand between our two cars until I know for certain the car is out of gear. To keep the driver at a disadvantage I will shine my spotlight into his side mirror and have my headlight high beams on to illuminate the interior. This way as I walk forward I can see better in the car, first checking out the back seat, then the front seat.

Once I have the driver roll down the window or open the door, I lean in to see if I can smell alcohol. I dread it but sometimes I have to have the driver blow his breath toward my nose. There have been times bad breath almost concealed the odor of alcohol.

I routinely ask for the driver's license and vehicle registration. Now I'll watch to see how adept he is in getting the license out of his wallet, and I watch him search through the glove box trying to find the registration. All the while, I keep the driver talking, listening to his speech. I want to hear whether or not there's any slurring or jumbling of words. If I'm satisfied I have a DWI prospect, I have him get out of the car.

Drunks do not exit cars gracefully. In fact, I need to be ready to catch them. I did not realize at first I should be prepared to catch a falling drunk. One of my very first DWI arrests fell out of the car. As soon as I opened the door, he fell out onto his face. The injury to his face and the bleeding looked so bad I had to take him to the hospital for treatment. I learned it is better to catch them than hospitalize them. Saves me a lot of time.

*   *   *

I need to feel comfortable when I remove a DWI from the road so I have a process I follow. If I'm satisfied the driver is possibly intoxicated, I have him exit the car and walk back to a point between his car and my patrol car to perform a few sobriety physical tests.

First, if at night, I have the driver face away from my car's headlights to check the eyes for dilation. If the driver is not intoxicated, the eye pupils will normally be enlarged in the dark to admit as much light as possible. When I hit him with a beam of light from my flashlight, his pupils will retract.

If a person is truly intoxicated, his pupils will not react when exposed to a bright light. So, I have the person look straight ahead while I take my flashlight and slowly raise it and lower, it passing over each eye. If there is no reaction to light, I now know he is under the influence and place him under arrest.

*   *   *

I use physical tests to further validate what I already feel—the person is too intoxicated to be driving. First, I have the person stand erect with both arms extended, and have him lift one leg, hold it up for ten seconds, then the other leg. An affected person will normally sway and have difficulty keeping his leg up at all. He needs to keep dropping his leg to maintain balance.

Of the three physical tests I use, my favorite is the finger to nose test. Before I have them do it, I first demonstrate how I want it done, and then talk them through it. This one I find the most entertaining.

The driver stands erect, arms stretched out to the side, head tilted back, and eyes closed. Just with this first command he often sways back and forth, and in a few cases, begins to fall. With the swaying I know he'll fail the rest of this test.

On my command I have him bring one arm around and touch the tip of his nose with his index finger. When finished, I have him use the other arm. If he is swaying too badly, I discontinue the test before he falls down.

Here's what happens depending on how much he's had to drink: sometimes he might be swaying so badly he forgets to touch his nose. It truly is hard to touch one's nose when swaying.

He tries to touch his nose where it had been before he started swaying. But the really funny part is where he touches. The areas of the face most often touched are the sides and top of the nose, the eyes, forehead, chin, cheeks, and lips, but most importantly, never the tip of the nose.

The last test I have him perform is the "walking the line test." I make sure we are on level ground, and I have a fog line or crack in the pavement for the driver to follow.

I first demonstrate how I want the test done. He must walk heel to toe; one foot is placed directly in front of the other so the heel is touching the toe of the back foot. Then, I have him walk heel to toe for say ten or fifteen feet, stop, turn around, walk back the same distance and turn around. At the same time he must have his arms extended outward. This should allow him to have a better sense of balance.

This test is also fun to watch. It doesn't require much coordination to do it; however, if one has had too much to drink, it will be very difficult. The bad ones will stumble on the first two or three steps, and just give up because they're too drunk to do it. The hard-nosed ones will give it the old college try and walk down the line, stepping off the line, not walking heel to toe, and stumbling on the turns.

After the tests, I inform the driver he is being placed under arrest for DWI and escort him back to the patrol car. I handcuff him before putting him into the back seat, and belt him in. No messing around, no argument.

Whenever I remove a driver from his car, it's necessary to impound it for safekeeping. A tow truck is dispatched to pick it up and store it in the tow company's storage yard. Before the car is removed, I will inventory the contents to show nothing is stolen, from the time the driver was removed to the time he picks up the car at the tow yard.

*   *   *

I had stopped a DWI, and as I walked to the car, I could see the brake lights were still on and the motor running, as if the car was ready to take off. When I approached the driver's door I could see this large man with both hands on the steering wheel and the gearshift lever still in the drive position.

The guy was just staring straight ahead. It was as though he didn't know I was standing by his car. I was concerned because the car was still in gear, so I needed to get him to turn the engine off.

I knocked on the door window with my flashlight and got no response from the driver. I knocked a few more times, just a bit harder, but still no response. The guy just stared straight ahead with no movement at all.

Suddenly, the guy took off driving straight down the shoulder, not back onto the road. Holy shit! I ran back to my patrol car and took off after him. It wasn't like I was going to have to get up to some dramatic speed to catch him, because the guy was only doing about 10 mph on the shoulder. I radioed for assistance.

It must have looked weird, running with my red lights and siren on, at 10 mph, with other traffic passing by us. A couple of minutes later, having traveled for about half a mile, the driver decided to stop again. This time I decided not to take any chances. I ran up to the front door, opened it, reached in, turned the engine off and removed the key. The car was still in gear and was beginning to roll away, but I was able to shift the lever into the park position. The driver didn't resist at all.

After I had the car stopped, I checked the driver out and he reeked of booze. Since he was not physically resisting, I pulled the guy out of the car, threw him to the ground and handcuffed him. I wasn't really feeling the love here.

I decided to leave the handcuffs on and dispense with the physical tests until I had backup. When another Trooper showed up, I had the subject perform the physical tests, but he failed them. So, off to jail we went to book him for DWI. While at the jail I tried to get the guy to take the Breathalyzer test, but it turned out to be a waste of time. He couldn't process what I was asking him to do. He wasn't all that drunk, just a strange duck. Oh well!

*   *   *

Drunks as a rule are friendly and cooperative. However, I will not take unnecessary risks when I encounter those few who could become combative. When I feel I have a DWI with potential issues, I immediately call Radio for backup.

Normally when I first contact a potential DWI, I can tell in the first few minutes whether or not this contact will be a bad one or not. I know I can avoid aggravating the situation, if I'm patient and take the time to talk the person through the process.

The reason a person is handcuffed is primarily for officer safety. Once the handcuffs have been put on, I quickly search the person for any contraband or weapons. When searching, I have to be careful so I put on leather gloves to avoid getting stuck with tainted needles that might have the HIV virus.

All DWI's are subjected to a Breathalyzer exam. I would guess 99 percent of the drivers consent to the test. The one percent who refuse are a win-win situation for me. Instead of having their driver's license suspended for 30 days, they will now be suspended for six months because of their refusal to take the test.

After the test, the subject is taken to the county jail to be processed and incarcerated. The whole process of the traffic stop, roadside test, breath test, and taking the prisoner to the county jail to be booked, can take from one to two hours to complete.

*   *   *

One evening I arrested a man for DWI and while waiting for the tow truck to arrive he complained it wasn't necessary for me to impound his car. I told him it was for safekeeping. He asked me just to leave it there and he would pick it up in the morning. I told him, "I don't trust that you'll wait until morning to get your car, and even with the car impounded, the tow company won't release the car to you until you have sobered up the following morning."

The car was towed away, and I took the driver to the office and conducted the Breathalyzer test. The test results showed him to have a .23 percent reading—way too high to be driving. I processed him through the jail, and went back to my office to finish with my arrest reports. About half an hour later having finished with the paper work, I went back out on patrol.

Once back out on patrol for about fifteen minutes I noticed this car weaving back forth in its own lane. As I got closer, I wondered if this wasn't the same car I had stopped a couple of hours ago. I thought, it couldn't be the same one because the other one was impounded. I quickly checked my Officer's Notebook to see if the license plates matched. Sure enough, they did. I couldn't figure out how this happened, but the car needed to be stopped.

The driver turned out to be the same guy I just booked at the county jail. I couldn't believe it. I asked him how in the hell he got his car back. He told me it wasn't that big a deal. He posted bail immediately then called his girl friend to pick him up at the jail. He then allowed his car to be released to her, and when she got it, he took control of it, and was now heading home, so no big deal.

I told him it was a big deal, because he was still intoxicated. He said he felt fine, and to leave him alone. Well, I thought, I'll have to prove him wrong. There's no way in hell his alcohol content will have lowered that much in such a short period of time. I had him perform the physical tests a second time, and this time I didn't have to explain how I wanted them done. He already knew the procedure. He wasn't that much better the second time around.

I placed him under arrest, impounded his car again, took him back to the office and he blew a .19 percent on the second Breathalyzer test. This DWI later tried to separate out the two charges of DWI with different court dates, but once the Judge heard the circumstances behind the arrests, he combined the two. Mr. Obnoxious spent five days in jail and his license was suspended for a year. These were the two quickest DWI arrests I ever made.

*   *   *

One warm weekday around noontime, I noticed a sedan ahead of me with a male driver pulling onto the highway in the same direction I was traveling. He had pulled out from a Mexican restaurant parking lot but I didn't think anything of it at the time. I continued on patrol.

I must have traveled a quarter of a mile behind this motorist when suddenly the car began to weave. It hit the lane divider line and then the white shoulder fog line a few times. This was somewhat surprising because normally you wouldn't see a DWI at this time of day. I continued to follow the car and became more concerned with the continued weaving. Obviously the driver must be intoxicated, so I thought I'd better stop him before he has an accident. I pulled him over.

I approached the driver and asked for his driver's license and registration. I leaned in the car to see if I could detect the smell of alcohol, but couldn't. The driver's speech was fine. The only thing out of the ordinary that I noticed was a small Poodle dog in the back seat.

I realized he was not intoxicated so I asked him why he was having trouble staying in his own lane, weaving back and forth. He said he wasn't aware he had been driving that badly. He then added it was probably because of "My God damn dog, that's probably why I was weaving." I was dumbfounded. I asked him what the heck he was talking about? How could the dog cause his bad driving?

It seemed this poor guy's wife had passed away a few months before, and one of her last wishes was for her husband to take care of her dog, a small toy poodle. The driver, the husband, hated the dog and the dog hated him, but he wanted to honor his wife's wishes so he tolerated the little devil, until today.

He continued, saying he had stopped at his favorite Mexican restaurant to pick up some take-out for lunch. After he got back into his car and was heading out onto the road, he noticed a mess of paper, fabric, and plastic all over the right front seat. He couldn't figure out where it all had come from. He looked back over in to the rear seat and saw the Poodle sitting there with fabric in its mouth.

The driver looked around inside his car and finally noticed where the right front windshield visor had been chewed to pieces. It had been totally striped of the fabric. Just the frame of the visor was left.

The dog had decided to show its displeasure while the driver was in the restaurant, probably getting back at him for some previous transgression. The reason he said he was weaving was probably because he was trying to kill the dog. I let him go. In hindsight, I should have cited the dog for vandalism.

*　　*　　*

I had just finished incarcerating a drunk driver at the county jail and was returning to my assigned area. I was on the freeway in Everett, traveling south in the inside lane when I noticed a car coming towards me in my lane. This could not be happening. It was midnight, a well-lit area, with very little traffic at that hour—so why in the hell was this car in my lane going the wrong way? I'm quite good at asking critical questions like this, but just then I decided I'd better get the hell out of the way.

I was in a 60-mph zone, but the car coming at me appeared to be doing around 20 to 25 mph. This gave me time to get my speed down and come to a stop. I flashed my high beams several times, but that had no effect. I quickly turned on the overhead red lights, but there was still no response from the other driver. I began to panic, and since the car was only a hundred yards or so away, I put the transmission in reverse and began backing up, while all my emergency lights were on and flashing.

The other traffic around me was heading to the shoulder to avoid getting hit. I blew the siren. The car kept coming. It was only a few feet away from the front end of the patrol car. If I were to stop, it would have hit my car. So there we were, two cars heading down the freeway, one going north backwards, and the other also going northbound.

It seemed like a life time, but it was probably only a minute or so, when the oncoming driver finally recognized the siren or the flashing red lights and stopped in the inside lane. Not wanting to leave anything to chance, I bailed out of my car and ran up to the driver's door, opened it, reached in, and turned the motor off. I was shaking so badly I wanted to punch out the driver, until I looked and saw a little 84-year-old lady. I was stunned.

She was drunker then a skunk. This lady scared the crap out of me so she was not going to get the senior discount. I didn't even bother with having her take a breath test; I placed her under arrest and took her to the county jail. When I arrived, the jailer asked me what my mother had done wrong this time. Funny guy.

We didn't really incarcerate her, we just held her in one of the supervisor's offices until a relative came to pick her up.

*   *   *

The Academy staff trained us to be aware drunk drivers will be out and about, day or night, and not to believe we'd only find them when it's dark. I never quite understood why they told us that, because for several months I never saw or even heard of other Troopers stopping a DWI during a day shift, that is, until I came across one.

Around mid-morning while patrolling the freeway near Lynnwood, I observed a full-sized school bus drive off onto the shoulder then back into its lane. Not a serious violation in itself, probably a simple mistake by an inattentive driver, it happens to all of us. A short distance later, the bus took the next exit off the freeway, and when it did, drove off onto the shoulder and this time almost completely into the ditch, but was able to steer back onto the shoulder.

I had also taken the exit and was directly behind the bus, because I was heading home for lunch. When I saw the bus go into the ditch, quickly turned on my overhead lights, and blew the siren to get the bus to stop, before it reached the intersection at the end of the exit ramp. Something was really wrong inside the bus and I needed to check it out. I suspected something might be mechanically wrong with it.

As I walked along side the bus I didn't notice any children on board. Apparently it was heading back to the school bus barn after dropping the kids off at the school. I could see a female driver and I knocked on the folding door to be let inside.

As soon as I walked up the steps to the main floor of the bus I was immediately overwhelmed with the odor of alcohol. I looked at the driver and noticed her eyes were dilated. I asked if she had been drinking. She said, "Yes." I asked if that's why she was having trouble staying on the road. She said, "Probably." I told her to turn off the motor and exit the bus.

When she stepped down, I had her perform the physical tests to see if she was physically impaired. She was. I placed her under arrest for DWI and put her in the patrol car. I had Radio call the school authorities to see if someone would come to the scene to take the bus away instead of my having to impound it. I did not want the impounding fees to affect my property taxes.

While waiting for the relief driver I asked the bus driver where she was heading. She said she just finished dropping off "the little fuckers" and was taking the school bus back to the storage yard until the afternoon pickup. Her speech was becoming more slurred, and I told her I thought she had had too much to drink and shouldn't have been driving the bus. She told me that was probably true; it was just that she couldn't stand the little monsters unless she had a couple of belts.

One of the school authorities met me at the scene of the arrest to find out why one of their school buses was a problem for the State Patrol. When the supervisor learned one of their drivers was being arrested for DWI, he was shocked. He told me this had to be a first for the school. It was a first for me as well.

*   *   *

To get a conviction at the current .15 percent blood alcohol, a person had to be really intoxicated. I knew from experience that anyone with a reading of at least .15 percent would be in terrible shape. He would be driving all over the road, speech impaired, and physically unstable.

In my day we really had to have an obvious drunk driver because the defense attorneys were tenacious and the judges were too wishy-washy. Even though the physical evidence might indicate the driver was inebriated without a .15 percent reading, the DWI charge more than likely would be reduced to Negligent Driving, HBD (Had Been Drinking).

We Troopers have always believed a person's reflexes were affected by alcohol with a much lower reading, but it took several years and deaths to wake everyone up and eventually reduce the legal limit of impairment to .08 percent.

Every year more people are killed on our country's highways then all the soldiers killed during the Viet Nam War. For this reason, I foresee the day the legal limit of intoxication will be lowered again.

*   *   *

I came to realize if a driver had a higher reading then .25 percent he would act like a wasted, stumbling drunk. Women with that high a reading would be in worse condition because of their lower body weight. This is not rocket science, the higher the reading, the drunker they appear. The higher you go over .30 percent, the more drunks will pee or shit their pants, talk incoherently, or be unable to walk for that matter, let alone drive an automobile.

The general opinion of the medical professionals is, if a person continued to consume enough alcohol to reach the level of .40 percent, that person's body will shut down and, and they will probably die from alcohol poisoning.

The State Patrol policy is if we have a DWI blow .40 percent or higher, we immediately conduct a second breath test to see if the alcohol content is still rising or falling. If it's on its way down, then we can incarcerate them. If still rising, then we must take them to the hospital to be treated for alcohol poisoning. I was of the opinion no one would survive with a reading of higher than .40 percent or higher. I was proven wrong.

*   *   *

One night, around one a.m., I noticed I had less then half a tank of gas left, so I filled the gas tank knowing the bars were beginning to empty out. I did not want to be caught without enough gas during the approaching witching hour.

Just after I filled up, I went back on patrol. A mile later, I came up behind a car driving about 5 mph under the posted limit. Only old people and drunks drive at this speed at this time of evening, so I pulled up closer to the car and followed. A short distance later the car hit the fog line once. Normally I would not have paid much attention to this mistake; however, as I said, this is drunk driver time, so I stopped the car. I explained the violation to the driver and when I smelled alcohol, I asked him to get out of his car.

The male driver appeared to be normal, standing all right, and his speech was fine, but the smell of alcohol was so strong I didn't feel right to let him go just yet. I checked his eyes with the flashlight to see if they were dilated, and when they didn't respond to the light at all, I knew he was inebriated.

I had him perform the normal physical tests, and he did well with all of them. His eyes not reacting to light convinced me he was a DWI. I was concerned I wouldn't stand a chance in court the way this guy had handled the physical tests, plus he had only hit the fog line once. However, I felt he should not be allowed to remain in his car. If I wouldn't let him drive, then I would have to place him under arrest for DWI, which I did.

The guy never complained at all and was more then cooperative. I imagined I probably would be laughed out of court with what little evidence I had at this point. I impounded the guy's car and headed to the county jail to conduct the breath test.

Once we arrived at the county jail I quickly warmed up the Breathalyzer. I had the driver blow in the mouthpiece, then sat back and waited for the results. Every time I run a breath test I try to guess what the reading will be. I'm pretty good at guessing, but in this case I wasn't even close. I was worried about this one. I guessed he would be around .15 percent, possibly lower. I also thought if he blew less then .15 percent, I'd have to reconsider the charge of DWI.

It seemed like it took forever for the machine to produce the result. Finally the green light came on. I turned the dial slowly as it moved to the right from .00 percent upward. I was holding my breath as it approached .15 percent. Please let it reach that number, I pleaded. The needle went past that number and continued on up. Well I'll be damned, my hunch was right; this guy was under the influence.

I continued to turn the dial upward, and the needle passed the .20 percent mark, and kept going higher. The breath sample was so strong the needle was telling me we had a way to go yet. It passed the .30 percent mark and I said out loud to the driver, "Jesus Christ, what have you been drinking?"

The needle continued on upward. I was absolutely dumbfounded. The needle finally stopped at .40 percent. I looked at this guy and told him, "According to this reading you're supposed to be dead." He actually laughed.

Everyone on the jail staff was aware of the high reading and came into the breath test room to see the results. My highest reading for a DWI up to this point was a .36 percent. Because of this high reading I was required to run a second test to make sure the drunk isn't still going higher. So I waited another twenty minutes before running a second breath test.

The second test results came back at the same .40 percent. I now wondered whether the machine was functioning properly. The driver was friendly and willing to cooperate so I ran a third breath test. This time the results had a reading of

John Young

.38 percent. I felt a bit more comfortable knowing he was somewhat stabilized and heading back down, and I could book him for DWI.

During the booking process I asked the guy why he wasn't surprised at the reading. He told me it wasn't that big of a deal because he was a terrible alcoholic and a very heavy drinker. He added he had consumed a half-gallon of Vodka and a case of beer that afternoon and evening.

He had been drinking heavily for so many years his body was accustomed to the high liquor content and had adapted accordingly, explaining why he did so well with the physical tests. A lesson well learned for me, and a better understanding of alcoholism.

*   *   *

A couple of years later I apprehended a woman driver who blew a .42 percent. Her second test had her one notch down at .41 percent, but I decided not to screw around with this because of her lower body weight. I had her hospitalized. She too didn't appear to be all that incapacitated, with a reading that high.

*   *   *

The second Sergeant I worked for had the innovative idea of putting five or six Troopers together on the same late evening shift for the purpose of conducting a DWI emphasis patrol.

All the Troopers would be concentrated in an area where we knew most alcohol-related traffic accidents occurred. The area included five

268

square miles of state and county roads. To accomplish his goal he had to borrow Troopers from other detachments to ensure there would be adequate coverage for his own area of responsibility during the day shift.

The Sergeant's idea had never been tried before and the Troopers were really excited about giving it a try, and more than willing to change their shifts to a later one. If it worked, we would be trendsetters for the rest of the department.

The detachment Troopers fondly referred to this exercise as the "Witch Hunt." As it turned out, this special emphasis patrol was so successful the Sergeant later received a commendation for his idea.

The Sergeant's instructions were simple—we should not concern ourselves with things like minor equipment violations, but instead concentrate on stopping the violations drunk drivers most often commit. That is, touching the fog line or centerline, going too slow, following too closely, jerky stops, brushing up against curbs, and running red lights.

When working this type of emphasis patrol, I felt that regardless of when my shift started—6 p.m., 7 p.m., or 10 p.m.—if I could nab a DWI right at the start, I would have a great evening. I always liked to put a little pressure on my peer group for them to step up to the challenge.

When I did arrest a DWI and had to take him to the county jail, I made sure everyone heard my transmission to radio saying, "I'll be enroute to the county with one for a test." The other Troopers knew what it meant, and that I would shortly be back out on the road looking for the next one.

Depending on the drunk's attitude and cooperation I could conduct the Breathalyzer test and booking process within an hour. Often the process could take up to two hours. The time I saved allowed me to get back out on the road to look for that second or third DWI. It was not unusual for all of us to end the evening with three DWI arrests. If one of us had less, he would hear about it from the other guys. If I ever had less then two arrests, I was disappointed. One evening I arrested five DWI's in one shift.

Over a period of three months of emphasis patrols, I worked eight late evening shifts. During those days, I apprehended and removed from the road, approximately twenty-two DWI's. I'm sorry to say I did not have the highest total DWI arrests. I believe I placed third. One of my buddies had a total of forty DWI's over the same period. What a show-off.

*   *   *

During one of the Witch Hunt evenings I had already arrested two DWI's and was starting to panic because I was almost at the end of my shift with the bars and taverns already closed. I wanted that third DWI before going off shift.

While on patrol I noticed one of my partners had a car stopped in a grocery store parking lot. I pulled over to see if he needed any help. No, he was fine he said. He had stopped a guy who appeared to be intoxicated and would probably have to arrest him for DWI. My friend asked if I would stand by while he had the driver do the physical tests. I said sure go ahead, I'd wait a few minutes.

While the Trooper was conducting the tests I looked over at his patrol car and noticed three men in the car, two in the back seat and one in the front seat. Who are these people and why is this one in the front seat of the patrol car? Policy does not allow anyone in the front seat other then officers. Now that I think about it, if my friend is going to arrest this other guy for drunk driving, where's he going to put him?

Finally my buddy walked over and told me he was going to book the guy and asked if I would stand by until the tow truck arrived to impound the car. I said sure I would, however, who are those people in your patrol car? Oh, those guys. I arrested all of them for DWI. I just keep stumbling across them on the way to the jail.

I said why don't you let me take this last guy in and you can work with the other three. No, no, he said, everyone is fine with this. They think it's a kick to see other guys getting arrested for what they just got nailed for. They're all laughing right now knowing this new last guy is going to jail with them.

He said, "I'll just squeeze this last one in between the two in the backseat." To kind of rub it in he said he believed this might be his sixth DWI arrest for the evening. Then I knew why he wouldn't give up the last DWI to me.

I have pride, and being the classy guy that I am, I rise above the situation. I called him an asshole. As it turned out this was some sort of record statewide for total DWI arrests on one shift by one Trooper.

*   *   *

I was working an early morning shift that began at 7 a.m. The traffic was heavy at this hour with Boeing workers heading to the manufacturing plant where they were producing the 747. Most employees were working constant overtime and putting in as much as 80 hours a week to help build the aircraft, filling orders as quickly as possible.

The workers earned tremendous wages with their overtime, but they were very tired and getting ragged around the edges. It was not unusual to find a driver going to or leaving the plant exhausted and committing minor traffic infractions. We had to be somewhat understanding but still stay firm, otherwise things could really get out of hand.

One morning I was traveling in the same direction as the Boeing workers, heading to work. I noticed the car ahead driving onto the shoulder a few times, like a drunk driver would. I was certain I wouldn't find anyone drunk heading to work this early in the morning. However, this driver kept driving onto the shoulder, not just touching it but sometimes completely onto the shoulder.

I watched him do it a few more times then decided I had better stop this car before something bad happened. Even passing traffic was reluctant to pass this car. When the driver acknowledged my emergency lights he stopped. He didn't even have to pull over onto the shoulder as he was already on the shoulder.

I went up to the car leaned in through the window to see if I could smell alcohol, but couldn't detect it. I asked the male driver why he was driving on the shoulder so often. He said he was probably distracted because of work issues and wasn't paying attention.

He elaborated he was employed by Boeing and had been working extraordinarily long shifts for months now and he was plainly and simply exhausted. He said he was very sorry and felt badly I was wasting my time talking to him.

I asked him if he was so tired why not get more sleep at night. He said there was never enough time to sleep, eat, or spend time with the family with these ungodly hours he was working. He was dreading going to work that morning, but there was pressure on all the employees to get this new airplane into production. I decided he had enough on his plate without me dropping a ticket on him so I told him to take it easy and get to work. No ticket.

The guy thanked me and said he would be more attentive. I went back to my patrol car and waited to let him get back out into the traffic before I went back on patrol. I waited and waited. After two or three minutes I wondered if he might have some other issues I was not aware of and just maybe I should go up and talk to him. But, at that moment he started up his car and left.

When I say he left, it wasn't back onto the road, but rather continuing straight ahead on the shoulder. What the hell? As I watched this I was wondering if he was ever going to leave the shoulder and get back on the road? But, he didn't, he was still driving on the shoulder, and he was approaching a bridge abutment about a hundred yards away. I was really concerned.

I began to drive forward to warn him of the bridge. As I neared the car, the driver suddenly swerved back onto the road and narrowly missed the abutment. Whew! Well fine, he would be all right, but I was going to talk to him anyway.

While I prepared to stop the car, the guy drove back onto the shoulder after passing over the bridge. Enough is enough. I turned on the lights and hit the siren to pull him over a second time.

I went forward planning to be harsher in my assessment of his driving skills. I had decided he would receive a citation for driving on the shoulder a second time. There was no excuse for this.

I asked him why he insisted on continuing to drive on the shoulder after I told him it was illegal to do so. His response was he didn't know that he had. Oh, oh, we have a problem Houston.

He was really, really sorry. I asked if he had been drinking because he was driving like he was intoxicated. No he had not been drinking; all he had this morning was coffee and couple of pills. "What kind of pills were they," I asked? "Oh, at night I take downers, something to make me relax. You see, the stress of the job is keeping me awake so I can't sleep anymore. Anyway, I took a couple of uppers before leaving for work just to keep me going."

He continued, saying he got more rattled when I pulled him over, so after I left him, he took four downer pills because he was really stressed out and needed to calm down before reaching work.

I realized I needed to get this guy out of his car and check him out. Even though it was daylight I could see his pupils were as large as dinner plates. He was looped. He had trouble performing the physical test, so I placed him under arrest for DWI.

I felt I was kind of out on a limb here because I never had come across a person before who had been under the influence of a drug or narcotic. I now better understand why the statute reads, "Driving a motor vehicle while under the influence and/or affected by an alcoholic beverage and/or a drug." This was my first DWI arrest where alcohol was not involved. I never suspected that in the near future drugs would become a problem as serious as alcohol in traffic accidents.

*   *   *

Probably the grossest story I have ever come across was one involving one of my fellow detachment Troopers with whom I had attended high school. He had come upon a car that was parked on a side road with a flat tire. He went up to check the car out and saw there was a driver inside and who obviously appeared intoxicated. There is another statute that states an intoxicated person cannot be in physical control of a motor vehicle.

In this instance, the driver reeked of alcohol, and was passed out behind the steering wheel. The car was drivable with the key in the ignition. The Trooper woke the guy up and had him get out of his car. He was placed under arrest for being in physical control of a motor vehicle while intoxicated.

While the Trooper was beginning to handcuff him, the guy explained, "I have colon cancer and I'm about to shit my pants from my recent radiation treatment." He then said, "No wait, I actually just shit them." The Trooper shined his flashlight down and could see shit running from inside the pants down over one of the shoes. Plus there was this repugnant smell.

The Trooper felt really sorry for the guy, but he could not leave him there intoxicated with his car, so he decided to transport him to the hospital instead. The problem now was, how to prevent the seat in the patrol car from getting soiled. The Trooper told the guy to wait a minute while he retrieved a blanket from the trunk of the patrol car.

While the Trooper was looking in the trunk, the DWI took off running into an adjacent field. The Trooper chased after him and stopped him in the middle of the field. My friend was trying not to get himself soiled so he tried to keep the guy at arms length to avoid getting any crap on his uniform.

The guy was restrained and convinced he was under arrest and might as well get in the patrol car, which he did. The driver was now going to jail rather then the hospital.

On the way to the jail, the Trooper had all four windows rolled down, and the air-conditioning on full force to get relief from the smell. It was a terrible, terribly long ride to the county jail. My friend was not the most popular Trooper at the jail that evening.

*   *   *

Here's another story involving the same friend. My buddy came upon a car actually stopped on the road, not the shoulder, with the motor running, on a city street in Lynnwood. There was a driver behind the wheel with his head slumped forward. The Trooper went up to the door and tapped on the door window with his flashlight to get the driver's attention. When the male driver didn't respond, the Trooper opened the door and was hit with an incredibly bad smell that almost made him gag.

The driver had vomited on his chest and it ran down and pooled in his lap. My friend's first thought was, this can't be happening to me again. Why can't this happen to Super Trooper or one of the other guys, why me?

His concern now was he simply did not want this guy in his back seat, like last time. He was thinking; No, I'm not going to go through this again. He had Radio dispatch the local city police to handle the drunk in physical control of a motor vehicle since this was inside the city. Afterwards my buddy continued on routine patrol feeling much better.

*   *   *

I did get caught up in two serious scuffles assisting other Troopers with drunk drivers. On both occasions the incidents involved ironworkers who were in extremely good physical condition. Both weren't trying to hurt us; they simply did not want to go to jail.

This one guy, whom we had pinned to the ground, was so strong we couldn't afford to release one of our hands to handcuff him because we would lose leverage and the guy could break loose. The only way we were able to subdue him was when two passing motorists stopped to assist us. While they sat on him, we were able to handcuff his wrists and hog-tie his legs. The struggle went on for at least ten minutes. I was so exhausted I couldn't catch my breath for several minutes.

Just to play it safe I rode with the Trooper when he transported this nut job to jail. In spite of his restraints, this prisoner was not going to go quietly. He kicked the back doors with his feet, thrashing about, and constantly yelled obscenities at the Trooper. Once at the jail the prisoner became more cooperative.

*   *   *

Whenever I worked an evening shift I would wear a cheap wristwatch. I knew the possibility existed I could get caught up in a scuffle with a drunk, so I never wore my best watch to avoid having it damaged. It doesn't take long to recognize the signs when a drunk driver's not going to be cooperative.

When I reached the point of a possible confrontation, I dramatically made a big scene out of removing my watch off my wrist and gently placing it on the trunk of the patrol car. The drunks always asked me what I was doing. I told them, since they were not going to be cooperative, I didn't want to damage my watch when I duked it out with them. "Oh, before I forget, after our fight I'm also going to charge you with felony resisting arrest." The DWI's always became cooperative at that point.

There was one time, however, when this technique didn't work. The driver said he didn't give a shit about my watch, and the minute he said that, I knew I needed to act fast. I immediately grabbed him around the neck and took him to the ground before he knew what was happening, and handcuffed him. No fight, end of problem.

*   *   *

One evening I moved behind an older sedan that was weaving back and forth from over the centerline to driving onto the shoulder. Obviously, I was following a potential DWI and decided to pull the car over. As I approached the driver's door I could see the car was leaning to the left. I was thinking, this old car is really in need of new shocks. The driver rolled down his window to present his driver's license. I could see this guy was very, very, very large.

Because I smelled alcohol on his breath, I had him get out of the car to perform some physical tests. Did I say he was large? I should have described him as a giant. After he extricated himself, I could see he was about six feet tall, and must have weighed at least 400 pounds. If he had headlights on his forehead I'd think he was a Volkswagen. In the back of my mind I was hoping, actually praying, he was going to be cooperative.

He failed the physical tests, so I placed him under arrest for DWI. Now what do I do. I needed to follow policy and handcuff him and place him in the back of the patrol car, but wasn't sure that would work. First, this guy's wrists were too big and the cuffs wouldn't fit. I had him put his arms behind to apply the cuffs but because of his size, the arms couldn't get close enough for me to even try to cuff him.

Since the driver was being very cooperative and was following my directions, I asked him if he would help me out a bit and just go ahead and get in the back seat for me. I probably should have asked him to try and wedge himself in the back of the patrol car.

My patrol car was a full-sized sedan with large doors. This guy was so large I knew he wasn't going to fit through the door. I even tried pushing from behind, but that didn't work. The guy apologized for being so fat. We were at a stalemate. I had to re-think this.

Finally, out of desperation, I asked him if he would try getting into the front seat. Sure he said, not a problem, and he did. Wow, am I good or what. I gave up trying to have the prisoner put on the seatbelt because it couldn't stretch out that far. I figured his stomach would act as an air bag.

As it turned out, the guy was cooperative, polite, and a very nice person, but he was still booked for DWI.

*   *   *

Radio directed me to a non-injury accident scene that was at the top of a long uphill grade. The accident involved a tractor-trailer rig and a sedan. As I approached the scene I could see that a car was wedged underneath the trailer, stuck almost all the way forward up to the windshield.

I got out of the patrol car, walked up and looked inside the car, and was surprised to see the driver was still inside, with the motor running. The car was wedged so far up underneath the trailer, the doors of the car were jammed shut and the driver couldn't get out.

I asked the driver if he was all right. When he said he was, his breath smelled of alcohol, his speech was slurred, and he appeared to be intoxicated. I told the driver to turn his motor off and hang in there until the fire department showed up to help extricate him.

What was strange was I couldn't find any physical evidence indicating where the accident had occurred. There were no metal parts, broken glass, or dirt anywhere pointing to a possible collision point. I finally went forward to interview the driver of the semi-truck and trailer.

The truck driver was up by the cab with a couple of witnesses. The truck driver told me he was going up this hill at a slower speed when a couple of cars passed by him, honking their horns, and there were people pointing backwards out their windows. The truck driver said he didn't understand what was wrong; he checked his mirrors but didn't see anything unusual behind him, so he continued.

However, more passing drivers kept honking and pointing backwards, so the truck driver finally decided to pull over to the shoulder and stop and see what might be wrong.

He thought, something must be wrong with his trailer—maybe the taillights weren't working. As he walked back he was shocked to find this car stuck underneath the trailer. The car's driver was yelling at him to get him the hell out of his car. From what the witnesses say, the truck and trailer had dragged this car for a half a mile or so.

The fire department eventually showed up and used their jaws-of-life equipment to cut off the driver's door and pulled him out. He was now mine to work with. The DWI didn't even remember driving up underneath the trailer. We went to the county jail for the Breathalyzer test.

*   *   *

Radio put out a report of a bulldozer illegally traveling down a secondary two lane county road just north of Monroe, at around 2 a.m. One of my partners received the call and was enroute.

The Trooper was able to get to the tractor's location quickly and actually caught it still moving. It was a large D-8 bulldozer driving down the middle of the road. Its width with the front blade was so great it almost covered both lanes. The treads of the dozer were chewing up the asphalt as it slowly worked it way up the road.

The Trooper was in a quandary, because even with his emergency lights on, the dozer's driver was not paying any attention. He was just moving along at about 5 mph. How in the heck do you stop this bulldozer, the Trooper thought? The only thing he could do was to follow it until it stopped.

Eventually the bulldozer driver realized he was being asked to stop, so he stopped the bulldozer in the middle of the road. He got down and staggered back to the patrol car, and asked, "What's the problem?" "Well for starters," the Trooper says, "you appear to be drunker then a skunk. Secondly, you are destroying this road big time with the dozer."

The driver said, "I know that, otherwise I wouldn't have stolen the bulldozer."

"You what?" The Trooper was dumbfounded. "Where did you steal the bulldozer from and why?" he asked. As it turned out, the driver had stolen the rig from a construction site about two miles away and was so pissed off about his ex-wife getting the house in the divorce settlement, he was on his way up to the house to bulldoze it down. The driver was placed under arrest for DWI.

There was still the problem of what to do with the bulldozer. It couldn't be impounded like a normal car. Who had the experience to drive one? The Trooper asked for assistance from the Sheriff's office and they dispatched a Deputy to help out. This enabled the Trooper to take the DWI in for a breath test.

The Deputy was fortunate enough to find a heavy construction worker who had experience with bulldozers, and was willing to come out to the scene and remove this one. This took time. Since there was so much damage to the road surface, a county road supervisor was dispatched as well, and upon his arrival he determined the damage to be around $20,000. Additionally, it would require closing the road for a few days until repairs could be made.

I have a feeling this DWI was going to spend quite a bit of time in the county jail. The ex-wife probably felt some sense of relief knowing her ex-bozo would not be a problem for a while.

Chases/Pursuits

It is extremely important to learn what speeds work best on any road on my beat when responding to emergencies or involved with a chase. When I first started working my patrol area, I had to familiarize myself with all the primary roads I would be required to patrol. Then, time permitting over the next few months, I would experiment with various speeds to learn my limitations for each and every curve on the beat.

I considered it part of my job to know how fast I could take each curve in the event I had to respond to an emergency. Eventually I felt I could, at a minimum, take any curve at 20 mph over the normal posted limit, not the recommended safe speed. Later on this proved beneficial when pursuing violators.

From my experience chasing drivers, I'm aware that if push came to shove, chasing someone into a curve often resulted in the runner sliding off the road and crash. I'm proud to say in the few chases I was involved in, not one runner ever escaped me.

Despite the time it took for me to learn the "beat," it took a few months for me to gain confidence with my driving skills. In the beginning I would drive like a bat out of hell, scaring the crap out of other motorists and some of my fellow Troopers.

One day, one of the old-timers asked me over coffee, why I had to drive fast all the time. I didn't have an answer. I asked back, "Doesn't everyone drive that way?"

"No," he responded, "you are the only one crazy enough to go that fast." That was an eye opener for me. If he was noticing my aggressive style of driving, then everyone else did. I was embarrassed. I slowed down. In hindsight I believe it's a maturation process every Trooper goes through.

I knew there would be times when I would be required to go fast responding to injury accidents, but being involved in a pursuit is a totally different matter, especially when speed is involved. Whenever this happened, I had to take into account my safety and that of other motorists and pedestrians. There was also the fear factor to overcome, not to avoid, but to deal with.

There have been many situations where officers should not have continued a pursuit. My problem would be deciding how or when to quit a pursuit. The pressure is tremendous; I did not want to hurt anyone or myself. I did not want the department to be liable for my actions, and I didn't want the runner to get away.

My Sergeant's advice was—"Just don't get hurt and make sure others don't get hurt." However, it's really hard deciding what to do when you're traveling in excess of a 100 mph. Pardon this pun, but once you start, you do get into the "thrill of the chase," and can't quit.

*   *   *

My first encounter with a chase situation involved a deputy sheriff who had radioed our department saying he was in pursuit of a car traveling at a high rate of speed on a secondary state highway south of Silver Lake. He was requesting assistance.

I talked to another Trooper on the radio and we both felt the runner was heading toward an intersection that we could reach in a couple of minutes, and set up a road block. We both arrived at the same time at the three-way intersection and set up with all our lights flashing. I had Radio notify the pursuing Deputy where we were, and that we were waiting with anticipation.

A minute later another deputy showed up to help us with the roadblock. We thought there was no way the runner was going to get by us now. Once he was caught in our trap, the tailing deputy would block his exit to the rear.

We didn't have to wait long; a minute or two later the running car came around a curve going pretty fast. The driver saw us blocking the intersection and knew he didn't have any hope of getting past us, so he came to a sliding stop in the middle of the three of us. The pursuing deputy had come up behind the runner and blocked him.

All four police cars, with their motors running and overhead emergency lights flashing, waited to see if the runner was going to shut down his car and surrender. We waited. Finally, one of the Deputies got on his PA and told the driver to turn his motor off and exit the car. There wasn't any response. I was wondering, what is this guy thinking; he's caught, so give up.

Maybe a minute had passed when suddenly the runner saw a slight opening between two of the patrol cars. He backed his car up a bit then drove through the narrow opening, just barely getting through. All of us couldn't believe this guy was actually getting away.

Off we went, chasing after this loser again.

The runner was now heading east on a county road at a high rate of speed. Needless to say we all went in pursuit after him. The runner couldn't have gone more then a mile when he apparently became distracted and wandered across the centerline hitting another car head on. The runner was killed instantly. Luckily the other driver and occupants received minor injuries because everyone was wearing seatbelts.

We, the pursuing officers felt bad that we hadn't rammed the car while we had him trapped, but later in reviewing the chase, we realized we were all a bit apprehensive. We did not know if we could legally intervene by ramming him. The State Patrol's policy wasn't all that clear at the time, so most Troopers were reluctant to ram anyone.

There had been a recent court ruling addressing this issue as to where liability rests in situations like this, but it was still not clear enough for an internal policy to be adopted to regulate police pursuits.

The four of us pursuing officers felt badly about this fatality, and questioned whether we should have taken responsibility to ram the runner regardless of the consequences.

*   *   *

One evening around midnight a fellow Trooper radioed he was in pursuit of a suspected DWI in Lynnwood who was refusing to stop. He reported they were leaving the state highway and entering a local neighborhood in Lynnwood. Was anyone close by who could assist? The city police responded they didn't have any units available at the moment, but to keep them posted.

I overhead the radio traffic, but I had a violator stopped. I couldn't do anything until I finished issuing the citation. I continued to listen to the other Trooper's progress, and when I did finish writing the ticket, I heard the runner was more or less heading in my direction. I got going and headed towards where I thought I could intercept the runner, who was at the moment, about ten blocks away.

The Trooper radioed the subject was now running at a higher speed. From the continuing commentary of the chasing Trooper I figured I might be heading toward the right spot if I picked up my speed a bit.

The runner was now heading down a narrow side street. I was only three blocks away from the chase so I set up at a four-way intersection. The runner was coming from my left so I blocked the road, forcing the runner to either go left or continue straight ahead. If he went straight, he would be going down a dead end street. I radioed the pursuing Trooper telling him where I was waiting. He said they were only one block away so I waited. The adrenalin was beginning to kick in.

Before the two reached my location, the running car drifted off onto the narrow shoulder and clipped off a large wooden power pole. The car literally severed this pole right off at the base. The pole did not come crashing down because the power lines were still holding it up.

However, a couple of hot wires did break loose and were dangling down and as the car passed underneath, the wires danced across the hood and trunk burning holes through the metal.

The following Trooper said he could see the sparks as the wires touched the running car. When I looked at the car later, the burn holes looked like bullet holes.

What was really strange about this situation was the car was an older, large Plymouth convertible. There was major damage to the front end but not bad enough to disable the car, so it continued running. The convertible top of the car didn't even have a scratch on it. Really weird! I will never understand why hitting the pole itself didn't disable the car.

Anyway, back to the chase. My partner knew I was blocking the path from the right, so he decided to hit the accelerator and pull along the left side of the runner. His thought at the time was to maneuver or force the runner to go straight down the dead-end street. Unfortunately for my friend, DWI's think differently, or not all.

There was the possibility the DWI didn't even know the Trooper was, at that moment, on his left side, because the runner turned left as they entered the intersection at about 45 mph. The DWI hit the patrol car broadside. The two cars spun around once before coming to a stop. The runner's car had stopped after the spin, and ended up facing my direction, and that's the way he went. He steered around me and roared by as if I wasn't there.

I took a few seconds to see what my partner was going to do, if he was still in the chase or not. When I didn't see him moving I assumed his car was disabled so I took off after the runner with red light and siren on. I radioed back to my buddy and asked if he was all right and he said he was and would be right behind me. I went in pursuit.

The other Trooper's car motor had died during the collision. I should mention this Trooper was considered the hotdog of the detachment. No one could out-drive him, especially the imbecile he was chasing. He felt he just needed to get the motor running and he'd be off to the races again.

It took a couple of tries to get the engine re-started, frustrating him more. His stress level was at the max. When the motor did catch, he rammed the gear lever into drive and floored the gas pedal.

Unfortunately, the Trooper did not know that from the impact of the collision his car's transmission was stuck in reverse. The patrol car accelerated backward at a high rate into a telephone pole totaling the patrol car. The whole rear end had been wiped out. My friend was so pissed off he couldn't talk to let me know what had happened.

Meanwhile I caught up with the runner in a few short blocks. We were running about 60 mph in a 25 mph zone. The driver was not responding to my siren or lights. I knew that about a quarter of a mile ahead we would reach a "T" intersection. The runner would have only two choices, to turn left or right. If he went straight it would be onto the front lawn of a church.

As we got closer to the intersection, I knew, at the speed we were traveling, the runner was not going to be able to stop or even slow down enough to make a turn. The driver didn't slow down at all. All I could do now was get my speed down and wait for the accident to happen. Thankfully there wasn't any traffic on the street at this hour.

At the very last moment the driver knew he had screwed up and locked up his brakes. The runner slid broadside through the intersection onto the front lawn of the church, really chewing it up badly. I continued to follow him onto the lawn waiting to see what the driver was going to do next.

He decided to continue running. I could see his rear wheels spinning trying to get traction. I said, to hell with this, I won't let this Looney Tunes keep running, so I drove forward and rammed him broadside. After the impact I just floored the gas and kept pushing against the sedan sideways until enough sod had built up underneath the car, incapacitating it so it couldn't move any further.

I rushed forward with my weapon drawn and ordered him out of the car. He was so drunk he literally fell out of the car on his face when he opened the driver's door. I handcuffed him and placed him in my patrol car.

Our Sergeant was called out because there was an intervention by use of force involving my patrol car, and the other patrol car accident. While he was investigating my incident he told me not to say too much to the other Trooper, who was sitting in the Sergeant's patrol car. I was told what had happened, and to let my friend cool down before I begin to harass him about his accident. Even though his accident was a fluke, there was no way I'd let this go without comment.

A few hours later after my friend's patrol car was towed back to the detachment office, the two of us met for coffee. I explained what had happened with my part of the chase and the booking of the driver. He was happy the guy didn't get away.

I added that in the future whenever he was involved in a pursuit and needed help, he should just pull over to the side and allow me to pass so I can finish the chase for him. He made me buy the coffee.

*   *   *

Late one night while home asleep I received a call from the radio dispatcher informing me a Trooper from the eastern Washington Wenatchee detachment, had been chasing a car for about seventy-five miles and they were now crossing over the Stevens Pass heading in my direction. I lived fifty miles away from the summit and I was the closest one who could help. There were no other Troopers or County Deputies on duty at the time.

I put on my uniform, jumped into the patrol car and took off heading toward the pass. While enroute, I was constantly receiving updates about the progress of the chase and where they were.

I calculated I'd have to run for about thirty miles before I could intercept them. After running hot for twenty minutes or so, I tried to reach the other Trooper by radio to see where he was. Because of the mountains, radio reception wasn't good. I was a little concerned because I didn't want to meet them head-on at the speed I was running.

A few minutes later I heard from him. He told me the guy was running around 50 mph, not any faster, not any slower. He didn't appear to be a DWI; it was just that he wouldn't stop.

The Trooper quit using his siren about seventy miles back for fear of burning it up. The car wasn't stolen and there were no active warrants on it.

Since I was more familiar with the area, I told the Trooper where the best spot would be for me to set up to interdict the driver. This would be a spot just west of Skykomish where the road passes through a short tunnel. On the other side of the tunnel there was a sheer rock wall to the right with no shoulder. On the opposite side was a guardrail with a drop off of about twenty feet into a river.

As I approached the tunnel, I had a few minutes before the others reached me, so I turned around and set up to partially block the road and waited. My plan was, when I saw them coming through the tunnel, I would speed up to stay in front of the running car and then gradually slow down forcing that car to do the same, and come to a complete stop.

I finally saw them coming about half a mile away. I turned on my overhead emergency lights, hoping this would discourage the guy from going any further. As they approached, the other Trooper told me to get going because this guy is flat ass not going to stop. So I hit the gas and got my speed up to the other car's speed of 50 mph.

The pursued car tried to pass me on the left so I moved to the left and blocked him; then he tried the other side, but I blocked him again. This is the way it went for the next half mile or so, so I radioed the other Trooper telling him I would start slowing down forcing him to either do the same or rear end me.

I slowly lowered my speed while still weaving back and forth, keeping this guy from passing me. Finally, after a short distance, he gave up and stopped. I jumped out of the car and pulled out my shotgun, jacking a round into the chamber and yelling at him to exit the car. The other Trooper pulled up behind the runner, and he too brandished his shotgun. The driver got the message and exited his car and lay down on the pavement.

I quickly got the driver handcuffed and walked him back to my patrol car. The other Trooper asked, "What the hell are you doing, he's my prisoner?"

I told him to go fish. "This is my jurisdiction and I will book him in our county jail." Get this, I'm saying this to a 15-year veteran and I have only been on the department about eight months. He knew I was right but he was still really pissed off at me.

It took several weeks before the driver was remanded to the other jurisdiction. This particular Trooper would never let me forget that it was his arrest, not mine. He always reminded me that I owed him one, even after he eventually out ranked me.

*   *   *

One Saturday evening while on routine patrol, I approached a popular hamburger joint where teenagers congregated. It was mostly a haven for those young morons who owned high performance cars with big engines. Needless to say, we were always receiving complaints of kids racing out from the parking lot, spinning their tires, making a lot of noise.

We tried to maintain a high profile by constantly driving by the place, but as usual, it was a matter of timing if we ever wanted to catch the kids screwing off. That is until one evening.

I was about half a mile away, approaching the drive-in slowly; when I saw two hot rods pull out from the parking lot. With my window down I could hear the kids revving their engines. No reason for me to be too concerned, nothing illegal had happened yet. That is, until they pulled along side each other facing the same direction as me. They were now blocking the road so I had cause to stop them, and bug them a little. As I got closer I could hear the engines revving to a higher pitch.

Well I'll be damned. We're in a well-lit area and I couldn't believe they hadn't seen me. I was only 200 feet away. I just couldn't get too excited because I thought they'd eventually realize I was directly behind them, and not race.

I finally had to slow down and stop about 50 feet behind them in the right lane, waiting to see what was going to happen next, because they were still stopped in the road. This was so strange.

I looked to my right and saw people standing around at the hamburger stand waiting for the race. However, they were now trying to get the attention of the drivers, warning them I was right behind. All to no avail, because off the two racers went. Tires squealing, the engines screaming, this was an honest to goodness race. First time I ever witnessed one since high school.

I was right on their butts, still fifty feet or so back, accelerating as fast as they were. I decided to let them go just a bit further to better prove to the Judge, the cars were actually racing. We run for another few blocks then I lit them up with the overhead emergency lights. This caused them to rapidly slow down.

The car on the right was heading to the right shoulder but the other guy was debating what to do and going slower in the left lane, but with no sign of wanting to cooperate. The car on the right stopped on the shoulder and was waiting to see what I was going to do. I pulled along side, but I still sensed the second car is going to run.

The minute I stopped by the first car, the other one took off. I rolled down my passenger window and yelled at this second driver, "I have identified you and recorded your license plate number, so remain here until I return." All I could hope was this driver would comply, because I was going after the other car.

I took off in pursuit. This car had a pretty good start on me and he was maybe a quarter of a mile away. There was no way I was going to let this driver lose me. I punched my speed up to 100 mph and began to shorten the gap between us. I then got a break.

The kid made the mistake of slowing down and turning right onto another highway leading down into Edmonds. He lost control and slid broadside. By the time he got his car straightened out and started back up again, I caught up and was now right on his back bumper.

We had entered the City of Edmonds, and the runner was taking several left and right turns in the belief I couldn't stay with him.

Even though I was pushing him by riding on his butt, I added stress to his cause by continually blowing the siren; I also had my headlights on high beam and the spotlight shining into his back window illuminating the interior. He had to have visibility issues with all this light. We ran for a few more blocks, and finally he gave up and stopped.

I quickly ran up to the car and told him to turn his motor off. He did. I pulled him out of the car and handcuffed him and escorted him back to the patrol car, searched him, and put him in the back seat. I told him he was under arrest for Reckless Driving and for eluding. I quickly locked up the kid's car and drove back to the first car hoping the driver was still waiting for me.

I lucked out. The first driver was still standing by waiting. I had him get in the backseat of the patrol car and explained to both drivers that racing cars constitutes Reckless Driving. I issued one ticket to the first driver and he promised to appear in court, so I released him. Before I let him go, I told him I was not impounding his car, a normal procedure for a situation like this, but he was free to go only because he waited for my return.

The second driver asked why he was not being released. I told him since he wouldn't take his medicine like a man, he'd be treated like any other serious arrest I made. I explained to him his car would be impounded for safekeeping and I would transport him to the county jail to be incarcerated until he posted bail. He screamed at me that I couldn't do this. All I said was, "Sit back please, and enjoy the ride."

*   *   *

While working a swing shift, I heard on the radio that a Trooper was southbound from Tacoma heading in my direction, chasing a car at a high rate of speed. I knew they were about five miles away so I quickly set up facing south in the southbound lanes just south of the Nisqually Bridge, and waited. While I was there, another Detachment Trooper pulled up and stopped behind me and waited.

Sure enough, here they were. The patrol car had its lights flashing and was right on this guy's butt. As they approached us, the other Trooper behind me began to pull out in front of them. We had talked on the radio and decided we should both try to get in front of the running car to block its path, believing the car might stop for the three of us. Wrong!

The runner steered around us by driving onto the shoulder and passed us probably doing around 90 mph. He now had three patrol cars behind him.

The order we're in had the original chasing Trooper in the number one position, my partner in position number two, and I was the trailer. Four of us were bombing down the freeway at 100 mph, and were now approaching the Marvin road freeway overpass. We're not sure if the runner would take the exit or continue underneath the overpass.

One Trooper stayed in the right lane in case the runner took the exit. The other Trooper and I stayed in the middle and inside lanes waiting to see what would happen.

Suddenly, the runner locked up his brakes and came to a sliding stop near the overpass in the middle lane. The Trooper on the right was caught off guard and shot past him before he could stop. The other Trooper and I were able to stop, and we waited to see what the runner would do next.

The runner took a few seconds then decided to turn left into the wide median and head back north, while traveling in the median. Oh well, off we go again. I was now in the number two position, cruising down the median at 60 mph. We were bumping and bouncing, throwing dirt and debris in the air making visibility difficult.

Suddenly, the Trooper I was following crashed into this culvert that was concealed by tall grass, tearing out the patrol car's transmission. He was out of commission.

It was then between me and the runner, who was about 400 feet ahead of me. This driver was tooling along as if nothing was wrong with driving in the median. He eventually worked his way back up onto the northbound lanes of the freeway and continued on. I was still right behind him.

A half mile later the runner took the next exit off the freeway to the right. We went down the ramp, slid through the stop sign and headed east on a narrow winding county road. The road was so curvy there was no way in hell the runner was going to survive this chase.

I was proven right when we approach a "Y" intersection that had two tight curves, one going left and one right. In the middle was a large power pole.

At our current speed of 50 mph neither turn would work. I was already braking, knowing the guy was going to can it up. The running driver finally recognized his problem, locked up his brakes and slid straight into a power pole. The car then rolled over onto its side. An end to a successful chase.

Surprisingly, the driver wasn't hurt at all; a few bruises and minor cuts. Knowing he was not seriously injured allowed me to handcuff the loser and put him in the back seat of my patrol car.

The driver was not on drugs nor was he drinking. He was driving his parents car for the thrill of it. The thrill of the situation continued while he spent the rest of the evening in the Juvenile Detention Center.

The Trooper who missed out on the last portion of the race caught up with me at the accident scene, and helped with the accident investigation. As for the third one, he had to wait for a tow truck to take his patrol car into the Detachment office for major repairs.

For me, everything turned out just fine. I made the arrest and enjoyed witnessing the accident. I did learn though, one should not chase cars while in the median—too dangerous.

Army Dust Off Program

The U.S. Army has a helicopter aviation battalion stationed at Fort Lewis, Washington. Part of this aviation group is a section called Dust Off.

This unit's responsibility during the Viet Nam War was to evacuate wounded soldiers to emergency first aid stations. A white circle with a red cross in the center on each side of the aircraft easily identifies a Dust Off helicopter.

During peacetime the unit at Fort Lewis performed rescue missions in western Washington. Our department approached the Army and asked if we could have their help evacuating seriously injured people involved in traffic accidents that were a great distance from urgent care facilities.

The Army liked the idea because of the humanitarian aspect, but also because it allowed the pilots to maintain proficiency under stressful circumstances. So, everyone benefited from this idea.

At the time I was fortunate to be assigned to the Olympia Detachment not far from Fort Lewis, and we frequently used Dust Off. We couldn't, on a whim, order up a helo—there had to be sound justification for it.

Before the Army would dispatch a rescue helicopter, the requirement was it had to involve a life threatening injury, time was of the essence, and the location of the incident was not within a reasonable distance for the injured to be transported to a local medical facility by a motor vehicle.

*   *   *

My first experience requesting Dust Off happened one cold night around 2 a.m. when a car had rolled over into a ditch. The driver was seriously injured but we were half an hour away from a hospital and it probably would take the ambulance thirty minutes or so to reach the scene, and another thirty minutes to reach the hospital. It was more prudent to have Radio call and see if a Dust Off helo was available to be dispatched to my location near Tenino.

The Army pilots were fast and good at what they did and they arrived twenty minutes later. From my military experience I was aware that a helo pilot's worst fears are telephone poles and power lines.

Accordingly I checked the surrounding area with the patrol car's spot light and saw telephone poles running parallel to the road so it wouldn't be prudent for the helo to land on the road. The only other alternative was to have the aircraft land in a vacant field next to the accident scene.

When I heard the aircraft approaching I went out in the field and lit a flare to show where the best landing spot was. As it got closer I used my flashlight to guide it in for the landing.

As the helo slowly lowered to the ground the pilot turned on a landing light that illuminated the field I was standing in. For the first time I realized I was not alone. I saw cows running in every direction, scared as hell and galloping away. I never gave it a thought that there would be livestock in the field. Oh well, no harm, no foul.

The following day I got a call at home from my Sergeant. He said he saw I used Dust Off the previous night, and asked how that went. I told him it was a success with no problems at all. I added it was the coolest thing and I couldn't wait to use Dust Off again. This is when my boss expressed his concern about my inattention to detail when using Dust Off.

Apparently our District Commander had received a complaint from a farmer who said he was going to sue the State Patrol because the helicopter landing in his pasture and scared his cows so bad, they wouldn't produce milk. The helicopter was not the culprit, I was.

*   *   *

Dust Off was dispatched to a rollover injury accident where a female passenger was seriously injured. This happened on Interstate 5 on a Sunday with heavy afternoon traffic near Maytown, south of Olympia. I was assisting the investigating Trooper and when I learned he had requested Dust Off, I prepared to set up the landing zone.

The car with the injured woman was upside down on the right northbound shoulder. We were able to channel the traffic down to one lane to allow it to pass by the accident scene. I looked around and noticed, because of high embankments on both sides of the freeway, the only level, unobstructed place for the pilot to set down was on the freeway, and in this case, the southbound lanes. There were no other choices.

When the helo arrived, we'd have to shut down all lanes. This couldn't be helped. To have the helo set down near the wrecked car would be best. The woman was already on a stretcher.

A few minutes later I heard the beating blades of the approaching aircraft, so I immediately began shutting down all freeway lanes. The stopped motorists didn't have a clue to what was happening. They could see the wrecked car but nothing else.

There must have been at least fifty cars backing up now in both directions. People started getting out of their cars when they saw the helicopter approaching, just a few feet above the ground. This was really cool. I was like a kid in a candy store, but I tried to act cool and look professional, like I did this stuff everyday.

This large brown military helicopter with a red cross painted on its side landed in the southbound lanes. The military medic jumped out, helped retrieve the stretcher and loaded the injured woman on board, strapped her in, and left. The show lasted a total of five minutes.

Usually, whenever we blocked traffic for a while and especially during peak traffic time, we'd receive hundreds of complaints of people being delayed. This incident didn't muster one complaint. That's show business for you.

Aircraft Enforcement

The Washington State Patrol's Aviation Division is located in Olympia, Washington. The Division has several Cessna aircraft primarily assigned to work traffic law enforcement. The aircraft work both in eastern and western Washington. Commissioned Troopers and Sergeants pilot the aircraft.

The aircraft work the most troublesome areas for speed violations such as those long stretches of highway where marked patrol cars are unable to work radar or are too visible to enforce the speed limit. This is where the WSP aircraft come into play and work best.

Whenever you see the posted signs alongside the freeway that read "Patrolled by Aircraft," we enforce the speed limit from above. There are white rectangular boxes painted on the road surface that have a small arrow pointing to the fog line. These boxes are posted in half-mile increments.

The pilot has a clipboard mounted with two stopwatches. When a car passes one white box, one stopwatch will begin timing the run to the next white box. After the car passes the second box, the first watch is stopped, while the second one begins timing the next half-mile.

The first reading is compared to a chart that shows time elapsed over a measured distance of a half-mile showing the car's average speed over that distance. When the second watch has recorded the next time, the first watch will be restarted for a third reading. How long the pilot is able to track the speed of a car depends on how long he's able to follow it.

The way the process works is, after the first reading, a reading may be recorded of 77 mph in a posted 60 mph zone. The second reading may be 76 mph. The third may also be 76 mph. These average speeds took place over the distance of one and half miles.

The pilot would radio the information down to a Trooper on the ground that's more than likely parked near a freeway overpass out of sight. When the offending car passes under the overpass, the pilot will radio, as an example, "Brown sedan, under now, inside lane, three readings, 77, 76,76." The ground Trooper starts his pursuit and enters the freeway behind the offending driver.

As the Trooper heads down the on-ramp, he'll get his speed up to 75 mph so when he enters the freeway, his speed should match that of the passing violator. If he can get a pace at that speed, then the pilot will not have to come to court testify to the previous speeds.

There have been instances where violators wouldn't believe they had been paced from the air, so time and circumstance permitting, I would radio the pilot and ask for a fly by. The pilot would fly as low overhead as he legally can, and wag his wings. Underneath the wings are the State Patrol markings. The fly by always makes the speeder a true believer.

*   *   *

I tried to set an example when I had a Trooper Cadet assigned to my care. But one day I was a terrible, terrible person. Radio had announced that one of our aircraft would be available to work traffic in about an hour, so all Troopers should make themselves available when it was in the air.

What a great experience for my Cadet. This was the luck of the draw, for him to actually see how the process works. I asked him if he was familiar with how the aircraft worked when conducting speed enforcement, and he said he was not.

The more I thought about it, the more I felt it would be even more of an opportunity to actually experience it from within the aircraft. I had Radio check with the pilot to see if he had space for two occupants during this air emphasis patrol, and he did. So I hurried over to the airport and we hopped aboard.

Before I go any further, I should mention I have had a lot of flying experience in small aircraft and even took lessons to be a pilot. I had also flown with our patrol aircraft working traffic a few times, so this was a bonus for me, to just sit back and enjoy the flight. One other minor thing to note; I was a chain smoker at the time.

313

It was a beautiful day for flying—I mean to catch speeders. The pilot was in the left hand seat, and the Cadet in the right. Super Trooper sat in the left rear seat, kind of supervising. Once airborne the pilot radioed to the local patrols where he would be working traffic, and for them to set up. It didn't take long for several Troopers to form up and wait for us to begin tracking speeders a few miles south of Olympia.

The pilot explained to the Cadet how he detected speeders and the way the speeds were calculated with the time and distance chart. He said they would be flying at 1,500 feet and at that altitude he could see for several miles. He looked for cars obviously weaving in and out of traffic, passing other cars, or better yet, just blowing by other traffic, indicating a dramatic difference in speed compared to the other traffic. Once he spotted a fast one, he'd wait until the car reached the white boxes on the shoulder and begin working with the stopwatches.

Since the pilot was sitting on the left side, we circle to the left. I could help spot traffic for him from the back left seat. The Cadet sitting up front watched how the pilot managed the stopwatches. As it turned out, we were quite busy spotting cars running fast, and relaying the information down to the chase patrol cars.

We had been airborne for about an hour when we began to encounter some air turbulence. Our ride was now becoming a bumpy one. This was not a big deal for the pilot, but for some reason, it was beginning to affect me.

The Cadet was fine because he was on an adrenalin rush, but I wasn't. The more we rocked the more I felt I was going to get sick. I was beginning to break out in a cold sweat. The only thing that I thought would keep me from puking was to light up a cigarette.

The Cadet looked over his shoulder and saw me fishing around in my shirt pocket and asked what I was doing. I told him I wasn't feeling well and I needed to have a cigarette. The Cadet, a non-smoker, pleaded with me to not smoke, or he would get sick too.

I told him in an unkind way I out-ranked him, and I went ahead and lit up a cigarette. Boy, did that help, I now felt a lot better. The Cadet's vomiting didn't even bother me. The flight ended prematurely.

*   *   *

My favorite story working with the WSP aircraft happened on a day when it seemed everyone was speeding. We were as busy as a fox in a hen house.

I just finished up with one speeder, pulled off the freeway down the ramp and went under an overpass at the bottom of the Nisqually Hill, to turn around and head back to the Marvin Road overpass where the other Troopers were staging.

As I was driving under the overpass, the pilot radioed asking if there was a patrol car near my present location. I responded I was just passing underneath the overpass. He told me to hold up for a couple of minutes. The pilot said he had several readings of 10 to 15 mph over the limit on this car heading my direction. He should be passing overhead shortly, and when he did, he'd call me out.

I waited for a minute or so when the pilot told me to come out from underneath. He added, "The car is a black sedan and is traveling at 75 mph in the inside lane. I have two readings of 73 mph and 75 mph." This was a posted 60 mph zone. I accelerated up the on-ramp and set my speed at 70 mph as I entered the freeway. At this speed if the other car was doing 75 mph, it should have been pulling away from me, good enough for a citation for 70+ mph.

I could see the speeding car in question was a black Lincoln sedan. As I held my pace at 70 mph, this car was pulling away from me, so I had the evidence I needed for court.

I increased my speed to catch up with the Lincoln to stop it. The pilot came back on the radio and said his last check had the car at 85 mph, so, I increased my speed to 85 mph and it still pulled away from me. Once again the pilot radioed down, he now had the black sedan at 95 mph.

What the hell, what was going on, did I have a possible runner here? It was strange because I didn't believe he'd seen me yet. I kept a low profile by running in the right lane parallel with him but in his blind spot. I was running at 100 mph and the car was still slightly pulling away from me at that speed.

The pilot reported the car's speed at 105 mph. This was getting out of hand, so I told Sky King I'm going to stop the target now. All I have to do is slide over to the left behind the Lincoln and hit the lights. I saw the driver jerk around and see me, quickly pull over to the right shoulder and stop. This whole pacing process took place over a 2-mile stretch.

As I walked up to the car, I could see the driver was a male and the only one inside. Everything appeared normal, except the driver was violently shaking his head as if he was upset with something. When I reached the driver's door, the window was down and I hear him saying, "I can't believe this, I can't fucking believe this is happening to me." I asked him, "What are you talking about sir, what happened?"

He pointed to the CB radio he has mounted on the dashboard, and said, "To stay awake I always have it turned on to the WSP frequency to listen to you guys stopping cars and responding to accidents."

"Today," he said, "I was fascinated listening to the radio when your aircraft reported this speeder and how the speed kept increasing, and how the chase car kept closing in on it." He said the more he listened the more he got excited, and unwittingly, increased his own speed without being aware of it. "I was the dumb shit you were after!"

It was only when I turned on my overhead emergency lights that he realized it was him the aircraft had been watching. Because of his honesty and since there are no other aggravating circumstances I cited him for a straight speed violation rather then Reckless Driving. The monetary fine would be the same but his license wouldn't be suspended. In my book, stupidity deserves a break every once in a while.

* * *

My first aircraft accident investigation involved an imbecile pilot who decided to land his twin engine Cessna without the wheels being deployed. The problem with not following this procedure is that the ground will bend the propellers and the bottom of the aircraft will be scraped off as it slides down the asphalt runway. The pilot did not realize he was in any danger until the sparks started flying when the props hit the pavement. This was an easy investigation.

* * *

The last aircraft accident I investigated was the most gruesome. The plane was a small two seat Cessna with two occupants. Initially the aircraft was approaching a small private airfield to land, but its approach was to low. Just before reaching the start of the runway, it clipped the top of two trees forcing the aircraft to crash nose first onto a road that ran by the end of the runway. When it hit, it immediately burst into flames.

I arrived at the scene a few minutes after the report was issued, but the fire department had already arrived and put out the fire. The plane had been fully engulfed and there wasn't much left of it. Most of the metal skin had melted, but you could still make out some of the frame and engine.

I asked one of the firemen if there were any survivors and he said no, but there were two fatalities in this crash. I looked around to see where the bodies were, didn't see any so I asked where the victims were. The fireman pointed towards the destroyed airplane and said they're still inside.

I walked over and look inside and all I saw were two shriveled up black charcoal lumps. Most of the legs and arms had been burned off; the heads were split open from the heat. The sight and smell almost made me lose it. If I hadn't walked away, I would have gotten sick. This was the first time I had ever heard the term, coined by the fire department—"Crispy Critters."

*   *   *

The morning and evening commute in King County is one of the worst in the country. We Troopers had our hands full wrestling with traffic to keep it flowing, and dealing with the traffic accidents when they happened. We were not alone. We were lucky to have KOMO radio's air traffic reporter radioing current traffic problems, slow downs, alternative routes, and traffic accidents.

This information proved to be very valuable to Troopers on the ground. The WSP communication's director made a concession, allowing the pilot to use our radio frequency to relay accident information to our dispatch center.

Receiving instant reports from the pilot, rather then having to wait for the report to come in by telephone, allowed us to respond to trouble in a more timely fashion.

At the time, our patrol cars did not have AM radios, so we carried our own portable AM radios for the express purpose of monitoring the KOMO traffic alerts. There were many times I learned of a traffic accident from listening to KOMO before our Radio received the information.

Radio would often call KOMO to confirm accident information. This was a great working relationship. I thought, what a neat life the KOMO pilot must have. I was envious, because I was taking flying lessons at the time, and thought there couldn't be a better calling then that of an air traffic reporter pilot.

Eventually, I got my courage up and called the radio station and asked whether the station allowed riders with the air traffic pilot. As it turned out, they would love to have a State Trooper riding with the pilot, so a trip was set up for me.

I arrived at the hanger at Boeing Field around 5 a.m. to meet with the pilot and learn what my role might be. I was told I would be introduced on the radio and during the course of the ride, and asked at different times my opinions of the flight and traffic conditions. I was not prepared for this. Anyway we took off at 5:30 am to be on station by six.

The flight went well, visibility was good, and the traffic was pretty much normal. It was fascinating watching the pilot work. He was working with four different radios; one to his supervisor, one for on-air broadcast, one for the FAA control tower, and the last to the State Patrol communications center.

Here he was with four mikes, two draped over each leg. I was beginning to wonder if he wasn't too distracted working all four radios. I was so worried; I felt my role, now, was to watch out for other aircraft.

I asked why he had a separate radio for the FAA control tower at the SeaTac airport. He told me he had to let them know whenever he flew across the north landing approach to the Boeing field, when flying west to view traffic in west Seattle.

Well now, I guess I'll have to watch out for landing aircraft along with everything else. It was turning out to be a bit too stressful for me. That was a hell of an experience I'll always cherish.

Use of Deadly Force

Almost every day I find an article in the newspaper or a television story involving shootouts between police officers and nut jobs. In my few years working the road, I never experienced anything like that.

Compared to today, my period of service was a safe time, and I now consider myself very lucky to have served when I did. I always felt I was mentally prepared to use my weapon if necessary, but those few times I did draw it, I never had to fire.

*   *   *

My first weapon experience happened only a few months after my graduation from the Academy. While on routine patrol working a day shift, Radio put out an all points bulletin of an escapee from a local prison work camp who was believed to be armed. The report stated this person was last seen in the area I was patrolling.

Hot dog, I finally had some action going here. Then, I remembered I had just passed a hitchhiker about a mile back who matched the escaped prisoner's description. I did a U-turn and headed back to get him. I informed Radio I believed I had seen the escapee and gave the location, and asked for backup.

The wanted subject saw me coming and left the road and ran off into the woods. Damn! There was no way in hell I could reach him in time to prevent him from getting away. Now that I'd seen him disappearing into the woods, I wouldn't chase after him until I have backup, especially if he's armed.

When a couple of city police officers and a Deputy Sheriff showed up, we surrounded the wooded area and waited for the guy to pop out. We waited for about thirty minutes but thought it fruitless and disbanded. The prevailing thought was no one was really certain this hitchhiker was the escaped felon, so why waste our time until we know for sure it was the same guy. I couldn't disagree so we all left our posts.

I was pretty frustrated because I was convinced this was the wanted person. I couldn't let go of it so I took a minute thinking this through and came to the conclusion; if the guy is running he might have continued on through the woods and might possibly pop out on the other side of the wooded area, which was about half a mile away.

What the heck, I drove around to the other side of the wooded area to an approximate point where he might reappear. I attempted to conceal my patrol car by parking it across the road behind a house; I walked across the road to a wood shed next to a farmhouse. The shed was unlocked, so I looked inside and the back wall had a window that had a view of the woods in back. I went inside and waited.

I hadn't been there for more than five minutes when sure enough this guy walked out of the woods heading towards my woodshed hideout, all the while looking back over his shoulder like he was looking to see if anyone was following him.

I left the shack, but remained hiding behind it, drew my weapon and waited. At about the time he reached the shack I stepped out, aiming the Magnum at him and said in a very serious Trooper voice, "Freeze fuck-head." I used strong profanity when dealing with escaped felons to emphasis my point, plus I was scared half to death. He surrendered. He was the escaped felon.

*   *   *

There were a few militant splinter groups causing havoc with law enforcement throughout the country. One such group was the Symbionese Liberation Army (SLA), which was conducting a war against the establishment. At one point the SLA had been involved in a bank robbery in Los Angeles and afterwards were on the run. One of the fugitives was supposedly the kidnapped heiress Patricia Hearst. She had been filmed holding an automatic rifle during the holdup.

Law enforcement through out the country was on alert to find and capture this very dangerous group. Rumors were rampant. They were sighted everywhere. I never believed they would head to my state. At the time I wondered who in their right mind would want to flee to Washington State, when they would be better off in Oregon where the taxes are lower.

Regardless, I continued follow the latest media reports, curious to see if the SLA were ever going to get caught. Then one day while I was driving around harassing drivers, a national intelligence bulletin was issued to West Coast law enforcement.

In the report the SLA group was believed to be driving a dirty looking green VW bus with California license plates, and they were last seen driving north towards the State of Oregon within the last twelve hours.

This news certainly perked me up. I did the math and figured if the fugitives were near Oregon twelve hours ago, and still heading north—possibly to Canada—they would have had more then enough time to reach Washington. With this time frame, they could conceivably be passing through my area at this moment. I was wide-awake.

Just to play it safe, taking into account the recent intelligence bulletin, I informed our communications center of the possibility the fleeing fugitives could be in transit through our county, and to notify the other local agencies. Meanwhile I decided to work the freeway's choke point on my beat. The choke point is where the freeway passes through downtown Olympia. I was totally committed to looking for the VW bus with California license plates, and nothing else.

I was mid-way through my day shift, traveling southbound on the freeway when I saw a VW bus matching the description of the SLA bus heading in the opposite direction. Not wanting to alarm everyone like Chicken Little, I did not inform Radio of this, but instead went to the next freeway overpass, crossed over and headed north just to make sure this was the same car we were looking for.

I kicked my speed up to 90 mph knowing I could over take the VW bus in short order. The VW did appear to be traveling at the posted speed limit when it passed me.

I felt the adrenalin kick in. If this was the SLA bus, and Super Trooper survived the next few minutes, I might get free donuts for a month from my Sergeant.

It took only a few minutes before my brain engaged, and I realized this was dangerous shit and I had better get my act together. It took three minutes to catch up to the suspect VW bus.

The VW bus was driving about 5 mph below the limit forcing me to slow down to follow. Everything checked out, the color was the same and the license plates were from California. I could see inside the rig and saw a few people, a couple of men and two females. Now I let Radio know what I had, and asked for backup. Radio acknowledged my traffic and put out an all-networks broadcast reporting my location, the circumstances, and the request for backup.

I continued to follow the VW, waiting for back up. Listening to the other units on the radio giving their locations I realized everyone was out of position or too far away to be of any help for many minutes. Even the local city police officers were unavailable to help. The situation was getting a bit more stressful now. What the hell would I do?

The bus was slowing down even more and most traffic was passing us. The occupants in the VW were beginning to look back at me, wondering why I was following them. Nothing felt right about this. I had read somewhere the SLA was reported to have automatic weapons, so I was feeling the pucker factor. I thought this was not going to end well. Radio informed me back up was still a few minutes away. Shit, I need to do something now because we getting closer to a populated area.

If there was to be any shooting, it probably should take place before we get any closer. I decided to act now and hope for the best. I let Radio know my location, the license plate number, and where I would be stopping the bus. I added I would hold the subjects at bay till help arrived.

The spot I had chosen was wide enough to get both my patrol car and the VW far enough away from the freeway to safely stop them. Now was the time, so I lit them up with the lights and the bus immediately pulled over to the side of the freeway and stopped.

I played it safe and parked about 20 feet away from the bus and in the driver's blind spot. I used my PA loud speaker and told them to remain in the bus until I said it was safe to exit. I wanted to wait a little longer hoping for back up to arrive.

My plan lasted only a couple of minutes when the driver decided to get out of his bus and started walking back to my patrol car. When I saw the driver's door open, it bothered me, so I immediately jumped out of my car pulling the shotgun out of its sleeve and jacked a round into the chamber. I leveled the weapon at the driver and yelled at him to lay down on the ground, now. I guess I scared the shit out of this guy and he immediately dropped to the ground.

I told him to spread out his arms and legs, which he did. The other occupants seeing this began jumping out of the bus wondering what was going on, why did I have my shotgun out? I told them to join their friend on the ground. I told everyone if I even remotely saw a move to retrieve a weapon, I would blast away. I believe I looked very menacing with the shotgun, so compliance was not an issue.

I had no idea when backup would arrive. I told these young kids to cool their jets until I had other officers back me up.

They obviously wanted to know why in the hell was I brandishing this shotgun at them, and why did they have to lie on the ground. I told them I had reason to believe their vehicle might have been involved in a robbery and if everything checked out, I would release them, "Be patient." That seemed to satisfy them for the moment.

It seemed like an eternity but two city police officers did arrive, and we handcuffed the subjects to stabilize the situation until we had time to check their ID's and search the interior of the VW bus.

Nothing. Everyone checked out. They turned out to be a free spirited group heading to Seattle for a rock festival. They were very understanding once I filled them in why I stopped them. When they realized their car matched that of the SLA group, they wondered how many more times they were going to be stopped on their trip. I didn't know the answer to that, but I did thank them for being very cooperative and told them to have a nice day.

*   *   *

The third time I drew my weapon involved the kidnapping of a seven-year-old boy. Radio reported a suspect had just kidnapped a young boy and was believed to be driving a blue mid-60's Plymouth sedan and last seen driving south on Old Hwy 99 in Edmonds. Wow, that's the area where I was patrolling. I tried to decide whether to stop and let traffic pass me, or turn around and see if I could spot the car going south.

Then, almost immediately I spotted the car passing me in the oncoming lane. I reported the sighting to Radio to let them tell the other authorities of my location. I turned around, and went after the car. I could see the driver watching me in his mirror and he appeared to be nervous but was driving legally. I couldn't see the kid in the car, but if he was, I had to be very careful not to alarm the driver until backup arrived.

I backed off a bit. We drove on for another mile when two city police department cars pulled along side me, and a Sheriff's Deputy came up from behind them. I hit the siren and lights to pull the suspect over.

When the car pulled onto the shoulder, the Deputy pulled further over on the shoulder, so he was on the right side of the suspect. I was directly behind the car while one of the police cars pulled forward and blocked the car's path. The last city officer stopped parallel to the suspect. We had the guy surrounded; he could not escape if he tried.

Events happened so fast, there wasn't any communication between any of us officers. We had all bailed out of our patrol cars brandishing shotguns. As I exited from my patrol car all I heard was the sound of rounds being racked into the shotgun chambers. All weapons were aimed at the kidnapper, mine included.

In one brief moment before anyone could speak, the thought crossed my mind that we all were inadvertently aiming at each other. I prayed for the driver not to make any false move, otherwise we were going to hurt each other really badly.

Fortunately, the guy put up his hands and allowed us to place him under arrest. The kid was in the back seat with his seat belt on and was all right. Later I promised myself never to get caught up again in front of another police officer's weapon. We had all aimed at the kidnapper, but also at each other.

*   *   *

Late one evening, I had a Trooper Cadet riding with me when I approached a car from behind while traveling south on the freeway. It was a brand new Oldsmobile Cutlass sedan. As I began to pass it, the car looked too new, as though it was right off the dealership lot. There weren't any license plates, no purchase agreement in the back window, and the dealership preparation and shipping stickers were still on the windows. There were too many red flags to ignore.

One other thing bothering me, the two black male occupants appeared too young to be driving any car. Call me a profiler, but nothing felt right. I can legally stop the car because no vehicle license is being displayed, so I had Radio check to see if there had been any recent reports of a car like this having been stolen.

Radio called back a few minutes later and said no one had reported any cars stolen for the past several hours. Oh well, I guessed I'd have to do a bit more digging.

Before I stopped the car I told the Trooper Cadet what I saw and felt about this car. I wanted to be very clear that I believed the car to be stolen and for him to have his weapon out when we exit the patrol car. I wanted him to stand at the right rear corner of the suspect car and be watchful. I knew he was a little shook up so I told him to please relax, and for him not to shoot me or anyone else.

I slowly approached the car from the driver's side while holding my weapon down along my right side so that it wasn't visible. I looked in through the window and told the driver to put his hands on the steering wheel. After seeing his hands, I had him exit the car. We walked back between the two cars and I asked for some identification. He didn't have any so I had him turn around to handcuff him just to be safe.

While I was searching the driver, the passenger was opening the door without being told. The Trooper Cadet reacted by yelling, "Do not come out or I'll blow your fucking head off!" This scared the hell out of me, but being the professional I am, I told the other guy to come out slowly with his hands raised. We handcuffed the passenger and placed the two in the back of the patrol car for safekeeping.

I checked the car's odometer and saw the mileage to be at forty-seven miles. This vehicle was so new it had yet to be serviced to be for sale on the lot. The shipping plastic still covered the seats. What surprised me most was that the keys were in the ignition. I would have thought the car's ignition would have been hot-wired. The only way to identify the car was to record the VIN number and have Radio run a check on it.

The mileage meant the car had to have come from a distance no greater then forty-seven miles. It had either come from Tacoma but more than likely from the Seattle area. The VIN report came back showing the car belonged to a dealership in Seattle. I had Radio call them

to see if they might have sold the car. Mind
you, it's around 1 a.m. in the morning now,
so we were going to wake some people up, but
I really didn't care.

The manager on call at the dealership did not
believe the car was theirs but would drive to
the lot to verify this. About an hour later he
let Radio know the car was missing. Apparently
one of the sales people left the keys in the
ignition by accident. We told him to file a
stolen complaint so that we could charge these
kids with a felony. All ended well, and no one
got shot.

*   *   *

Patrol Car Accidents

Patrol car accidents can happen in a variety of ways. Most occur with Troopers not paying attention when backing up. That aside, the Department seriously investigates all patrol car accidents, especially when liability might be an issue, and if it involves a civilian.

There is an accident review board for every patrol car accident. If there is any one thing that can really screw you up for promotion it is an accident that you caused. Sometimes Troopers drive too cautiously just to avoid having an accident, risk takers they are not. In a way it can affect your job performance. Not me, I tried to be careful, but I did not worry about whether or not I would get promoted. I was having too much fun.

I was personally involved in a few accidents, two of which I discussed earlier, but it was the minor ones that bothered me the most. They happened only because I was stupid. If I had simply engaged my brain, they never would have happened.

*   *   *

Radio directed me to contact a person who was standing by at a service station east of Lynnwood who had been involved in a one-car accident. Once I meet with the driver, he would take me to the accident scene. It sounded like a simple car in the ditch type of accident, so I really didn't feel the need to rush to the station.

As I pulled into the parking lot, I looked around for someone who looked like they were waiting for my arrival. No one stepped forward so I stopped the patrol car, put the transmission into park, and got out leaving the motor running. As I was walking up to the station office a guy came running out and yelled at me, "Hey, there goes your patrol car!" What the hell, I turn around and sure enough my patrol car was going backwards at about 5 mph.

I started running after it, but quickly realized the car would soon stop on its own because some dummy left the driver's door open. The open door struck another parked car crunching the door up to half its size, forcing the patrol car to come to a stop. The person I was supposed to contact realized I had a problem worse then his, and left.

My role of accident investigator had changed to that of stupid victim. All I could do for the moment was wait for the Sergeant to be called out to investigate my accident. He would not be happy to see me.

Despite my carelessness, there was an extenuating circumstance. It was later learned my patrol car, a Ford, had a history of the transmission popping out of the Park position into the Reverse position while the motor was running. Obviously, when this happened, as I learned the hard way, the car moved backwards. My accident, however, was deemed a violation of policy resulting in a written reprimand.

The reason is, Troopers are instructed to always put the emergency brake on whenever we exit the patrol car. I forgot to do that because I was in too much of a hurry. My bad.

*   *   *

I'm probably repeating myself when I mention that 80 percent of all patrol car accidents are due to improper backing. It's true because Troopers do not pay attention when backing, or are too lazy to turn their heads around and actually look to the rear when backing up. This is why you'll always see police cars backed into parking stalls at any restaurant just in case they have to leave in a hurry to respond to an emergency.

I'm not proud to announce I am a member of the lazy 80 percent. My first mistake happened when I had stopped a violator. When I finished with the driver, I had to leave in a hurry for some reason. I looked into my review mirror and did not see anyone behind me. I backed up fast to get some separation between me and the car I had stopped, so I could enter the freeway quickly.

What I could not see, unless I actually turned around and looked back, was a small road reflector marker. You see them all the time. They are small aluminum posts about three or four feet tall with a reflector tag at the top to alert motorists that the post is at the very edge of the road.

When I backed up as fast as I did, I drove over the post bending it backward, flat to the ground. No big deal, they are not that expensive, however, if you hit them hard enough, they will put a sizeable dent in your plastic bumper to the tune of around $250. In this instance, my Sergeant treated the accident as a fatality because, without question, I had killed the reflector post. The written reprimands were beginning to accumulate in my personnel file.

*   *   *

One of my fellow Detachment Troopers had a DWI stopped on the right shoulder of the freeway. He had all his warning lights on, and was in the process of waiting for the tow truck to show up to remove the drunk's car. Suddenly, another drunk driver drove onto the shoulder and rear-ended his patrol car.

Apparently the second DWI had become mesmerized with the flashing emergency lights on top of the patrol car and drifted over on to the shoulder. This is not an unusual occurrence. Fortunately no one was hurt in either car. Both DWI drivers were booked in the county jail for drunk driving.

The patrol car rear-ended in the accident was declared a total loss. The Trooper assigned to this patrol car was ecstatic because this meant he probably would be issued a brand new patrol car. He was excited because the

Department was beginning to issue the new, hot Chevrolets, the current winner of the bidding process.

All Troopers were lusting after this new patrol car. This Trooper borrowed another patrol car until he would be issued a new one. The process could take up to a month because the new ones hadn't arrived to be outfitted before being issued.

As a general rule to qualify for a new patrol car, a Trooper must have accumulated 80,000 miles on his assigned patrol car. When it reached that milestone, it could be turned in for auction. Once we turned in the old patrol car, the new one was issued.

The normal turn-around time could be anywhere from two to three years, depending on how many miles you put on a year. In my case, I was putting that much mileage on my car every year and a half, so I was getting a new one more often. As for the rest of the guys, it was irritating to see this Trooper getting a new one when he had just been issued one a year before.

About three weeks later the Trooper was told to report to Olympia to receive his newly assigned patrol car. We, his detachment mates, were jealous. A few hours later he returned to the district office in his new car, and when I looked out the window, it looked exactly like his old patrol car.

The Trooper climbed out of the car and walked into the office. I could see he was really pissed off about something. One of us asked what the problem was, but he wouldn't talk to anyone. Others in the office were beginning to give him a hard time about his new patrol car, which did not appear to be a Chevrolet. Finally the Sergeant came into the office and asked what was going on. The Trooper had calmed down enough to tell us what had happened.

Apparently somewhere else in the state, a patrol car had rear-ended another car, and it was declared a total loss. All totaled patrol cars are returned to fleet operations in Olympia to be cannibalized. In this particular case the car was of the same manufacture as that of our Trooper's.

The fleet supervisor felt he could easily save money by having the two cars cut in half at mid-point, and take the rear end of one and weld it to the good front end of the other patrol car. It was an easy fix for our shop guys.

The beauty of this story is our Trooper friend got his old patrol car back, at least the front half. Did I mention he was upset? Well, he was, but it got even better.

This "new" patrol car turned out to be a piece of shit. He continually had problems with it. It was never the same again. I never did like this Trooper because he was a blowhard, and I truly believed the haunted patrol car was the reason he resigned a couple of years later.

*　　*　　*

One sunny warm afternoon Radio kicked out a report of a two-car injury accident about eight miles from where I was patrolling. Once I received the call, I acknowledged my location and said I would be enroute. From hearing the other Troopers' locations, I knew I was the closest to the accident scene and would be the first to arrive.

I was on the freeway at the time and figured it would take me a couple of minutes to reach the off ramp to get on the secondary county road where the accident was. I hit the gas, picked up my speed, and turned on the lights and siren.

As I was approaching the exit ramp I took my foot off the gas pedal to slow down a little. When I did the patrol car suddenly accelerated. What the hell! I hit the brakes and the car's speed kept increasing. I kicked around with the gas pedal and somehow got it dislodged and the patrol car began to slow down again. Everything was back to normal, or so I thought.

I exited the freeway, turned left onto the county road and took off. The accident scene was now about three miles away. As I began to accelerate I noticed in my rear view mirror one of my fellow Troopers had caught up with me and was following with his red lights and siren on. We were running around 90 mph and everyone in front of us was yielding and pulling over to the side of the road to let us by.

When I was about a quarter of a mile away from a set of curves, I knew I needed to get my speed down to around 60 or 70 mph to negotiate them. I took my foot off the gas pedal to let the car's compression begin to slow the car down without having to hit the brakes. The patrol car accelerated. Oh shit, the stuck gas pedal problem had resurfaced. I hit the brakes hard locking up the tires. The smoke coming from the tires alarmed the Trooper behind me and he backed off.

Even with the brakes locked up, the motor was screaming—it wanted to go faster. I was running out of room. I might be able to take the first curve at 90 mph, but there was no way in hell I'd survive the second one. I was chewing up real estate real fast.

When I kicked at the pedal like I did before, the car accelerated, so I locked up the brakes again to slow it down. I didn't have a clue of what to do. I knew if I turned off the ignition I'd lose my power brakes and steering, so I didn't want to do that. I knew this was not going to end well.

At the absolute last second I noticed a dirt road angling off to the left. At this exact point the main road begins to curve to the right. All I had to do was steer straight to make the dirt road. This road led to a private home about 500 feet away. I took the dirt road. I had no idea what my speed was because I was too busy trying to steer the car. I assumed I was still doing around 80 or 90 mph.

Once on the dirt road, I hit the brakes again. Because I was running on dirt and gravel, the patrol car went broadside. I let off the brakes and straightened the car out. The car accelerated. I hit the brakes again and it went broadside. I lifted off the brakes and straightened out. That was all I could do, hit the brakes and then correct my steering, repeatedly. At the same time, whenever I took my foot off the brakes, I kicked at the gas pedal trying to dislodge it.

The Trooper who had been following me said later all he saw was a cloud of dust when I took the dirt road. He assumed I was taking a short cut, but he decided to stay on the paved road rather then follow me.

Somewhere, sometime during my journey the gas pedal came unstuck. Once the engine's power dropped down to an idle speed, I hit the brakes and came to a sliding stop about ten feet away from a giant fir tree. A couple of minutes passed for the dust and dirt to clear before I could see around me. Then it took me a few more minutes before I quit shaking.

Just before I came to a complete stop the patrol car slid through and sheered off a part of a large shrub in front of the house. When the owner realized the State of Washington would pay for any damages to his property, this shrub suddenly became a rare Japanese specimen and was very expensive to replace. The owner did ask me if I was all right, which was nice of him. He said, "I heard you coming. What a racket you were making."

The Sergeant didn't quite believe my story until he looked inside my patrol car and saw the tangled wire holding the gas pedal to the metal arm that extends down from underneath the dashboard. Somehow the gas pedal had worked loose, and caused the gas pedal to wedge against the transmission housing, sticking there until it could be dislodged by kicking at it. This incident became a concern for our fleet supervisor who checked all patrol cars similar to mine to make sure this didn't happen again.

This special trip of mine I figure took five or six seconds, but my body and mind believed it lasted four hours. Thinking back, this was probably the closest I had ever been to being seriously injured. I relived this accident in my dreams for several years.

*   *   *

One afternoon there was a lot of ice and snow on the ground. I was directed to a multiple car accident with no injuries. Due to the terrible road conditions it took me a while to make my way to the scene, and when I did arrive I noticed the accident involved three cars. They were all together facing in different directions half way up a very steep hill.

I looked up the hill at the accident scene, about 400 feet away, and wondering if I could make it up the steep hill. I certainly didn't want to walk that far up and not have access to my car's radio. I decided, with my vast wealth of experience driving in ice and snow, and being a professional driver that I could make it up the hill.

My patrol car had studded tires so I was not too worried about having traction. I took a run at the hill and make it up just past where the other accident victims were parked. I stopped the patrol car and attempt to turn around to park behind them.

After I made the turn, the patrol car lost traction and I began to slide down the hill. Oh Shit! Not a damn thing I could do but wait for whatever was going to happen next, because I had no control of the car. What happened then—I struck each of the other three cars and we all went spinning down the hill, coming to a stop at the bottom. It was like real life bumper cars at the Puyallup Fair. No one was injured. But my pride was seriously damaged.

Since I no longer could be the investigating Trooper, the Sergeant had to be dispatched. He showed up and approached the scene from the top of the hill rather then the bottom as I did. I walked up to meet him and explained what had happened. The devil in me made me tell my boss, the road was safe now, why don't you drive down and park by my patrol car. I then realized my Sergeant had great common sense, he said he would wait for the sand truck to arrive and sand the hill before he went down. Chicken shit. So we waited.

The highway department truck finally arrived, and we explained what the driver needed to do. The truck started down the hill spreading sand out behind. Suddenly, the sand truck lost traction and began spinning down the hill.

Fortunately the truck didn't strike my patrol car or any of the other cars at the bottom. My boss turned to me and said, "that's why he's a Sergeant, and I'm not."

Unusual events and
embarrassing moments

Every workday was different. I knew without a doubt something, sometime, would happen that I would find incredible, humorous, or bizarre. I couldn't wait to jump into my patrol car to go to work. The following stories are part of what I experienced; the humorous cop stories I loved telling.

*   *   *

One of my partners and I had arranged to meet for lunch at a drive-in where they deliver the food to your car. This was convenient for us because we could eat in the car and listen to our patrol radio for emergency traffic. On this occasion I got into my buddy's patrol car and we ordered hamburgers and milkshakes. This hamburger joint was at the top of a "T" intersection. We were parked facing in the direction of the bottom of the "T".

We had just received our order and begun to eat when we noticed a motorcyclist running up and down the bottom of the "T" road that was a dead end. The driver was not wearing a helmet, the motorcycle had no muffler for his exhaust system, and there wasn't any vehicle license displayed.

My buddy said, "if this guy comes back up the road close enough to us, I'm going after him. If he does, grab your food and get out." The kid hadn't noticed our patrol cars so we knew he would be back. My buddy started his engine to be ready. We ate our food with the motor idling.

Sure enough, the motorcycle arrived again, roaring up to the intersection, stopping and turning around to head back. I didn't need to be told what to do, I grabbed my food and bailed out of the patrol car and got back into mine.

My buddy set his hamburger to the side and rapidly backed up, turned on his overhead emergency lights and accelerated as fast as he could to catch up to the biker who was already heading back down the dead end road. My friend hadn't gone more then 50 feet when he came to a complete stop.

What the heck, what's wrong, why did he stop? I started up my car and drove over to where he was stopped. I pulled alongside him, rolled down my window and asked what happened, why did you stop your pursuit? I could see my friend was seething, so I knew he was pissed off about something. He told me he had to go home now to change his uniform.

I got out of my patrol car, walked over and looked inside his car. The front of his patrol uniform shirt was now pink, and there was a big clump of pink ice cream in his lap, on his gun belt and in his cartridge cases. He had forgotten he had left his milkshake on the top of the dashboard and when he took off after the biker, the shake fell back and hit him in the chest, then spilled down into his lap.

I was laughing so hard I couldn't catch my breath. As he drove away, my first thought was, I couldn't wait to tell the other Troopers in the detachment that Mr. Perfect, wasn't.

*   *   *

A similar situation happened to one of my partners when he became annoyed with a motorcyclist who was operating an unlicensed motorcycle on a public road. This Trooper tried a few times to catch him, but the kid was elusive. If the motorcyclist ever saw a patrol car, he would pull off into the woods to avoid getting apprehended.

Then one day, as the Trooper was passing by the same dead-end road, he saw the same kid heading down the road on the same bike, not wearing the required helmet. He took off after him.

The kid didn't see the patrol car coming up behind him until the very last moment. When he finally did, he cut off into the woods like before. There was no way a patrol car could enter the woods on the narrow trail the kid had used. The Trooper stopped at the trailhead, steaming mad.

About this time another motorcycle rider pulled up alongside the patrol car and asked what was wrong. The Trooper told him what happened and then asked if he would help by letting the

Trooper hop on his bike and take him into the woods to find this kid. "Sure, no problem," he said, "hop on the back."

The Trooper took off his patrol jacket and left it and his campaign hat in the patrol car. The biker gave the Trooper an extra helmet and his own coat to wear over the uniform, and they went into the woods.

A hundred yards or so into the woods they spotted the other motorcyclist and pulled up along side him. The other rider was beginning to say "What's up dude?" when the Trooper tackled him off the bike before he could get it started. This reminds me of the old Canadian Mounted Police saying, "We always get our man."

*   *   *

There are many days on patrol when it will be so quiet, I would start looking for action, for something to do. Normally I didn't have to look for it, but this particular day I did. What little traffic I saw was moving safely. There were no accidents to respond to. I was basically wasting gasoline, not earning my keep, and I was bored. I couldn't stop speeding cars because there weren't any. Like I said, everyone was driving legally.

I finally decided to pick on those drivers who fail to signal. Drivers are required to signal prior to a making turns, when they change lanes, and when they enter a freeway from an entrance ramp, or complete a pass of another car.

These signal requirements are simple to follow, and are basically a courtesy extended to other motorists. I rarely write a citation for this infraction unless there are extenuating circumstances, or the driver has personality issues.

On this day, I began looking for those drivers who repeatedly failed to signal. There are drivers who are either too lazy to push the lever up or down, or they're just plain rude and inconsiderate to other motorists. I feel I can accomplish a lot more by illustrating to a driver the need to signal by simply taking the time to work with them.

Here's how I go about it. I approach the driver and ask for his driver's license. Normally he'll ask, "What's wrong officer?" I tell him, "Well apparently you have defective taillights." The driver would be shocked, "are you sure?" they'd ask me? "Well," I'd tell them, "just to make sure, let me check them out for you."

I instruct the driver to wait until I get back behind his car and when I do, ask them to turn on the left turn signal. Then I have them turn on the right turn signal. "How about hitting the brake pedal a couple of times," I ask. After this, I go around to the front of the car and go through the same procedure with the front turn signals.

I walk back to the driver and tell them, "It's strange, but I find your lighting system in proper working order. I'm at a loss why the turn signals weren't working when you made several lane changes back down the road.

I assumed you were signaling, but the taillight bulbs were defective." The driver slowly digests this information, and then suddenly, the light comes on.

I tell them that I'm not issuing a citation because I figure I've made my point by taking the time walking around the car checking everything out. "Just think of the time you might have saved by using your turn signals. Have a nice day."

*   *   *

I eventually asked for a transfer to my hometown. Once assigned there, I figured I would eventually cross paths with old friends and high school classmates. It concerned me somewhat that I might encounter them while working.

It didn't take long for everyone to realize Super Trooper was back in town, and to drive safely while I was on duty. This didn't mean I was Mr. Serious all the time. I did have this little devil inside that would surface every once in awhile.

There were two very close classmates who had married who I stayed in contact with on a regular basis before moving back home. Since my return I hadn't had a chance yet to catch up with them.

One day on the freeway I saw a car being driven by the wife of this couple. She was driving legally, but what the heck, since I hadn't talked to her in a while, I thought I would stop her and say hello. I turned on the lights and pulled her over. She was immensely relieved to see it was me. I told her I only stopped her to say hello, so not to worry.

She said she had heard I had returned to town and was glad to see me and hoped we could get together soon. We visited for a few minutes and she left. About four months later I saw her again and I pulled her over to say hello. We had a nice visit.

A few months after our last visit, I was assigned a Trooper Cadet from the Academy for his two-week coaching trip. While on patrol with the Cadet driving, I saw my lady friend driving. It looked like she was close to where she lived and was probably heading home. I thought what the heck, I'll give the Cadet some practice stopping a car, and at the same time say hello to my friend.

I told the Cadet I knew for a fact the driver had a suspended driver's license, and to pull her over. What I failed to take into account was my friend was in a hurry to get home.

When the Cadet turned on the lights, she thought to herself, it's my Goddamn friend, Super Trooper. Screw him, I'm in a hurry to get home, I'm not stopping. The Cadet was worried because the car wasn't stopping, so he turned on the siren. Now my friend realized it might not be me, so she pulled over.

I knew I'd bitten off more than I could chew, so I told the Cadet "I'll handle this violator," and to stay in the car. I got out of the car, walked up and told her I'm sorry. She told me, "Don't ever do that again, because you scared the shit out of me". That was the last time I felt the need to bond with my classmates. I will never stop anyone unless they have done something wrong.

*   *   *

Late one evening a Trooper who was working south of me on the Interstate, advised me by radio there was a 1960 Ford sedan northbound in my direction with a defective taillight. He advised me I should check the car out.

My first thought was, he wouldn't have recommended this unless something else was wrong with the car or driver. There was very little going on at the time, so I pulled over to the side of the road and waited for the car to pass by me. Eventually it did, and sure enough the left taillight was burned out.

I pulled out and got in behind the car to pull it over. Once I turned on the emergency lights, the driver quickly pulled over to the side of the road and stopped. As I approached the car I could see the driver was female and the only occupant in the car. The car radio was playing loudly.

When I reached the driver's door I looked down at the young lady and was surprised to see she was topless—I mean, wearing nothing on the top. She had shorts on, but no top or bra. She didn't even try to cover herself up—she acted as if everything was normal.

She smiled at me and already had her driver's license out. Once I got over my shock and found some words, I informed her the taillight was out and she should get it fixed the first chance she had. She thought that was the reason for me stopping her, and said she would fix it when she got home. I released her and she took off.

As she drove away, the other Trooper radioed me and asked if I had made contact with the car with the defective taillight. I said I had and just released her to be on her way. He asked me how the view was, and I said it was great.

This Trooper suggested I should inform other Troopers further up the road in the next district, of this car with defective equipment. I thought this a prudent idea and so relayed the information by radio to the next batch of Troopers. This was a very serious situation. The car definitely had a defective light.

I listened to the background radio chatter for the next couple of hours while on patrol, and I would guess this poor woman was stopped at least seven more times before she reached home. It's nice to have a perk-me-up moment like this once in a while.

*   *   *

One day my Sergeant asked if I would be interested in working a spot check north of my current patrol area. Normally, I would shy away from working outside of my beat, because if I arrested someone, I might have to spend my day off attending court in a different jurisdiction. However, this day I needed a change of pace, so I volunteered.

Our group consisted of seven Troopers, a fun bunch of guys I've worked with in the past. One of the participating Troopers was an old-timer, kind of gullible, but a nice person. Troopers were always playing pranks on him, but he was good-natured about them. He normally didn't get the jokes until they were explained to him, then he would laugh. We thought they were funnier when he didn't get the jokes. For the sake of this story I will call him Dan.

As I said, Dan was part of the team working the spot check. I hadn't worked with him for a while so it was good to see him again. We worked for about three hours stopping almost everyone we saw. We found a lot of equipment violations, a few arrests for expired driver's licenses, and that was pretty much it, so it was time to wrap it up and head to the Detachment office to fill out our activity reports.

We all had pretty much finished together, except for Dan. He was still involved with a violator, but knew when he finished; he too would head to the office to meet with the rest of us.

With Dan out of view of his patrol car, one of the jokesters picked up a dead skunk from the ditch, popped opened the front hood to Dan's patrol car and placed the skunk on top of the air cleaner, then closed the hood.

In hindsight, it was not very funny considering this could have damaged the patrol car to the tune of a few thousand dollars. I guess the thought was when Dan smelled the skunk he would immediately remove it. Not!

We were in the parking lot at the detachment office waiting for Dan's arrival. A short time later he finally showed up. We waited with anticipation for his reaction—you could feel the tension in the air.

He got out of his patrol car like nothing had happened. We looked at each other and were puzzled by his demeanor. Finally, the jokester asked him how it was going. Dan said, "Well, there's something wrong with my patrol car because it really smells bad."

He said that on the way into the detachment he had to roll down all his windows because of this stench. He was asked, "Did you stop to check it out?" "No, I didn't have time, I just wanted to get back to the office." Someone said, "Let me check your car out," and walked over to the patrol car, pulled the latch to the hood and popped it open. Sure enough the skunk was still lying on the air cleaner.

No real harm done to the car as it turned out. Very funny at the time, but as I write about it now, I realize this prank wasn't in very good taste.

*   *   *

I had a Trooper Cadet riding with me one night when Radio kicked out a report of a stolen car sighted northbound on the interstate coming my way. I was also northbound and figured I was about two miles ahead of this suspected stolen car, so I pulled onto the shoulder and waited. Sure enough the car passed by me. I pull out behind the car.

I turned on the lights and the suspect car immediately pulled over to the shoulder and stopped. I used my public address system to order the driver out of the car. I exited with my weapon drawn and told the male driver to lie down on the ground. I had the Cadet handcuff him. We searched him and placed him in the back seat of the patrol car.

After requesting a tow truck to impound the car, I began my interview of the subject by first informing him of his constitutional rights. After that I asked why he stole the car. He shocked me when he said he had not stolen the car. He said he didn't know what I was talking about because he was just walking down the freeway, hitchhiking, minding his own business when I arrested him.

"What the hell are you talking about, I just pulled you over in the stolen car," I told him. The suspect said he had no idea what I was talking about. He knew nothing about a stolen car. I couldn't believe this. I had never heard of anyone denying something when caught red-handed. This was ridiculous. Whatever this guy said or believed, he was going to jail. I informed him of this.

I needed to figure out a way of calling his bluff. We all knew he was guilty. If he had admitted his guilt I could avoid having to go to court on my day off. I thought what the heck, let's wing it and maybe we'll have a little fun at the same time.

I asked the Cadet to hand me the mirror that was attached to the right visor. I took the mirror and got out of the patrol car, opened the back door, took the prisoner's left hand and touched his fingers to the mirror. I told him now I had his fingerprints and I would match them with the prints left on the steering wheel. Mr. Stupid said, "Damn, you got me, I stole the car—just take me to jail so I can get some sleep."

Needless to say, I impressed the Cadet. I will be a legend in his mind as I am in my own. No one messes with Super Trooper.

*   *   *

The state highway passed through the small town of Goldbar, a community of about 500 people. The speed is posted at 50 mph until you reach the city limits, and then drops down to 35 mph.

The State Patrol constantly receives complaints of motorists speeding through the town. Most motorists who travel this highway know there's very little enforcement so why reduce their speed when passing through?

Trying to enforce the speed limit in a marked patrol was hard for me. So, one day I decided to use the radar unit. The day turned out to be very windy when I decided to set up the unit. I parked on the west end of town to work the traffic traveling east. Lo and behold, five cars traveling close together passed through the radar at 50 mph. They never slowed down to the city speed limit. I pulled out and went after the cars.

Stopping a car for speeding takes time and distance and a little cooperation from the offending driver. To make matters more interesting, I was going to try and stop all five cars.

The speeders didn't notice me until I pulled up alongside the trailing car, blew my siren and directed the driver to pull over to the shoulder. He did, so I pulled ahead and did the same with driver number four, and on and on until I had all five cars stopped together. I couldn't believe my luck. All five cars were parked right behind each other in a row. I was very proud of myself.

After the leading car stopped, I turned the patrol car around and went back to park behind the last car. I got out of the patrol car, put on my Smokey the Bear hat and walked forward to tell them why they had been stopped. I told the last driver he had been stopped for speeding and to remain there until I contacted the other four drivers informing them of the same thing.

As I went forward I asked each driver to be patient and I would have him on his way shortly. After talking to the lead driver I walked back to the patrol car to write up the first citation.

Just about the time I reached my patrol car a gust of wind hit me and sucked the campaign hat off my head and it flew away. If you are not familiar with this style of hat, it's like a Frisbee with a large bump in the middle, and it will actually fly. That day the hat did not fly but instead rolled down the highway on its brim.

The hat must have been doing 10 mph when it passed the five stopped cars. As I chased after the hat I happened to notice the drivers laughing as I ran by them.

I finally trapped the hat by stepping on it by the lead car. With what little dignity I had left, I walked back to my patrol car, and on the way I stopped at each car and told the drivers if they quit laughing they could be on their way without a ticket. I worried for a couple of weeks word might get out about what happened, but it never did.

*   *   *

After being on the road for a few years, I was interested in promotion to the next rank of Sergeant. I felt I had performed well up to that point and my evaluations were very good. I began taking self-improvement college courses in preparation for the next promotional exam. Meantime I continued doing the job as best as I could, being careful not to screw up.

There were eight evaluations, one every quarter, over a period of two years. I had already put together seven good ones, with one remaining. I knew my scores were the best of the detachment and felt pretty good about myself until I got careless.

I had been very busy issuing quite a few tickets. I was almost at the end of my shift, so I decided to stop by the local district court to drop the tickets off. The court was located in a large strip mall where there were about 200 cars parked. As I pulled into the lot, luck was with me, there was one open space directly in front of the court's entrance. I couldn't believe it. I wouldn't have to park half a mile away.

I quickly pulled into this vacant stall. Since I was parked directly in front of the court office I could see directly inside because the front was all glass. It would only take a minute to walk in, drop the tickets off and walk back out to the patrol car. I felt safe enough to leave the motor running, so I jumped out of the patrol car and went inside.

Just as I dropped off the tickets, one of the clerks asked me about another ticket I had left earlier, something about the date of the arrest being incorrect, a minor issue I quickly resolved. I turned to leave, and as I approached the door I could see outside where my patrol car should have been—instead I saw a tan Chevrolet station wagon.

What the hell! I went outside thinking, I've lost my mind; didn't I just park my car at this spot? Ok, I'm a State Trooper, stay cool, don't panic. To make sure I hadn't lost my mind I looked out into the lot at the tops of the other cars to see if there was one with overhead emergency lights attached to the top—nothing.

I was at a total loss about what had happened. I went back into the courthouse trying to figure out what to do next. I felt like I was having a bad dream and I couldn't wake up. If the patrol car were stolen, I'd be in a big world of hurt. I could kiss off any chance of getting promoted. The only thing left for me to do was to call Radio and report it stolen.

About this time while trying to find a phone to use, my Sergeant walked into the court's office, came over and said hello to me. We made some small talk. He noticed I was somewhat uptight, and asked me, "What's wrong you look worried?" I explained what had happened and he said eloquently, "You left your fucking keys in the patrol car with the motor running—what the hell were you thinking?"

He told me, "You better call Radio and let them get a report out right away; just maybe the patrol car is still close by. After you call them, let's get in my car and we'll go and see if we can find it."

I thought maybe he was pulling my leg, so I called his bluff. I pretended to be talking on the phone to our dispatcher telling them what happened. The Sergeant didn't seem to care if I was faking the call or not. He said, "Let's hurry up and get going."

We took off but first drove through the parking lot to see if my patrol car might be in the lot. The lot was packed with cars. We drove up and down each row looking and I was getting more pissed and wondering why we were wasting time like this, but I didn't say anything.

After a couple of minutes we finally reached the very last portion of the parking lot when I spotted my patrol car. Like a little kid I yelled out, "There it is!"

The Sergeant pulled up by the car and said, "We're really lucky to find it so quickly. I wonder how it wound up over here." I was so happy I was not going to question how it got there. At least my car was not stolen.

I hopped out and walk towards the patrol car, fishing around in my pocket, looking for my keys when I suddenly remembered I left the stupid keys in the stupid ignition. I turned around and walked back to the Sergeant's car and he rolled down the passenger window and said, "Are these yours?" holding up my key ring. I reached out and took the keys and he asked me, "Do I need to say anything more about this?" "No sir," I responded, lesson learned." He drove off.

Apparently I must have been in the court talking to the clerk longer then a minute. How could the Sergeant park his car, take my car and park it out in Timbuktu, then come in and talk to me within that short period of time? When the last quarterly evaluation came out I anticipated about as low a mark as one could get. I was wrong. There never was any mention of my mishap in my personnel file, nor was my evaluation down graded. I'm forever grateful.

*   *   *

At one of our Detachment Trooper's meetings we were informed of a series of break-ins of local volunteer fire department buildings throughout the county. Nothing was stolen, however, there had been extensive interior damage by the vandals. We were instructed, when working a late evening shift, to find time to drive by these stations to check them out.

The following week while on patrol, maybe around 2 am, I had passed by one small volunteer fire station and happened to notice the outline of a rear bumper and taillight of a car behind the building. The car's lights were off. Well I'll be damned I've caught one of the burglars.

I quickly turned the patrol car around and went zooming towards the back of the building to catch the perpetrators red-handed. I rounded the building, turned on my high beams, spotlight and overhead emergency lights. Then I saw a figure getting back in the car on the driver's side and closing the door. I could see another occupant in the car and advised Radio to send back up, just to be safe.

I carefully walked up to the car and told the occupants to put their hands on the dash and not move. As I approached the driver's side I saw the occupant to be a female. The passenger was a male. I asked the young woman to roll down the window and tell me what she was doing.

She said they weren't doing anything. "If you're not doing anything then why were you out of the car?" I asked. "Really nothing," she responded.

"I know what I saw—so don't lie to me. What were you doing before you got in the car? If you don't level with me, the both of you will be placed under arrest for trespassing and the car impounded."

"Well, Officer, this is really embarrassing, but I had to pee so bad I pulled in behind this building so I could go to the bathroom." I surmised they were being honest since I found myself standing in her puddle of urine.

*   *   *

One outpost Trooper, who worked near Goldendale in eastern Washington, was on call after midnight. Sure enough he got the dreaded phone call from Radio around 3 am with a report of a car-cow accident. There were no reported injuries, so the Trooper mumbled to himself, got dressed, and headed off to the accident scene.

When he arrived at the scene there wasn't any damaged car around, but he did see a dead cow on the shoulder of the road. There was some broken glass, perhaps from a headlight, but nothing else. The Trooper figured the driver must have clipped the cow's head just right, killing it on impact. Apparently there must not have been enough damage to the car to disable it, so the driver left the scene.

The Trooper got out of his patrol car and went over to check on the cow. He saw the cow had suffered a severe head injury but the rest of the carcass was intact. This Trooper was a farmer and figured the carcass was worth saving. His plan was to put the cow in the patrol car, take it home and butcher it. He'd then freeze the meat until the cow's owner could be identified.

This Trooper was a big guy. He walked over and grabbed the cow by a hoof and dragged it over to the back of the patrol car, opened the trunk and then realized, the cow was too big and wouldn't completely fit inside the patrol car. The cow must have weighed around 300 pounds. So the Trooper decided the cow would fit if he removed the back seat cushion. He removed the cushion and put it down low in the ditch to conceal it, planning to come back later in the day to retrieve it.

He tugged and pushed the cow in through the back door, and when he had it propped up, climbed in from the other side, reached out to grab a hoof and pull the rest of the carcass into the back seat area. He later told me he must have sweated off ten pounds getting the cow into the patrol car. His uniform was sopping wet and soiled, but he was bound and determined to save this cow's meat.

After a few minutes he caught his breath and got his strength back, and was ready to head back to his home. One little problem though, he couldn't close the back doors. Oh what the hell, he thought, no one would see him at this hour, so he drove home with both doors open. The hooves were sticking out one side of the patrol car and the head out the other side. God, I wish I had a photo of this. He made it home, salvaged the meat, and froze it. Strangely, no

one ever reported a missing cow. The Trooper
returned to work the following day.

Here's the kicker—three days later he arrested
someone and had to take the person to the
county jail. As he began to place the guy in
the back seat, he noticed the seat cushion
missing. Oh shit. He forgot to go back to
retrieve the seat cushion.

He put the prisoner in the front seat, hurried
back to the scene of the accident that wasn't
that far away, found the cushion down in the
ditch and installed it back in the car. The
Trooper never told anyone this story until at
his retirement luncheon.

*   *   *

Port Townsend has an annual Rhododendron
festival that is very popular, and thousands
of people from all over the state attend.
One year a notorious California motorcycle
gang announced they were going to attend the
festivities for the second time, and they would
be there in larger numbers.

The year before the gang created quite a bit
of trouble, so it was assumed this year could
be worse. The local police department and the
Sheriff's Office asked the State Patrol if
they could provide a gaggle of Troopers to
help out.

The department sent a contingent of twenty
Troopers. I was part of that group. The
motorcycle gang was notorious for being armed
and dangerous. They also had a reputation up

and down the west coast for trafficking drugs. To keep a tight rein on them we were not going to take chances with this gang.

Our primary concern was always for officer safety. Normally we had one Trooper per patrol car; however, for this event we were going to be more careful, and have two Troopers in each patrol car.

To convey the message of how serious we were when dealing with gang members, if a biker was stopped for a violation, no matter how minor it was, the Trooper riding as passenger, would exit the patrol car holding a shotgun at port arms as a show of force. The other Trooper would make the contact with the operator of the motorcycle. We believed if the bikers understood we were serious about our business, they would be more cooperative and be less inclined to cause trouble.

To better illustrate how serious were in promoting a safe event, we were instructed to stop every motorcycle no matter how minor the violation might be. The charges could range from a defective exhaust, brake light not working, or someone who failed to signal when making a turn. No matter how minor, that motorcycle rider would automatically be placed under arrest and taken to the county jail to post bail. Additionally, his motorcycle would be impounded.

The day before the festival began, the bikers began arriving in small groups. They were trying to look mean, but mostly they were just dirty and ugly. In my opinion, they are a waste of skin. Boy, were they in for a surprise. Before they reached the city limits the real celebration began. It really wasn't that difficult for us to find something legally wrong, so the bikers were easy pickings.

Our Troopers were concentrated at the city limits and as the bikers entered the city, we found something wrong with each one, and stopped that rider. As with each stop, one Trooper hopped out brandishing the shotgun while the driver went up to contact the motorcycle rider.

The bikers knew they would receive some sort of harassment but were surprised to learn, if they did something wrong, they were going to jail for that violation. Then tension would get worse when they realized their motorcycle was being towed away for safe keeping until they were able to post bail.

This was unheard of in any of their previous travels. Generally in the past, law enforcement gave them more leeway.

There was one thing we hadn't planned on. The biker gang was better organized then we gave them credit. They had their own attorney and bail bondsman traveling with them. When the biker was booked, finger printed, picture taken, he was immediately released on bail, back out on the street before we could even complete our reports. This was very discouraging.

The gang members were told if they know what was best for them, after being released from the jail, they should leave town. If not, they could be cited for the same infraction, and booked again.

One of the Troopers and his partner had booked a biker at the jail, and as soon as they finished their reports, went back on patrol. No sooner were they back in position when the biker they just booked returned. He had already paid the fine and was released. As soon as he was out of jail he retrieved his motorcycle and was heading out of town.

This is when the proverbial shit hit the fan. This arresting Trooper saw the biker they just booked leaving town. He stopped him a second time. He approached the rider and said, "I thought I told you to leave town if you got out of jail, didn't I?"

"Yeah, you did shitbird, and that's what I'm doing, leaving town," the biker responded. His language might have been a bit more racy then this, but you get the point.

The Trooper was offended by the biker's attitude, so he pulled a coin out of his pocket, and turned to his partner and said, "Heads he goes back to jail—tails, we let him continue out of town." The other Trooper riding shotgun was saying to himself, oh no please don't do this, but before he could complete his thought, the other one flipped the coin in the air and caught it in his hand. He looked at the coin and said, "Well I'll be damned, it's heads. Off to jail you go."

The biker was arrested and his bike impounded for a second time. When word got out about this

Trooper's conduct, everyone was upset with the
State Patrol, especially the local Sheriff. He
blew his stack, and rightfully so. An internal
investigation soon followed.

*   *   *

One supervisor I have a lot of respect for,
loved working with his subordinates. He was a
happy-go—lucky, fun-loving guy. Always looking
for a challenge, always active. That would
change during his ride one day with one of
his subordinate Troopers. This Trooper was
assigned to an outpost that was considered in
the middle of nowhere, in eastern Washington.

There really wasn't much traffic and the two
were bored with nothing to do. As they were
driving down the highway, the Sergeant saw a
small baby coyote in the ditch that appeared
to be injured. He told the Trooper to pull
over.

After the Trooper stopped and backed up, the
Sergeant got out to check the pup to see if it
was hurt. The Trooper said, "This might not be
a good idea boss man," but the Sergeant was
too excited to be denied.

The Sergeant went down into the ditch to examine
the Coyote and said, "This animal is not hurt
all that bad, I just think it's in a state of
shock. I'm going to take it home and nurse it
back to health and keep it as a pet."

The Trooper again mentioned this was not a good
idea because the damn thing was wild. "Oh quit
being a worrywart. I'll just hold it until we

get back to my patrol car and take it home with me." The Sergeant picked up the Coyote pup without any resistance, walked back to the patrol car, cradling the pup, and hopped in. "Let's go."

The minute the patrol car started moving, the coyote went bonkers. No matter how strong the Sergeant held it, it wanted nothing to do with this ride-along. The coyote tried to bite, and the Sergeant was fearful of getting bitten so he released the animal. The pup went underneath the front seat, growling and snapping. The Trooper quickly pulled the car over to the side of the road and everyone bailed. The Coyote looked around and seeing the coast was clear, ran off into the bushes.

Later the Sergeant asked the Trooper not to tell this story. Get real—The Trooper couldn't wait to reach a phone.

*   *   *

Our State Patrol cars have a public address system installed. We have the ability to switch from our radio to this P.A. system to address crowd control issues, rather then getting out of the car and yelling. The policy is, it's not for personal use. This rule is sometimes ignored.

One Trooper became so flustered or should I say he was pissed off at one driver who refused to yield. Finally, after several minutes of blowing the siren, the Trooper turned his public address system to its highest volume and said, "Pull the hell over asshole." Unfortunately, a few hundred other motorists heard the same command. Of course, you can't do this without getting suspended with a loss of one day's pay.

*   *   *

Speaking of improper use of the P.A. system, I was assigned to work this one intersection where people were running through a stop sign. There had been a few injury accidents in the past at this intersection, so I was assigned there to arrest the stop sign violators. Easier said then done.

It was a very warm day during the summer and the only place I could conceal the patrol car was underneath a large fir tree whose branches hung out over the shoulder of the road where I was parked. Perfect spot. I sat there for two hours without seeing one car fail to stop for the sign. I was totally bored.

While sitting there for an eternity I happen to glance over to the right at a pasture. There must have been twenty to thirty cows grazing. I looked around and didn't see anyone so I turned on my P.A. system and mooed into the mike.

A few cows looked up. Hey, this is kind of fun. I mooed again, this time most of the herd looked in my direction. I did it a third time. Now the whole heard was wandering over to my spot. A few stuck their heads through the barbed wire and looked at my patrol car. Stupid cows.

*   *   *

I'm an animal lover. Over time I had two dogs and two cats. All became close members of my family. Each one knew they were in charge. There were times while on patrol I came across abandoned pets that I was able to find homes for or return them to their rightful owners.

While working a early morning shift on a cold wet day, I was passing through the freeway interchange in Olympia by Capitol Lake, heading south. As the freeway curved left I noticed a small pup that looked to be a mix-breed of a spaniel and poodle huddled up against the center cement barrier, shivering.

Oh no, I have to rescue this poor thing. Forget about patrolling for the moment. I rushed forward and exited off the freeway to turn around and back track so I could retrieve the dog. My problem while heading back was, how can I do this with the traffic as heavy as it is? Will I be able to turn on my overhead emergency lights while semi-blocking the inside lane without causing an accident? This would be almost impossible to do, but I was determined.

As I returned to the location where I last saw the pup, I began to slow down looking for it. I did see it finally, but unfortunately it was now as flat as a pancake. It's taken me years to get over this.

*   *   *

I hadn't been working all that long, but while on patrol on Stevens Pass my Sergeant decided to visit me to see that I was okay working alone in this unusual environment. After meeting up with him he asked whether I had ever been up to the restaurant at the top of the ski lift. I hadn't and was somewhat not interested. He insisted we take a ride up and have a cup of hot chocolate. What the hell, he's my boss so I might as well humor him and go up with him.

The staff at the ski lift got a kick out of two State Troopers taking a ride up while in uniform without skis, as I did. We took the ride up and it was a spectacular view from the chair lift. We eventually reached the summit and went into the lodge for refreshments. After having been there for a half hour or so the Sergeant said, "lets head back down".

What we didn't know at the time was the staff radioed down below that two State Troopers were coming down. No one rides down the ski lift because everyone is supposed to ski down. Obviously this gave everyone coming up a warning of what they are about to see. In our case as we traveled down, those skiers coming up were prepared. They had snowballs ready for us. We got hit, I'm guessing, thirty times on the way down. It was all in good fun and everyone was laughing. My dumb Sergeant thought it was funny, but I didn't.

*   *   *

Finally, I'll finish with a story to end all stories. One of the first things I learned was to find a gas station where I can have my patrol car serviced. It's very important to find the right station where the employees are trustworthy enough to work on the patrol car without vandalizing it.

I found such a place about a mile away from my home. The owner was really an outstanding guy. Most of my fellow Troopers serviced their cars at his station. He and I eventually became everlasting friends. I even serviced my personal car there as well.

I was on my day off and decided I needed to pick something up at the hardware store for a project I was working on. I have a small dog who loves to ride in the car and whenever he senses I'm leaving, he'll wait by the door waiting to tag along. He does notice the difference between my civilian clothes and uniform, so when I'm in my civvies I'll find him waiting. This day was no different.

We got in the car and my dog buddy, Leroy, hopped up onto my shoulders. He would ride there between my head and the headrest while looking out the door window. So, here we are, the happy couple heading down the road.

Before returning home I noticed I was low on gas. My favorite service station was only half a mile away so I decided to go there and fill the tank. Before I left the highway, the owner, my friend, saw me coming so he ran out from the office and hid behind one of the gas pumps planning to scare me as I pulled up to the pumps.

As I came to a stop the owner jumped out and yelled "Boo," scaring the crap out of me. He also scared the pee out of my dog. My dog, my buddy, peed down my back. I was sopping wet. I would have killed my friend but he was laughing so hard and hopping around, I couldn't get off a decent shot.

Epilogue

My job was an educational experience, and at times it could be a lot of fun. Often I would encounter some lost soul with personality issues making things more difficult for me. However, I was taught Troopers must stay cool regardless of the situation.

We Troopers constantly have to remind ourselves we are in charge, no matter how bad the contact might become, stay the course, and do our job. When finished, allow the driver to continue on his way. As irritated as we might be afterward, the one way we could show our displeasure with the person, without getting into trouble, was to finish our conversation by saying, "You have nice day, now." You know, just a slight dig to get rid of some frustration.

This salutation eventually pissed off so many people, the Department got sick and tired of responding to their complaints, so, we were ordered to refrain from using those words anymore. No more lashing back with kind words.

Have a nice day